Brewster,

to Charlie Kelly

Porkekey

AKA

McSmith

# Early Poke

*...a great southern humorist looks at life's pitfalls and pinnacles*


by Vic Smith
aka *Poke McHenry*

edited by
Vicki Smith
aka *Little Poke*

illustrations by
Steve Bridges

ISBN 0963046349

Published by:
Smith & Daniel Marketing and Public Relations, a corporation.
4500 Phillips Highway, Jacksonville, Florida 32207
*For ordering information, please call 800-330-1325*

Volume 1 of a 6 Volume Series

to
all my
faithful readers…
if it weren't for your love
of Poke, he would have died long ago

# INSIDE

## Tales that Defy Belief



## Football and a Bit of Nostalgia



## Something for Everyone

## Tests, Temptations and Critters



## Playing and Eating



## Of Fishing, Fame and Other Things

# Introduction

Poke never confesses. Poke simply "explains." And when the explanation is made, whatever impropriety may have been committed is at once forgiven... such is the power and charm of Poke McHenry, nee Vic Smith.

The written word, the spoken language, these are the foundation of his character, the tools of his trade, the weapons of his battles, the fuel of his fires, and the endless ground-spring of his power and charm.

Using only words, carefully configured into an even-flowing stream of uncommon thought, Poke will delight and entertain you. "Early Poke" is his first collection of favorites, and will take you back to his early years as a popular columnist in the *Florida Times-Union* newspaper of Jacksonville.

In this collection, mostly written in the late 1970s, you will learn how "Poke" was born, meet many of the more interesting folks he interviewed, and travel around the south to places you might never have known existed were it not for his intrepid interest in and exploration of the out-of-the-ordinary. You will also quickly realize that Poke is, perhaps above all else, opinionated. He may be right, or he may be wrong, but he will never be indifferent.

Poke has written a brief introduction to each column and, when possible, brings you up to date on the people and topics involved. Although there have been myriad changes along the way, you'll find Poke's observations of past events a timeless treasure.

Be careful as you read these pages, for you will doubtless be captured by the riveting allure that is Poke McHenry. From that happy prison, there is no escape.

# FOREWORD
## BY THE AUTHOR

"Poke McHenry" may never take a place alongside such noms de plume of literature as Mark Twain (Samuel L. Clemons), Boz (Charles Dickens), Elia (Charles Lamb), O. Henry (William Sydney Porter), and others of such stature. Indeed, (or forsooth, as Poke would say), perhaps he never will deserve such a lofty perch, at least on a national or international scale.

But during the many years in which he wrote the Poke McHenry column three times a week for the *Florida Times-Union* daily newspaper, Poke hit a pinnacle of popularity with hundreds of thousands of Georgia and Florida readers unprecedented in the annals of the hallowed old newspaper. And the love of the people for Poke kept growing and spreading constantly until he retired from the paper on January 2, 1992.

Even today, nearly three years since he left the T-U, not a single reader, seemingly, has forgotten Poke. Everywhere he goes, and he still perambulates considerably, people greet him with great warmth and fond memories, and tell him how much they miss him and ask "why don't you still write for us?"

And he is still asked, almost daily, where and how and why he came up with the name "Poke McHenry."

The full story of that already is a classic, and it may one day become a legend, if indeed it hasn't already, at least on a limited scale.

It began about 40 years ago with a letter to the editor of the Albany, Georgia, Herald, a daily newspaper for which I, Vic Smith, toiled as a reporter at that time.

The letter-writer was an elderly gentleman of the community who had been rendered irate anew by another silly action of some sort by the Albany City Commission, a commonplace occurrence everywhere in those days, too.

Among other things, the old man exhorted the governing body to get the machinery in motion and straighten out the city. At least, that's what he tried to say. The way he wrote it, in longhand with a pencil, he thundered that, "The mayor and the commissioners have got to get the McHenry in motion and straighten this town out!"

From that day forth, "McHenry" became a byword around the Herald. Whenever someone would be dragging his feet or goofing off somewhat, some superior would yell at him, "All right! Let's git the McHenry in motion and git this paper out!" In the Saturday night poker game, you could often hear the losers holler "Get the $#!@&** McHenry in motion! Deal!"

I never forgot McHenry, and when the time came for a pseudonym, there was old McHenry, still lurking in my brain, ready to be born into full glory after a 40-year gestation hiatus. We put the McHenry in motion, so to speak. And he completely took over Vic Smith, shoving old Vic all but completely out of the picture and the memory of most folks, including some members of my own family.

The Poke McHenry column was started after a Times-Union newsroom shakeup resulted in Fred Seely taking over as managing editor. Seely promptly promoted me from copy editor to chief of the news desk and installed a young man named Frank Ranew as Georgia editor. At that time, we were putting out three daily editions — the Georgia edition, the Florida, or state, edition, and the Metro, or local, edition.

Ranew, anxious to make a good impression in his first prestige job in Jacksonville, set about trying to hire a Georgia columnist, to write solely for the approximately 9,000 subscribers we had in Georgia, hoping thereby to increase that number substantially.

But he had no luck. Everybody he tried bombed out, and Seely, a past master at putdowns, was gleefully riding Ranew pretty hard.

Finally, Seely suggested privately to me that we give Ranew a Georgia columnist just as a joke, keeping the writer's identity secret. Seely wrote the first experimental column, supposed to have been penned by a South Georgia red-neck pickup truck driver named Billy McCoy. I countered with a column by Billy McCoy's catfishing buddy, Poke McHenry.

Seely loved that name, as did everyone else who was in on the plot, so that's how Poke was born. Poke, with its myriad connotations, was the one word that naturally fit the exact image we were trying to create. No name other than Poke McHenry could have conveyed so perfect a mental picture of a sleepy-eyed, easygoing philosopher with the sagacity of the ages accumulated in a nimble brain which also accommodated an enormous endowment of uncommon sense.

Poke didn't always live up to those expectations, but with a name like that, nobody noticed.

We wanted to give our Georgia readers a sort of mystery man that everybody loved but nobody, including the Georgia editor, knew. We succeeded better that anybody could have possibly foreseen.

But while Poke was being put together, Ranew remained in the dark as to his identity. I would write a batch of columns and mail them to Ranew, who would read them and tell Seely, "Hey, this guy is pretty good," and Seely would say, "Well hire him, if you think he's the man; don't bother me with it. That's your job."

Then Ranew, always sensitive to criticism and remembering the stinging sarcasm of Seely over his early efforts, would teeter and totter, unable to come to a firm decision. Ranew had contacted practically everybody he could think of in the newspaper field in Georgia trying to get some sort of line on old Poke, to no avail.

"This guy Poke is supposed to be a veteran Georgia newsman with a wide reputation, but I'll be danged if I can find anybody who's ever heard of him," Ranew complained to me one day. We worked at the same big desk with the Florida editor, the metro crew and the news desk copy editors.

"Gee," I sympathized. "I sure wish I could help you, old boy."

Finally, Seely got one of his friends in town to pose as

Poke and call Ranew, from some joint where you could hear the glasses tinkling and the girls giggling, and demand that Ranew quit fiddling around and hire him.

Ranew and the ersatz Poke made a deal over the telephone, and to this day I believe Ranew had no inkling as to who Poke was until he saw my picture on the first column to appear in the Times-Union.

The whole thing started out as a joke, and we fully intended to let it sort of peter out and fade away after a few columns appeared, but it grew like the national debt and not only wouldn't die but got lustier and stronger until management decided to try it in all editions, and found out the paper had accidentally come up with a major winner.

For the first two years or so, I had written the column on no particular schedule and just as an unrequired and unpaid-for adjunct to my regular duties as news desk chief. I did it for fun, and I loved it.

But when the paper began running it three times a week in all editions, the response was so overwhelming it became obvious that this was a full-time job. So management told me to forget the desk and just ride and write, wherever I wanted to travel and whatever I wanted to write about.

And that's how Poke became such a significant part of the lives and lifestyles of so many folks in our corner of the world and so many other places. I hope you enjoy this sojourn into a few of the early adventures of Poke McHenry.

# DICK BEAT THE DEVIL

*There was some question as to whether Uncle Dick was a barbering preacher or a preaching barber, since he was pretty good at both, especially when he was running an occasional "protracted meeting" on the side. But he could tell a good story, even if some folks were inclined to disbelieve him. This is from a Poke memory of long ago, first told in print in 1978.*

ST. MARYS RIVER*

A few days ago I read a wire story from up north some place where the only barbershop in town had closed its doors and fellows who wanted haircuts had to drive 15 or 20 miles to get them.

I have noticed over the past 15 years or so (dating from the time the first longhairs [hippies] hove upon the scene) that barbershops have been getting scarcer everywhere. Some of the barbers, particularly the younger ones, have gone into "hair styling," and a lot of men have gone in for getting their hair "styled." The old-fashioned barbershop rapidly is becoming a thing of the past, along with so many other institutions we used to know, and this got me to thinking about some notable barbers I have known.

Probably the most memorable one of them was my Uncle Dick, a handsome rascal who not only was a barber but also a part-time preacher who could whip a sermon on you that would make the Devil himself mend his ways. Dick used to, periodically, run what was called in those days a "protracted meeting," usually held nightly in a tent and guaranteed to send

** Editor's note: Most of the newspaper columns reprinted from the Florida Times-Union were datelined "St. Marys River." Poke never actually lived there, but he sure did have a lot of folks thinking he did. When the Poke McHenry column first appeared, and for many weeks, people would travel up and down the river, trying to find him.*

the congregation into a frenzy of rolling in the sawdust aisles and chattering in "unknown tongues" every night.

In those days people of that religious persuasion were referred to as "holy rollers," a cognomen of disrespect which, fortunately, has been frowned upon for a long time now.

It was customary in those days for members of the congregation to provide food and shelter for the evangelist for the duration of the "revival" meeting, with various families having the preacher (in our case, Dick the barber) at their homes to spend the nights.

Now one day right after the closing of one of those protracted meetings conducted by Uncle Dick, he was back at his chair in Dock Deese's Barbershop, trimming away on somebody's hair, and telling of his most recent experience in soul-saving. Here is the story, as told by Dick:

"Every night during the revival, this gorgeous young widow just begged me to visit her house for late supper and to spend the night after the services.

"Well, I was sure she didn't mean any harm, but I knew it wouldn't look good and might cause unpleasant talk if I stayed at her house, so I made every excuse I could think of to keep from going.

"Finally, on the last night of the revival, I just couldn't refuse any longer without hurting her feelings, so I agreed to go.

"We had a wonderful supper, prepared by her cook, and she showed me to my bedroom, where I turned in for the night.

"Well sir, I had been in the bed but a few minutes when she came into the room, carrying a lamp turned down low and wearing the sheerest kind of flimsy nightgown you ever saw, and nothing else, as I could dimly see. I had never seen a more deliberately seductive move, and I am a World War I veteran and I have seen some seductive sights in France.

"She got right into the bed with me.

"Now I'll tell you what — I've done a lot of praying in my life but right then I prayed harder than I ever had before, for the Lord to help me prevail over this tremendous temptation.

"I lay there and sweated blood, almost, agonizing and

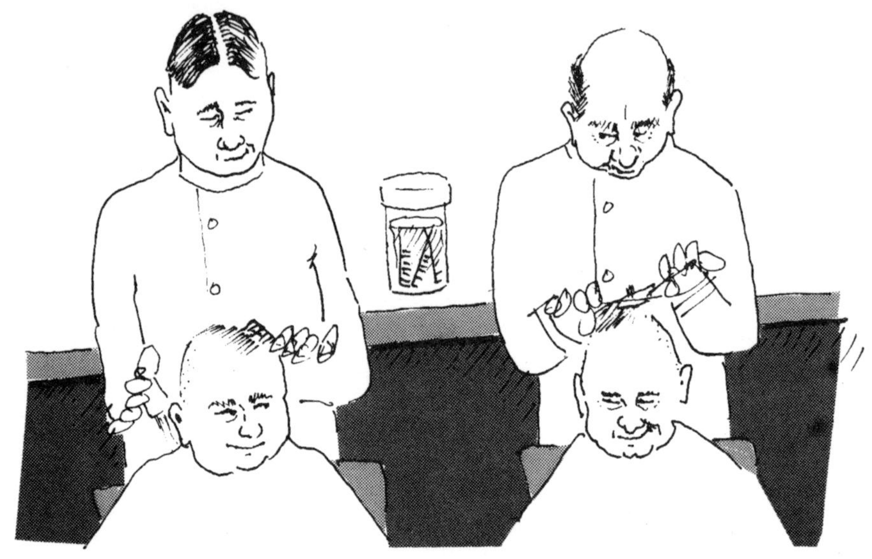

fighting the lusts of the flesh, and praying for this poor woman, whose goodness had been overcome by a passion she couldn't control.

"It was a terrific struggle, but eventually I won. I successfully fought the temptation, and she finally realized that nothing was going to take place, and so with a sweet smile she left my bed, bade me goodnight and went away, carrying her lamp."

"Now I ask you, Dock," said Dick to the crusty, droll old owner of the barbershop, "just what would you have done under those circumstances?"

"I'da done the exact same thing you did, Dick," said old Dock, never missing a snip himself at his customer's hair. "Yessir, I would have treated her just like you did. Ida give her a good lovin' and then told a damn lie about it."

*(Columnist Poke McHenry tried to get a haircut on credit the other day, but the barber told him that if he had no money he had already been clipped.)*

# Henhouse Blues Laws

*Figuratively speaking, the "blue laws" of our communities put us in the holiday position of a poor fellow whose wife saw to it that he didn't have himself any "to-do" on Christmas Day. How many of us have had experiences comparable to that of the hero of this tale by Poke?*

ST. MARYS RIVER

I've been watching the papers lately and it has been amusing to see the weeping and wailing and gnashing of teeth over Christmas Eve coming on Sunday this year.* What is upsetting so many people is the laws that prohibit the sale of alcoholic beverages on Sunday.

It is amusing to me and it is also very irritating, because any "blue law" forcing the general public to conform to certain religious beliefs is clearly unconstitutional, under our Founding Father's plain language concerning separation of church and state. Our Constitution guarantees not only freedom of religion but freedom from religion, for any person so minded.

Yet we continue to elect representatives to govern us who ignore these simple facts and put and keep laws on the books hamstringing a lot of people. I think anybody who wants to buy a drink on Sunday should be allowed to do so, whether or not it is Christmas Eve.

I'm not advocating drinking or not drinking, just advocating letting everybody have the freedom to choose what he wants to do.

Of course, there are some people who will go to any sort of extreme lengths to see that certain other people can't do what the do-gooders don't want them to do. I am reminded here of the sad fate of a fellow I knew years ago back in my hometown.

**Editors note: The year is 1978 in Jacksonville, Florida*

This happened on Christmas Eve, when the hero of this yarn was in the grocery store of a crony (drinking crony, I might add) and the grocer informed our hero that there was to be a little "to-do" down at the store on Christmas morning.

"You know," the grocer said. "We ain't gonna be open for business tomorrow (Christmas Day), but a few of us are going to gather up down here and open up a keg of nails and have a little to-do. Why don't you join us?"

"Why, I surely will," said our man, with enthusiasm. "I'll be right on down. What time does the to-do start?"

I haven't mentioned it, but our hero's wife was standing alongside him, listening to all that conversation and never saying a word herself. But she was wearing what could be described as a calculating look.

Well, our hero lived sort of on the fringes of town, and kept some pigs and a cow and a flock of chickens. And this being during Depression times, everybody who had chickens had a sturdy lock on the henhouse door, lest some less fortunate citizen let his hunger get the better of his conscience. Some folks just would steal an unprotected pullet or two.

On Christmas morning, our hero was up real early. He busied himself in every way possible to please the missus, since he knew she frowned on the bottle and that she had heard his plans for the to-do. But neither of them mentioned the matter during breakfast. Then, as she was clearing away the dishes, she said:

"Dear, would you mind going out and gathering the eggs? I need some fresh eggs for the pound cake I'm going to make for Christmas dinner."

"Why, sure, sweetheart," said our hero. "I'm glad to do anything you want done, my dear. I'll get it done right away."

So he bounded out to the henhouse and began probing around in the nests, gathering up the eggs. The madam, meanwhile tip-toed out to the henhouse door, eased it shut and snapped the padlock, effectively trapping our man.

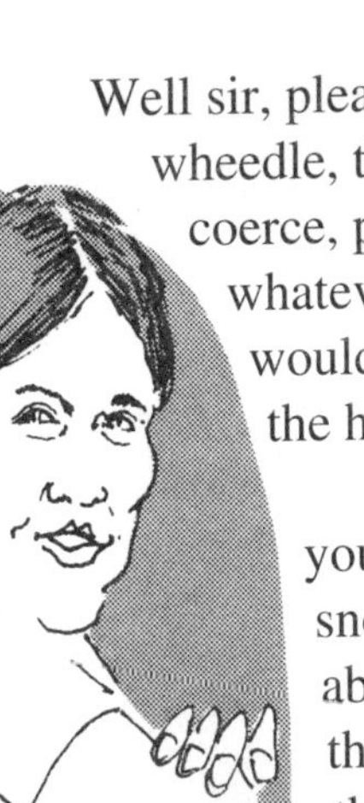

Well sir, plead, beg, cry, wheedle, threaten, cajole, coerce, proposition or whatever he might, she would not let him out of the henhouse.

"I'll show you and your to-dos," she snorted. "You ain't about to go down there and carouse with them drunks on Christmas Day. I'm seeing to it that you stay here today, and that's that."

She never let him out until long after the "to-do" was over and there was no chance for him to get into any other mischief.

That's sort of what these lawmakers do to us free spirits with their silly law about Sunday closings — they sort of lock us in the henhouse on Christmas Day. And like our friend, there doesn't seem to be anything we can do about it.

*(Poke could change all this if he were elected president. If that happened, then every other day would be payday and the next day a day off.)*

# Coffee County Charlie Can Sure Reel Off the Hyperbole

*Coffee County Charlie sure likes old Poke's way of writing, and most everything else about him, but vows that Poke is the spittin' image of a Charlie in-law who is so ugly he could hire out as a week-old July road kill.*

ST. MARYS RIVER

There is a newspaper columnist over in Douglas, Georgia, who claims he is a great fan of mine but I don't know whether to believe him or not, since he appears to be an even greater practitioner of hyperbole than I am. He obviously doesn't chew tobacco, since he keeps too much tongue in cheek to allow room for anything else.

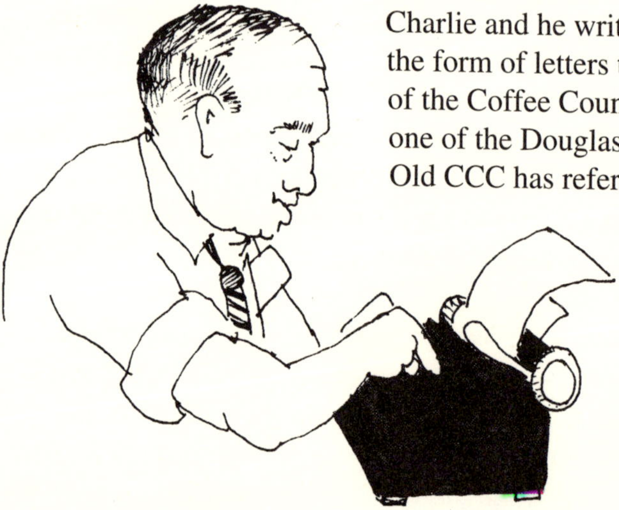

He calls himself Coffee County Charlie and he writes his stuff in the form of letters to the editor of the Coffee County Progress, one of the Douglas newspapers. Old CCC has referred to Poke before, but the latest was a few weeks back when I was over in his town at the behest of Douglas banker and Rotarian J.B. Olliff, who asked me to talk to the Rotary Club. I'm not sure whether the other club members ran J.B. out of town after that or not.

Anyway, under the assumption that old Charlie won't care, I'm going to reprint a couple of his columns. Here is one:

"Somebody tole me that one of my favorite writers is acoming to town right shortly, maybe this week, to make a talk to one of the local clubs, civic club that is. I'm speaking of one Poke McHenry what writes fer the Floridy Times-Union. Poke is one of the names he uses, another being Vic Smith.

"They is several things I admire about this world traveler such as: He just writes his column sorta when he feels like it which shore ain't every day, that could wear a fella down in a hurry. He writes about any subject he wants to it seems, without any clubs held over his head.

"He ain't ashamed to point out his weaknesses whereas so many people don't admit to having any. And I like that fact that he ain't ashamed to tell folks about him being born a Georgia boy. He loves his younguns and grand-younguns as evidence by some of his artickles which any fella with any spunk would do and he loves to fish and tell about it.

"But everybody has a flaw so I've heard and bout the worse thing I know about this fella Poke is that as I have said before, pore thing, he shore favors my Old Lady's brother which ain't no feather in nobody's cap. 'Course I know neither one can't help how he looks, but if my brother-in-law is on his feet the day Poke comes to town I'm shore gonna try to git the two face to face and see just what the reaction is."

Well now, Charlie, that must be one more ugly feller, sho' nuff. He may be the guy who goes squirrel hunting and is so ugly he never takes a gun, just knocks them dead off the limb by giving them his ugly look. The only person uglier than this guy is his wife, whom he won't let go squirrel hunting with him on account of she is so ugly she tears up the squirrels too badly when she squares off at them. Ruins the meat.

Now here is another recent Charlie effort:

"Eddication is a good thing to have and I shore wish I had more of it. Some folks have it but don't know how to use it and some need a little more wit or just plain old horse sense. I've seen some with years of schoolin' that couldn't read nor write, yet you couldn't outfigger them of a thin dime.

"My story today is about an eddicated lawyer and uneddicated farmer and it happened years and years ago.

"The farmer got accused of stealing some goats that accidently got in his herd but the lawyer promized that he could get the man off scot free for $50. The farmer agreed and the lawyer advised his client that when he got in court he wuz to answer every question asked of him by just bleating, baa-aa, like a goat.

"So, that is just what he did. When they asked him his name he would answer baa-aa. When they asked if he stole any goats he'd answer with a baa-aa. The judge told them to put that man out, he was crazy.

Later, the lawyer met the farmer and wuz bragging about how smart he wuz to get the man off so easy. Then he asked the farmer for his $50 fee.

"The farmer looked at him and bleated, baa-aa, turned around and walked away."

Charlie, I tell you what. I like your style. And if you can find that brother-in-law I'll come over there* and we'll compare mugs, and if he's really as ugly as I am I'll buy you the best steak in Douglas.

** Editors note: Poke has been back to Douglas numerous times since this column first appeared, but claims he never had to pay off on the steak dinner.*

# Hitchhikers Seem to Lack Intelligence

*"Help! I'm in the hands of an escaped lunatic and swerving left and right across a major highway at 80 miles an hour! Get me outta this!"*

ST. MARYS RIVER

Rambling around South Georgia and North Florida roads lately I've noticed an unusually large crop of hitchhikers, it seems, and some of them don't appear too intelligent.

For instance, the other day I rode by one and watched in amazement as he tried to thumb a ride from the most unlikely spot, probably, he could have picked. He was in Jacksonville, Florida, on 20th Street Expressway west, just beyond the Myrtle Street intersection, at a place where there was barely enough curb to keep him off the street and where it is impossible to pull a car off the road and out of what is bumper-to-bumper traffic most all the time.

How, I wondered, does he think a guy could stop and pick him up, even if one yearned in his innermost heart to do so? To stop there for any reason would be inviting chaos, at least. Your car would be rammed in the rear by some other speeding vehicle, run over and flattened by seven 18-wheelers, and compacted and baled, driver and all, by the following flood of traffic.

But it got me to reminiscing about the days when I did a lot of what was called "hitchhiking," covering a great portion of the whole United States during that time, when the whole country didn't include Alaska and Hawaii. I could write a manual on do's and don'ts of hitchhiking.

One of my doggonedest fingernail-chewing experiences of those days occurred in Florida. It was right after World War

II and I was beating my way up the coast after some unofficial business down at the Boca Raton air base. I had spent a week with my younger brother, who was still in the Air Corps, and I would have stayed longer except his wife ran me off, declaring me a menace to society and a villainous rogue leading her poor innocent husband plumb totally and completely astray. She had no couth, that woman.

At Sebastian, a guy wheeled a little Willis Americar over and motioned me to hop aboard. I threw my cardboard satchel over behind the front seat and settled down as he roared off up U.S. 1.

"How far ya going?" I asked, and was horrified at his reply, which went something like this:

"Flunf flauflufleen!" He said this with what I'm sure he intended to be a friendly grin, but which I immediately perceived to be a menacing leer.

"Oh Lordy," I thought. "What have I got into? I'm in the hands of at least an escaped lunatic with mayhem on his mind!"

Seeing my look of utter consternation, the driver cut loose with something like "Flurf, flyllflfluuff flo flaff!" and bent over me to open the glove compartment. Meanwhile, the Americar careened wildly down the highway at 80 miles an hour, probably all it would do.

Here we went, freewheeling it all over that coastal road as a 15-knot wind off the paralleling Atlantic Ocean was doing little to stabilize the situation, and big trucks were blasting us with angry air horns and swerving skillfully to avoid squashing us like a bug.

"Good grief," I sweated inwardly. "He's gonna bury us under a truck, split us in half with one of those power poles or head straight out across the Atlantic Ocean at any minute!"

Finally, after scrambling through a stack of stuff in the glove compartment, the driver came up with a little memo book, thumbed through it — still at 80 miles an hour and glancing at the road only about once every three hours — and pointed with obvious glee to "St. Augustine" printed in the book. "Flahnff! Flaunff Flufmph!" he said in triumph. I took this to mean he was going to St. Augustine and mentally made my last will and testament, certain that we could never last for the approximately 150 miles to St. Augustine.

I finally figured that the guy was simply a deaf-mute and meant me no harm personally, but likely would kill us both with his reckless driving. So by dint of a great many gruntings and rollings of eyes heavenward and pointing with one hand at the speedometer and the other at my chest I made him believe that I had serious heart trouble and that speeding and reckless driving confounded and exacerbated the situation. Actually I was just trying to tell him I was a coward but he interpreted it as a heart problem, and in respectful deference to my infirmities slowed down to 78, glancing at the road every two hours.

Then, glory be, the engine coughed, sputtered, backfired and quit. We were out of gasoline somewhere just north of Melbourne.

"Hallelujah! I exulted inwardly. "Somebody up there is looking out for me."

Grabbing my bag, I started scrambling out of the car and telling the man how much I had appreciated the ride and all that stuff, but lo! "Flunphff!" he said, nodding and grinning vigorously, and motioning me to keep seated. Whereupon he opened the trunk of the car, withdrew a five-gallon can of gasoline, poured it into the tank, and with many a "Floonfph" and "Flaumphflafffloof" cranked 'er up and off we whizzed anew.

Like the drunk who stumbled into the telephone pole, felt his way around it and dropped his arms with the comment, "It's no use, I'm walled in," I resigned myself to my fate and hung on.

Miraculously, we made it to St. Augustine without incident, although it took considerable quantities of a relaxing, soothing potable to calm my bejangled nerves, and but for employing that immediate cure, I might have sworn off hitchhiking forever.

# Old Bone's Mill Pond Has Come a Long Way

*The bones of old Bone are lying somewhere around what is now one of the most popular and prettiest recreation spots in South Georgia. Bone was a killer who was handed some of the old-time, on-the-spot swift and permanent punishment, as meted out in the old days. Some called it "rope justice."*

IRWINVILLE, Georgia

Old Bone wouldn't recognize his mill pond today. But if he should awaken at the site of it, known for the last century or so as "Crystal Lake," he might allow as to how, murderer or not, he had gone to heaven.

Bone, whose surname may be lost to history, was the first recorded owner of "Bone's Pond," which is about six miles west of Irwinville on Georgia 32 and which came by its present name sometime after old Bone was hanged for the messy murder of one of his neighbors.

The full and fascinating story is told in the late J.B. Clements's *History of Irwin County*. Bone, according to Clements, "proved to be a criminal of the vilest kind."

It seems that Bone, an incongruous Union-backer eye in a hurricane of Rebels during the fading days of the Confederacy, owned a steam corn mill on the shore of what is now Crystal Lake. He was not only a strong Union sympathizer but also an active supporter of the Northern cause, pulling such stunts as hiding escaped Federal prisoners and runaway slaves on his farm.

It was one of the latter actions that led to Bone's untimely demise. The neighbor, Jack Walker, discovered a runaway slave hiding on the Bone place and endeavored to recapture him. They scuffled, and while this was going on, Bone, bringing food to the runaway, came upon them.

Clements' history shows that Bone shot Walker, then beat him with a gun butt until he was assumed dead. Then Bone and the runaway buried Walker in mud near the north end of the old pond. All this came out at a trial held immediately after Bone had been arrested and Bone's teenaged son, Tayler, under threat of otherwise being hanged, told investigators how his father had disposed of Walker.

Justice (or maybe retribution), like everything else in those days, was primitive — but swift, certain and permanently effective. A court composed of Irwin County citizens who had helped search several days for the missing Walker was hastily convened, a judge appointed on the spot, and Bone was tried for murder.

"After hearing the evidence," Clements' account goes, "he was promptly and properly convicted and sentenced to be hung." Right then and there, too.

Walker's sons, Sam and John, were allowed to fashion the noose after a scaffold was erected under a big oak tree on the edge of the pond, and Sam shinnied up the tree to throw the rope over a large limb.

"Then Bone," Clements recorded, "was made to mount the scaffold and told that he had 15 minutes to make any statement he desired. These were his last words, 'Take warning from me and don't come to what I have.' He moved and the scaffold fell and launched Bone, the murderer, into eternity."

Bone's family members then were told to wind up their affairs, dispose of their property and get out of Irwin County, which they promptly did.

The Crystal Lake property eventually came into possession of Dr. W.L. Story of Ashburn, Georgia, and subsequently to the present owner, Tifton, Georgia businessman A.N. Adcock.*

Lewis's daughter, now Mrs. Bob Harp of Irwinville, Georgia, was kind enough to share with me a wealth of pictures taken during bygone days at Crystal Lake. Unfortunately, no pictorial recording of the Bone trial and execution was among them.

The popular Crystal Lake recreation spot was improved over the years while Lewis owned it, but has really been renovated and revitalized under Adcock to the point that old-timers who used to take their girlfriends there for outings (such as I did many moons ago) wouldn't know the place today.

Perimeter roads now run all the way around the 100 acre, sparklingly clear waters, and pure white "sugar sand" beaches now encircle the whole thing. There is also access by road to most of the 2,000 acres surrounding the lake, and those acres are nature lovers' delights. Botanists have told Adcock that the sand ridges support between 600 and 700 species of flora, among them the almost-extinct myrtle oak.

Adcock has planted more than 300 palm trees around the lake; installed sun decks on the waters, built the "highest water slide in this part of the world," pushed thousands of tons of sand to cover the entire 40-foot-deep bottom of the lake from three to five feet deep; scattered scores of picnic tables

** Editor's note: The Crystal Lake property is still owned by Adcock and Associates. Unlike much of south Georgia, it escaped damage in the summer floods of 1994.*

and other outdoor-living conveniences throughout acres and acres of shade trees; installed hookups, rest room and shower facilities for scores of campsites; built a modern pavilion; and made dozens of additional improvements.

He has turned old Crystal Lake into a true oasis and given landlocked South Georgia a touch of the tropical seas — or as nearly akin to that as seems possible. And he isn't through yet.

For one thing, Adcock plans to turn those 2,000 acres into a flower garden that may eventually rival such other great Georgia attractions as the Masters Golf Course at Augusta or Callaway Gardens at Pine Mountain. It shouldn't be hard to do, with the start he already has.

The place is attracting thousands of folks from all over South Georgia and even more distant points.

Yessir, old Bone probably would think he'd been forgiven for all his Yankee-lovin' sins if he could gaze upon Crystal Lake today.

# Notes from an Old Soldier and a 'Former' Smoker

*Things weren't much different in 1980, as shown in this piece, which highlights a letter from a reader disgusted with the way things in Washington were going. The reader even made up his own joke and paid for a supply of T-shirts to spread the word.*

ST. MARYS RIVER

Today I'm not going to spread any great wisdom, but rather try to tie up a few loose ends and get around to doing something about one of the many good letters I've been letting accumulate.

But before getting into the letter, I want to mention in passing that I have successfully hurdled the two-year mark in my experiment at quitting smoking. I had my last Chesterfield on the night of September 10, 1978 — so I've got a 10-day start on the third year. This leads me to believe that it just might barely be possible that there is a glimmer of hope that I could be about to make a start on beginning to think about trying to quit permanently. In short, I'm still not guaranteeing anything. But I've been off the things long enough now to realize how badly an ash tray in a car stinks. And that, I guess, is progress.

Still, it never pays to jump to conclusions. Being the realistic sort, I never judge anything prematurely, figuring that, in this instance, if I start bragging about quitting smoking it might turn out differently.*

Reminds me of the time when one of my daughters asked me, "Daddy, will you always be broke?"

**Editor's note: To date, Poke has never again taken up the habit, successfully lengthening his life long enough to get this book out.*

"Heavens no, child," I told her. "A condition that has lasted for a mere 40 years cannot by any means be considered a permanent thing. I'm sure I'll be rich any day now."

(I didn't tell her then, perhaps because I didn't realize it then, that by having her and her mother and sister, good health and all the world's outdoors to ramble around in, I was already richer by far than I deserved to be.)

And now for that particular letter I've been trying to get around to. It is from old soldier Albert Foster of Keystone Heights, a community a few miles south of Jacksonville, Florida. Albert is pretty doggone good at coining jokes, as you will see:

"Your recent column, 'Year of the Politician', was quite amusing. I would add a joke, originated by myself, to your collection.

"Seems this fellow was so distressed at the Washington goings-on that he began to have this nightmare every night. In it he was standing up on Capitol Hill just at daybreak, looking down Pennsylvania Avenue towards the White House. All was very quiet with no movement of either vehicle or pedestrians, and the sight he beheld was indeed a ghastly one.

"From every lamppost along the avenue was hanging a politician of some sort or another — senator, congressman, bureaucrat, cabinet officer. Then the dreamer would awaken and find himself laughing hilariously. Well, now, our dreamer was not by nature a man of violent passions, and it disturbed him exceedingly that he always awakened laughing at such a gruesome nightmare.

"He became convinced that such a reaction indicated that he was somehow mentally ill. So he sought out a psychiatrist and told him the whole story.

"That gentleman heard him out and finally told him there was nothing he could do for him. Dismissed, he dejectedly started from the office. Just as he reached the door, the psychiatrist called out to him, 'If you ever wake up crying, hurry back to see me!'

"I am, myself, much distressed at the seeming incompetence, greed, indifference, corruption amongst our elected and appointed officials of all parties and at all levels. I am an old retired professional soldier, belong to no party, and have never been a political activist.

"Nevertheless, I have given much thought to the problem. I am certain that I have at least a temporary solution.

"In an attempt to bring this solution to the attention of the public I have written an essay of just 10 words and spent a not inconsiderable sum of money to have it imprinted on T-shirts. I enclose one with my compliments and in the hope that you may wear it at your pleasure and in good health."

Albert did indeed send me one of the T-shirts, which is imprinted with "Vote TA-BOO - to Throw All the Bums Out of Office." It also has a picture of what I assume to be a fat politician.

I have worn the thing around a few fish camps and other places and it really gets some attention.

He tells me further that he is advertising the shirts nationally — not for any profit motive, since he's offering them at or less than his cost for producing, packaging and mailing — but just to spread the word.*

**Editor's note: Poke has been unable to locate Mr. Foster, so you may not be able to get a shirt like this, even though the message is still timely. (Albert, if you're out there, let us know.)*

# "SEE, YOU CAN CALL OFF A CIRCUS."
## ...*HUEY LONG*

*The facts as presented in this version of a famous old southern story are as they were given to Poke many years ago, and some of them may be subject to dispute. But this is the way Poke remembers the story, and he insists only that the thing happened, roughly as he remembers it here, and he does not guarantee the absolute accuracy of each quote; only the general truth.*

No account of the exploits of Huey Long, the famed flamboyant former governor of Louisiana, could be complete without mention of a famous confrontation between the late Governor Long and John Ringling North, a long-ago president of Ringling Brothers Barnum and Bailey Circus.

The time was in the 1930s, and Huey was riding the absolute crest of his power and popularity in the Bayou State. His pet love, pride and joy was Louisiana State University in general and its Bengal Tigers football team in particular.

Huey was determined to make the Tigers a national powerhouse, and he was well on the way toward success.

The confrontation referred to came about when it was brought to Huey's attention that on a certain Saturday the circus was scheduled to appear in New Orleans, in direct conflict with one of LSU's biggest football games of the year. This, Huey decided without hesitation, would never do.

So he got John Ringling North on the telephone and told him he was "sorry and all that, Mr. North, but you will just have to call off your circus."

"Governor," said Mr. North. "There is just no way one

can call off a circus. These bookings are made months, sometimes years in advance. Contracts have been signed, agreements made, arrangements for housing and feeding people, vast publicity programs set in motion - billboards, posters, newspaper advertisements and stories, business commitments and no telling what all else is involved. I'm sorry, sir, but there is just no way you can call off a circus."

"Well, Mr. North, I've got something to tell you. Mr. North, did you ever hear of a stock-dip law?"

"No, governor, I can't say that I have."

"Well now, Mr. North, it means that every animal that crosses the state line in Louisiana must be dipped in a vat for ticks.

"Mr. North, did you ever try to dip a tiger?"

In the face of such a cogent argument, Mr. North had no choice but to call off a circus.

# FISHING

*Here, in a late 1978s column, Poke recalls his first, and last, experience as a member of a two-man expedition bent on dynamiting Ocmulgee River catfish, bream and all other fishes that happened to be in the vicinity of the explosive. The method worked, but with somewhat less than happy results. Read on:*

FOLKSTON, Georgia

I dropped in at the Charlton County Herald newspaper office recently and had a chat with editor Doyle Lewis. We got to talking fishing, and he told me a story I hadn't heard, although most of the people I've been talking with since have heard it, so I guess it must have gotten around and passed me by while I was someplace else.

In case you haven't heard it, I'll pass it on, mainly because it reminded me of a long-ago experience with something of the type. Here it is:

This game warden lived next door to a guy who was a constantly successful fisherman, never coming home without a cooler full of fish. Wanting to learn his secret, the warden went with him one day, and when they got anchored on a lake the warden started to rig up when, to his consternation, he saw his neighbor take up a stick of dynamite, light the fuse and pitch it overboard.

After the resulting explosion, the neighbor took his dip net and started scooping up dead fish all over the place. When he cleared them up, he lit another stick of dynamite and dropped it in, repeating the collection process afterward.

The slack-jawed warden couldn't stand it, and said, "Look here, you and I are friends and neighbors and all that, but I can't sit by here and watch you break the law like this. I'm gonna have to make a case against you..."

The neighbor stared at the warden for a moment, then picked up another stick of dynamite, lit the fuse and shoved it into the hand of the flabbergasted warden.

"Now then," said the neighbor briskly, "are you gonna talk or fish?"

And that brings me to the tale of the only two times I ever went dynamiting fish — my first time and my last, both wrapped into that misadventure of about 40 years ago.

It began when an old river rat friend of mine invited me to go with him and paddle the boat while he handled the explosives. He promised we'd load the boat with choice Ocmulgee River redbellies and catfish.

Well, he had me row the boat up under some willow branches at the edge of an eddy about 30 yards in diameter, and told me to hold the boat right there until he said "git," and then to back out of there like the devil himself was after us.

He fumbled around up front for a bit, then I heard the fizz and sputter of a fuse and he dropped a bundle of something over the side. It was dynamite tied to a good-sized rock, but how much dynamite I had no idea. It might have been half a stick or half a dozen sticks.

"Now git!" he yelled as the package slid under the muddy waters.

I tried my best to "git," but to no avail. The boat was stuck so fast to an old treetop barely submerged — an obstruction impossible to see and aligned just so that you could get a boat stuck on it and never know it until you tried to get off.

"Git back! Git back!" the old man was screaming as I

frantically fought the water with the paddle. But we didn't move, except to rock gently.

Then came the great upheaval. I do not know if there was any noise or not, but suddenly the water erupted upward as if some giant spout had cut loose from the bottom of the river.

The treetop rose out of the water as if in slow motion, carrying me and the boat skyward with it and rolling us slowly over as we went up. The old man either was hurled from or leaped from the front end of the boat onto the bank beneath the willows, but the boat and everything in it wound up upside down and sinking halfway across the river.

As soon as I was clear of the boat and surrounding debris, which included a great many dead fish of assorted types and sizes, I just sort of treaded water and let the current carry me along till I beached two or three hundred yards downstream and on the opposite side from our great experiment.

After surviving that, I figured there were simpler and less perilous ways of procuring a mess of fish, and thus ended my fish-dynamiting career.

*(Columnist Poke McHenry swears that one of the catfish they dynamited that day was so big that after he floated to shore they had to put him in two piles.)*

# Fish Stories

*True stories from an incredible fishing site as it was in its beginning, many years ago. This column includes the fantastic story of a four- or five-acre congregation of shellcrackers Poke and a buddy discovered. In one week, more than 37,000 fish were caught by hook and line in the area. There were some disagreements, too.*

FORT GAINES, Georgia

On the way back from a Mississippi trip I stopped in this old stomping ground for the first time in about five or six years, and found there have been some changes with one of my old fishing buddies, Lindy Bryant. Lindy runs a store, restaurant, fish camp, some sort of combination of it all — what exactly it is is a place to really relax and enjoy yourself.

Lindy is pretty much the same as he was back when we used to patrol the waters for speckled perch (crappie), shellcrackers, bass and catfish. Except there is a lot more of him now. Old Lindy's done got fat along with getting rich.

Chatting with him brought back many fond memories of how things used to be the first few years after completion of the Walter F. George Dam across the Chattahoochee River at Fort Gaines and the impoundment of vast acreage of great fishing waters. When folks first started fishing there in earnest, there were literally bejillions of small bream in the place.

During the era of the little bream, many good stories came out of the area. One of them concerned an old man who had been piddling around fishing here, there and everywhere for most of his life and had never caught anything to speak of. He had plenty of money and was generous with it, but he just never could seem to hit it right anywhere he went.

Then he discovered Fort Gaines and those little bream. It was fabulous. He caught fish beyond what he had hoped for in his wildest fantasies. True, they were small, but they were many. So he fished and he fished and he caught and he caught one day until he completely filled a cooler with those bream and returned to the landing beaming like a spring-morning sun.

He button-holed passers-by to show off his fish, and among those he attracted was the resident game warden. "Look at that catch!" the old man crowed, opening his cooler. "Ain't that a bunch of 'em?"

"It sure is," said the warden. "Looks like you got about $35 worth more than the law allows." (He was quoting the standard fine for exceeding the limit.)

"All right! All right!" said the old gentleman, whipping out his wallet. "I don't mind that a bit! Worth every penny of it! I'll pay you right now!"

On one memorable day about 10 years ago, Lindy and I discovered the most monstrous concentration of shellcrackers I ever heard of anywhere. It was along in the tail end of winter and before the beginning of spring. The best of the crappie fishing was over and the best of the spring bream fishing had not yet begun, and we were just cruising around trying to pick up what we could.

We drifted into an area about 400 yards from a fish camp and suddenly each of us had a hand-sized shellcracker on. As soon as we got the lines back out, we had two more. We anchored the boat and as quickly as we could pull them in we loaded both our coolers.

At the camp they could see we had some action and when we got in there was quite a crowd swarming around the boat to find out what we had.

The fact was we had stumbled into a gathering of shellcrackers in three-foot deep water that covered four or five acres of just about solid fish. The next day it was impossible to get near the place. Game wardens were out there "directing traffic" — chasing off boats which had caught the limit and allowing others in.

Tempers flared several times, and more than one fistfight broke out. A woman in one boat became so irked at another in a nearby boat that she jumped out, sloshed over to the other boat and turned it over, spilling a screaming woman, worms, poles and all into the lake.

The game wardens told me later that during the week following our discovery, they checked out 37,000 shellcrackers taken from the mammoth "hole," and of course many others were taken that didn't get checked.

I had never before seen anything like it, and never have since. But in those days nothing was surprising at Fort Gaines.*

*(Poke McHenry writes columns when the weather is too rough to go fishing.)*

**Editor's note: There are still fish camps at Fort Gaines, but if you go, don't expect this kind of good fortune.*

# Ace Adams Won't Throw You Any Curves

*This 1979 column is concerning the competitiveness of, and friendship with, ex-New York Giants relief pitcher, hunter, fisherman an all-around good sportsman Ace Adams, who always caught one more fish than whomever he was fishing with on any particular day. Ace, a long-time buddy of Poke, was one of those major leaguers who was lured to Mexico in 1946 for a bundle of Yankee dollars.*

ALBANY, Georgia*

About a dozen or so years ago, Ace Adams and I went fishing in one of the Patrick's Fishing Paradise ponds over at Brookfield, Georgia. We had a pretty good day, stuffing a cooler with nice bream. En route home, I asked Ace how many fish did he reckon we'd caught.

"I don't know," he replied with a mischievous grin. "But I do know I caught one more than you did." In short, he had to be the winner at whatever he did.

The incident was typical of the competitiveness of the old New York Giants pitcher, who was a premier relief man on a staff that included, at one time or another, such illustrious gents as Carl Hubbell, Hal Schumacher, Cliff Melton, Harry Gumbert, and Bill Voiselle.

Ace is 69 now**, but still carries his playing weight of 190 pounds on his 5-10 frame - although it is obvious that some of the poundage has shifted position considerably.

Nowadays, he is one of Albany's most successful businessmen, still an avid fisherman and hunter and a gardener of considerable note. About six months ago he opened an

**Editor's note: Poke lived in Albany for many years (people knew him by the name he used in that former life, Vic Smith).*

*** Mr. Adams is now 84 years old.*

expanded package store that is nothing short of fabulous. It is stocked with just about every type of legal alcoholic beverage in existence, including full complements of foreign and domestic wines. He also owns some apartments, among his other holdings.

With a 16-horsepower tractor, he tills a garden on about an acre near the apartments, and it was in full flourish when I talked with him the middle of June.

For his fishing excursions, he has an excellent lake and river boat at a place on Lake Talquin, near Tallahassee, Florida, a 25-footer at Panama City, Florida, for flats (shallow water areas) and offshore junkets, and a bass-chaser he hauls wherever he takes a notion to go. He often is accompanied by his wife, Ellie,* and she is a fine fisherman in her own right. Together with their son, Alvin, they see to it that there is never a shortage of fresh fish around the Adams abode.

Ace was born in Willows, California, and came to Georgia to play baseball, specifically to pitch baseball, a thing he did considerably better than anybody else in the old Georgia-Florida League. Hurling for Cordele in 1937, he won 26 and lost 13 in the regular season, garnered two more wins in the playoffs and led the league's pitchers in practically everything. The Georgia-Florida League wasn't ready for Ace Adams.

The next year he went up to Winston-Salem and won 16 games of 34 the club had won when he departed. He finished the season with Nashville in the Southern League,

*Editor's note: Ellie Adams is now deceased.*

spent the 1939-40 seasons with the Vols and then was bought by the New York Giants. With the major league club he appeared in 302 games from 1941 through the early part of the 1946 season, when he joined some other select company in jumping to the Mexican League for a bundle of pesos.

Other outstanding pitchers who joined him in Mexico included Sal Maglie and Max Lanier. Old Brooklyn Dodgers catcher Mickey Owen also was among the 19 players who took the Mexico gold.

Adams played only one season in Mexico, then came back to South Georgia (he still has a fine farm down in Decatur County on Spring Creek.) He dabbled a bit more in baseball before settling down to business in Albany in the mid-1950s. He bought a piece of land at the intersection of Slappey Drive and Palmyra Road, which wasn't much of a deal at that time, but now it ranks among the most valuable packages of real estate in Albany.

With the Giants, Ace was renowned as one of the toughest competitors in the business, and he had the stuff to handle major league hitters. He was 41-33 overall for the Giants, where he was used almost exclusively as a relief pitcher. He was 4-1 in 38 appearances in 1941; 7-4 with an earned-run average of 1.84 in 61 games in 1942; 11-7 in record-setting appearances in 1943; then 8-11 and 11-9 in 1944-45, appearing in 65 games each season.

He played in only three games in 1946 before leaving for Mexico.

His top salary with the Giants was $15,000, which was in the range of top salaries for most pitchers those days. He got that after he held out, wanting to be a starter pitcher rather than a relief man, until the front office finally asked, "Will you continue to relieve, if we double your salary from $7,500 to $15,000?"

"I told them that for that I'd not only relieve but also be the bat boy and groundskeeper," Ace recalled with a wide grin.

Despite having been out of the game as long as he has, Adams still gets an average of five to 10 fan letters a month from fans who still remember him or autograph collectors who know him only by reputation.

In 1952, he ventured out on his own as owner, manager, pitcher, utility player, bus driver, business manager and a few other little duties with the Fitzgerald club in the old Georgia State League.

"I lost $5,000 that season," he said. "And it would have been worse if I hadn't been able to develop and sell a couple of young players."

Much of his trouble that year, he said, was brought on by a general indifference on the part of some of the city fathers.

"I just couldn't ever seem to get full cooperation from the city," he said. "They just didn't seem interested enough."

We have been on many a fishing and hunting trip together, and old Ace is still one of the top sportsman I know, despite having a somewhat acquisitive way about him at times. Once he borrowed my Igloo-brand 48-quart cooler, one of the first of that type to show up around Albany, and about six weeks later I remarked that he must have really liked that cooler.

"Dang right," said Ace. "That's a pow'ful fine cooler. I don't see why you don't get you one just like it."

# OLD DAN: A COLORFUL CHARACTER

*Old Dan is recalled by Poke as one of the most colorful characters he ran across in a long career in the newspaper field. Dan had a prodigious memory, but he also had some glaring faults in other areas. He knew, however, exactly what a "bagatelle" was.*

ST. MARYS RIVER

Somebody asked me recently if I could remember personally any legendary colorful characters of the newspaper business. Well, I crossed trails from time to time with many of the guys with fabulous reputations, mostly undeserved, according to my observations. A lot of those characters are more forgettable than otherwise.

But the question did set me to thinking about one particularly unforgettable reporter — old Dan Gibson — who worked for me and the same paper I did for 12 or 13 years.

Dan had been a number of things in his long career. He started in newspaper work about 1917, stayed in it for eight years or so, opened an insurance agency and ran it until being appointed to a postmastership, and remained postmaster until forced into retirement after nearly a quarter-century and when approaching his 70th birthday.

That is when he talked the publisher of our paper into hiring him, a fact accomplished before I, the paper's city editor, had any inkling of what was afoot. I roared in protest at being saddled with a 70-year-old reporter, and had my usual success in an argument with the publisher. Old Dan was a member of the staff and stayed on active duty until dying in his sleep at age 82, as best I remember.

It wasn't long before I changed my mind about old Dan, for I found him to be more industrious than staffers one-third his age, plus the fact that he knew everybody who ever thought about being born in or connected with the community, and had an absolutely prodigious memory. He could not only tell you the score of an obscure 1924 football game, but also the name of the cheerleader who broke her ankle tumbling from an aborted pyramid with eight minutes to go in the third quarter.

But old Dan did have his foibles, not the least of which was an uncanny propensity to distort names. He wrote a feature story once about a guy named Breckenridge (I think), and he must have referred to the poor guy in 15 different ways throughout the story. He was "Breckenfridge," "Brokenfrap," "Brackenbrack," "Brokenbridge," "Brenenrackige," and no telling what all else.

By the time I finished reading that piece of copy I had no idea how to spell Breckenridge's name, if indeed it was "Breckenridge."

Old Dan also had a singular hang-up with the name of a hospital administrator who went by the name of O. Brackett Hardy.

With Dan, Hardy became "O.B. Bracker," and that, by golly, was that. He would consistently refer to the man as "O.B. Bracker," despite all my remonstrances to the contrary. In fact, every time I'd chide Dan about mistakes in his copy, he'd snort that "That's what they pay you for, to catch all that stuff."

Once Dan wrote a story about a civil suit and began it in this manner:

"Joe Jones, a local barber, today sued James Smith in City Court for…"

Then the second paragraph, detailing the suit:

"Mr. Barber claimed…"

Dan was one reporter that carried his curiosity to inordinate extremes. He worked in an office adjacent to the publisher's, and his sense of hearing was uncommonly acute, so very little that went on in the publisher's office escaped his ears. The publisher, of course, knew this.

One day the publisher, who owned the local television station, had his station manager in for a conference over some new equipment they were buying, and after a lengthy conversation the publisher waxed indignant over the way he had been treated by some salesman.

"Do you know what that S.O.B. said to me?" thundered the publisher. "He said (at this point he lowered his voice to a whisper, mindful that old Dan was listening, and muttered something indistinguishable, purely to get Dan's reaction)."

Almost instantly, Dan's noggin appeared around the publisher's door.

"What did that S.O.B. say?" he demanded.

Old Dan also was a monumentally poor poker player, and suffered the consequences in our regular Saturday night newsroom games.

One Monday, just as Dan was strolling by, I asked the managing editor how much he had won the Saturday night before.

"A bagatelle," he replied airily. "A mere bagatelle."

"How much is a mere bagatelle?" I asked.

"Thirteen dollars and 40 cents," growled old Dan, without breaking stride. "That's how much a mere *&%$#@@!! bagatelle is!"

Among his many other achievements, old Dan was the only reporter I ever knew who could declare positively what a "bagatelle" is.

He was truly an unforgettable character.

# Oyster Bar is an Institution

*Poke called her "Tugboat Annie," and she was rough, tough and gruff, but the way she could prepare oysters was indescribably good. And she had a good heart, even though she would not, under any circumstances, accept a check or credit card, no matter who you were or how trustworthy she knew you to be.*

ALBANY, Georgia

Mae's Oyster Bar has been an institution in Albany, Georgia for more than a score of years, and if it isn't already a legend, also, it is well on the way to becoming one.

The owner and operator is Mae Tyre, and the interior of her place somehow strangely reminds me of Kipling's description of Gunga Din's attire: "And the uniform he wore was nothing much before, and rather less than 'arf o' that behind."

In short, Mae's place ain't much to look at, but if you like oysters as I do, there is no better place to go. The ones she cracks open and serves on the half-shell are always icy cold and have that fresh, salt-sea tang almost like dredging them up off the bed in January and cracking them in the boat. And where fried oysters are concerned, I don't believe there is any way to make a fried oyster taste any better than Mae can.

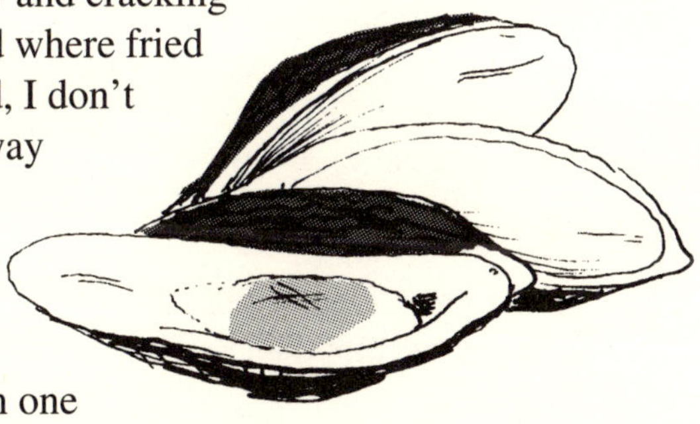

I don't know how Mae would do in one of those oyster-shucking contests, but she can open them faster than I can eat them, which is, I assure you, swift.

The place used to be located as an adjunct of Ace

Adams' package store on North Slappey Drive in Albany, but when Ace expanded Mae had to hunt other quarters, and wound up on West Broad Avenue, where she has been for the past dozen years or so.*

When the place was on Slappey a bunch of us used to congregate there almost every afternoon and solve the world's problems with brilliant bursts of suds-inspired intellect. We also consumed mountainous quantities of oysters and an occasional smoked mullet or two.

One can still do the same things in her place now, but she has added other little delicacies such as small, fried channel catfish and the like, coming from a "kitchen" about the size of a poker table.

Mae was born in Ocala, Florida, and migrated to Albany about 1952. I don't know exactly when she was born, but she has been a grandmother for 20 years now, so like the rest of us old customers she is no youngster.

Neither can I say just what size Mae is. I would not be ungallant enough to say she is obese, but if she was a lady wrestler (and she could be) she would be in the heavyweight class. And, although she has a reputation for being rough, gruff and tough, she actually has a heart bigger than she is. I call her, although not within her hearing range, "Tugboat Annie."

Not too many people besides me know it, but I saw her pay the insurance premiums for a dying and nearly destitute friend, because she knew he couldn't keep up the insurance, as much as he wanted and needed to.

Mae is as sharp as they come, too. She once opened up a new avenue of thinking for me, when a guy came in to her place soliciting contributions for a Boys Club.

"I'll be glad to donate something to your little Boys Club," Mae told him firmly, "just as soon as you also organize a little Girls Club. There are just as many little girls out there that need help as there are little boys."

Up to that time the truth of what she said had never dawned on me, but there was then and there, and are now, "just as many little girls" who should be cared for and helped as there are little boys.

** Editor's note: Mae's Oyster Bar is no longer in operation.*

One of the many things Mae is famous for is that she operates her business on a strictly cash basis. The only way she'll take a credit card, she told one customer, is "down to Penney's or someplace and get me a new set of tires for my car, if you wanta give me a credit card."

And President Reagan himself couldn't get a check cashed in Mae's place. She absolutely refuses to take anybody's check.

As a for-instance, I went in there once without a dime on me, just looking for someone. Immediately, one of my inebriated friends began insistently demanding that I allow him to buy me a drink. I finally gave in, after five or six seconds of fierce resistance, and when we finished the drinks he discovered he, too, had no money.

"Mae," I said, "I haven't got any money on me either, but if you'll take my check I'll be glad to pay for these drinks, even though I don't owe for them."

"No!" snorted Mae. "I won't take your check, no way."

I was in her place the other day and they were still laughing about a pretty important fellow and his wife who had eaten and had a few drinks and when it came time to pay up he didn't have enough cash with him. Customers swear that Mae made him leave his wife there whilst he went off and withdrew some money from one of the bank night machines.

The couple, incidentally, hasn't been back — but that worries Mae not one whit.

"He knew I don't take credit cards or cash checks," Mae said.

Seldom does anyone cause any trouble in Mae's place, but if they do Mae handles them herself. She needs no bouncer.

I personally watched her once go into the men's rest room and drag out a couple of oversized bruisers, one of whom was flashing a switchblade knife on the other. She gave them such a tongue-lashing that in 30 seconds they were as humble as third-grade schoolboys jerked up before the principal.

She is an unforgettable character.

# HEBER JONES

*Poke recalls with great respect and fondness his late friend Heber Jones, a real southern gentleman, who once called a would-be robber a sorry dog for holding him up with a handgun that wouldn't fire. "If Ida known that," Heber said, "Ida shot him with my own gun, instead of trying to shoot him with his." Heber was overseer of Blue Springs Plantation south of Albany when President Eisenhower used to hunt quail there, and we used to watch him. This column appeared in the Jacksonville, Florida Times-Union daily newspaper in 1978.*

ALBANY, Georgia

I was over here on a Sunday afternoon of late, after a long absence from this town, and I had forgotten how absolutely dead the downtown area is on the Sabbath. Since I've been writing this column, I've been spending a good many Sunday afternoons across the line in North Florida, where you can't tell the difference what day of the week it is.

But a visit to Albany, dull as it was, got me to thinking in general about old friends I had there and in particular about Heber Jones, now departed this existence for several years.

Heber, despite a rustic background, had all the attributes of a true Southern gentleman. That is, he was mild-mannered, easygoing, kind to all people, gallant and chivalrous with the ladies, a deadly shot with rifle or shotgun, a master fisherman with anything from a cane pole through a fly rod, and had a limitless capacity for good bourbon. The last-named item was about the only thing I could match him in.

After he retired, Heber took some part-time work as a clerk in a liquor store owned by Dan Graham, another old friend of ours.

Heber was on duty one night when a guy on crutches,

and already fairly well into his cups, came into the store and bought a pint of cheap whiskey. About 30 minutes later, he was back, this time minus one of the crutches.

"Friend," he said to Heber, "I seem to have misplaced one of my crutches since I was in here, and thought maybe I might have left it here. Have you seen anything of it?"

"Son," said Heber in that soft Mississippi drawl, "why don't you git you another pint of that stuff and throw that other crutch away?"

That is one of my favorite Heber Jones stories, but there are many others.

Heber and several of his cronies used to spend a lot of time sitting around in Pappy Bryan's poolroom, The Sportsman. One day Heber announced that he was tired of watching all those old men loafing around and had decided to take vagrancy warrants for everybody who didn't have a visible means of support.

But this time the late Hobson Gregory, a retired salesman whose wife was principal of an Albany elementary school, stopped old Heber cold.

"I got a visible means of support," declared Greg. "My wife. She works. She's visible."

At another time in the whiskey store, a guy came in and ordered a bottle of some sort of off-brand booze.

"We don't sell much of that," commented Heber. "Hardly ever anybody calls for it. What do you like about it?"

"Confidentially," said the customer in almost a whisper, "It works wonders with your sex life.'

"Really?" said Heber, snapping to full attention. "Is that a fact?"

"Sure is," replied the man. "Most amazing thing I ever saw. Works great with me all the time. Wouldn't be without it."

"Well, well," smiled Heber. "I sure wish I could sell you a bottle, but we just don't have any left."

"Whatta you mean you don't have any left? There's a whole shelf full right behind you!"

"I know," said Heber. "But I've just bought all that myself."

Heber once was held up while working in the liquor store. The guy, a white fellow who was sort of nervous, held a gun on Heber and demanded all the money in the cash drawer.

Heber dutifully emptied the money on the counter, and in his haste to gather it up, the man laid the pistol down between them. In an instant, Heber had the gun scooped up, pointed dead center at the bandit and was working the trigger with the speed of a Jim Hardy, a television-western hero of that time. Jim once drew and fired one shot and piled up a stack of bad guys big as an entire winter's supply of cordwood.

But all Heber got was a series of clicks. The gun, although fully loaded with .38 slugs, wouldn't fire. And on about the fourth click, the robber realized he was in a heap of trouble, abandoned the project and bailed out the front door in full panic flight, leaving money, gun and all behind.

"The dirty, lousy, lowdown sorry son of a female canine," Heber growled. "Too damn sorry to have a gun that would fire. If I'da knowed that, I'da killed him with my own gun which was right under the counter."

That was my friend Heber, always that true Southern gentleman. He was a good man, one of the best I ever knew, and I still miss his ever-ready wit and his true good fellowship. We need more like him.

*(Georgia columnist Poke McHenry also once worked briefly in a liquor store, but for some unexplained reason the arrangement was not entirely satisfactory with the proprietor.)*

# ARTIST-HISTORIAN HAS KEPT HER WIT, SENSE OF HUMOR

*This is all about a birthday party celebrating the 75th anniversary of the birth of a great and talented lady, Mildred Huie of St. Simons Island, Georgia.**

ST. SIMONS ISLAND, Georgia

My good friend Mildred Huie, the widely known and popular artist and historian, had a little to-do given for her by her children at her place on St. Simons Island recently in celebration [in 1980] of her 75th birthday, and I went over to join scores of others in paying proper homage to this unusual woman.

The children are son John, of Table Rock, N.C., and daughters Carlton, of Dallas, Georgia, and Mildred, of St. Simons. Mother Mildred had not seen them all together in 17 years.

A good time, naturally, was had by all, in the terminology of days gone by. And now comes a letter from Mildred in which she proves that she has certainly lost none of her sharp wit and great sense of humor. She also sent me a few of the pictures made at the party by Skipper Riggins, a commercial photographer on the island.

Here are excerpts from Mildred's letter:

"Dear Poke:

"Enclosed are some shots made on *my* day, which turned out to be *your* day — from the number of pictures you managed to push yourself into. Out of a hundred shots, you managed to get in 99. I was in a few, mostly from the back.

**Editor's note: At this time, Mildred Huie is into her 89th year and is still active as an artist, historian and community leader on St. Simons Island, where she has lived for many years.*

Not you. Cameras seem to automatically seek the handsome, as you often said. Not to mention the crowds that surrounded you for your autograph.

"Your handsome face and your Brooks Bros. clothes plus your journalistic abilities ranked you No. 1 at the picnic. However, I was so happy to see you and all the Albany (Georgia) crowd, swapping tales of our Albany days. I know you loved seeing all the Albany crowd. Did you know eight couples came down here when they heard you were to be here?

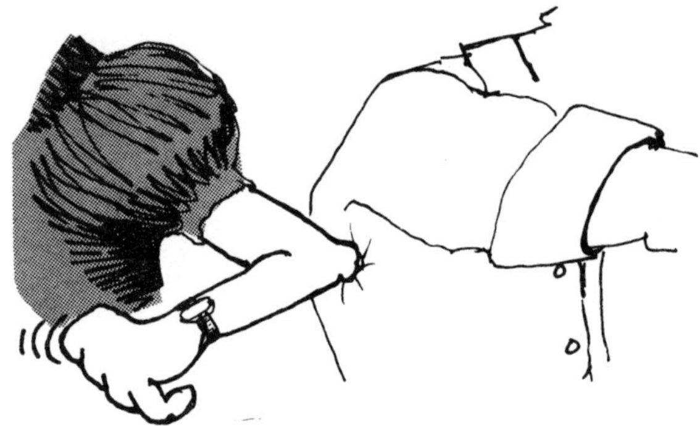

"It was a super day. I had slept with the Bible, praying for no rain, and it worked.

"We all enjoyed Bessie Jones and the Sea Island Singers (this group provided entertainment), and the food you brought was the big delight. Everybody wants your recipe for barbecued ribs and Brunswick stew and that special sauce of yours.

"Your fans were here en masse. That column of yours is the talk of these islands. You have no idea how many thousands look for your column.

"Most people can't believe you have lived through all those experiences in only 70 years.

"I hope you can come up soon and let us arrange some fishing outings for you. Right now, we keep the crab traps busy at Mildred's docks.

"John and Carlton will never forget what they learned 'journalistically' when you steered them with writing for the *Albany Herald*."

See what I mean about that sense of humor? Seventy

years, indeed! Well, she isn't too far off the mark, at that.

And all that stuff about Brooks Bros. clothes and signing autographs — ahem, we celebrities have to live up to our public's expectations. By the way, what is a Brooks Bros. clothes? And the last autograph I can remember signing was at the 1972 Major League All-Star Baseball Game in Atlanta, when some kid mistook me for Connie Mack, who had died 16 years earlier just a few days short of his 94th birthday.

But we had a lot of fun and it was good to be with the St. Simons people, and it is true that they had some mighty kind words about my barbecued ribs and sauce. One fellow, in fact, wanted to go get a few slabs and have me cook them on the spot. I pleaded other pressing engagements, fearful that I wouldn't be so lucky with the next batch.

One of these months, honestly, I am going to take a week or so and just laze around that Golden Isles area and see how much of the tradition, legend and lore I can absorb and possibly translate into deathless prose.

Mildred says she will gladly be my guide and tutor, and I'm sure I couldn't have a better one.

# THERE WAS NO RASSLIN', AND IT WAS VERY "TROOMATIC"

*Here's how dear old George, a harmless and innocent man, fell victim to what, for him, was a truly "troomatic" experience upon entering the place where the weekly "rasslin'" matches normally were held. It was enough to drive a man back to drink, it was.*

ST. MARYS RIVER

Somebody told me the other day that old George, an unforgettable acquaintance of years gone by, was dead, but I don't believe it. Old George was too unlucky to die.

George was one of those snake-bit creatures who go through life with misfortune seemingly forever dogging their heels. When George was in the Army, if he ever got at the head of the chow line, they began serving at the other end.

Once George won a new Buick at the American Legion's raffle, but got drunk celebrating his good luck and totaled the car on the way home the night he won it, breaking his leg in the process. He had a long record of shining hours of that type.

But just hearing about old George made me remember the last time I saw him, which must have been about 15 years ago. I dropped into a favorite oyster bar for a nightcap and found old George sitting at the end of the bar, pale and obviously badly shaken.

"Why, George!" I exclaimed. "I've never seen you so shook up! You look like a rattlesnake might have run up your britches leg. What's the matter?"

"Cap'n," said George, who called everybody "Cap'n" because he could never remember anybody's name. "Cap'n, hit wuz worse than that. Tonight I had me one of them trooly troomatic experiences, as them head shrinks would call it. It wuz troomatic, Cap'n, and I don't mean maybe."

"Well, tell me about it," I said.

"All right," said George. "Y'know tonight's Thursday, and that's the night of the rasslin' matches. And they ain't nuthin in this world I love more than the rasslin matches.

"What I do, every Thursday when I git off from work about 5 o'clock, is rush down here to the oyster bar and have me a few beers to git in the right mood for the rasslin'.

"Well, that's what I done today. I come down here and had five or six beers and left about a half-hour before they started — you know they have 'em right down the road apiece here at the Shriners' Hasan Temple — and I have just time to walk down there in plenty of time for the first match.

"Boy, I tell you I figgered this wuz really gonna be a good 'un tonight, cause they wuz cars backed up and parked along the road for three blocks on each side of the temple. 'Hot ziggety,' I thought, 'I'm gonna enjoy this 'un tonight.'

"I went into the foyer of the temple, reaching for my wallet, when a nice young feller standing there grinned at me and said, 'No sir — they ain't no charge tonight — go right on in.' 'Hot dang,' I thought, 'this is really something! Free, too!'

"Well, I noticed they wuz a heap o'folks standing around in there mighty dressed up, nuthin like the regular rasslin' crowd, but I didn't pay it too much mind. Then I got into the main arena, and they must have been two or three thousand folks millin' around in there. I never seen sich a mob for the rasslin' before. They wuz chairs set up all the way to the walls all around.

"About the time I set down in a chair next to the wall, I noticed that where the ring wuz supposed to be they wuz a platform with a bunch of dressed up folks settin' on it, and a speakin' place with a microphone and everything. I begin to think I wuz in the wrong place or had had a beer too many, so I decided to sidle on out."

"'Scuse me,' I said, as I started to git up outa my chair. Then I heard a loud 'SSSHHHHHHHHhhhh' of somebody shushing me, and looked around and there wuz a great big fat woman who smelled like a talcum powder factory and she wuz glarin' at me with about the fiercest look I ever seen.

"Well sir, Cap'n, that woman plumb locked me in that chair and pinned me to the wall with that look. I never seen sich a look. I wuz froze.

"So there I set. They begin to preach and pray and sing and shout and you don't know what all else, and there I had to set, in my dirty old work clothes and smelling like a wrecked beer truck, till the whole thing wuz over. Ever time I'd cut my eyes around, thinking to sneak out while that old biddy weren't looking, she'd be glaring at me harder than ever.

"It must have lasted for an hour and a half or so, but it seemed like a month to me. Why, Cap'n, they even passed around a collection plate sometime along in the proceedings and all I had to my name wuz a pair of five-dollar bills, and blamed if that old woman didn't plumb look me into giving up one of them! You never seen sich a look as she could put on a man. It wuz troomatic, I tell you.

"Them folks had plumb desecrated that temple, that's what they'd done. And I don't know if I'll ever be able to enjoy another rasslin' match. Troomatic, that's what it were, Cap'n."

It turned out old George had stumbled right into the middle of the opening night of the citywide Youth Crusades for Christ, which had preempted the "rasslin' matches" that week.

I'm sure that truly it was a "troomatic" experience for old George, bless his heart.

# Flying Catfish

*Never own up to anything, saith the Catfish, who always played the percentages. He also played a mean game of pool and was a wizard with a deck of cards... a true southern gentleman.*

ST. MARYS RIVER

The recent hijackings of American airliners, the first in several years, brought back some memories to me of the days when the practice first broke out and quickly became commonplace, at least for a while.

During those days of a dozen or so years back, my friend The Catfish, a sort of institution over at Albany, Georgia, had a lady friend in Valdosta (Georgia) and upon occasion hopped a plane in Albany and buzzed over to call on her. And sometimes upon these courting trips old Cat was not exactly the soberest person around, although not what one would call inebriated or anything like that.

On one such journey, old Cat boarded a small commuter-type commercial plane for a short hop to Valdosta, and scarcely had the flight gotten airborne before Cat made a remark at which a stewardess took umbrage. She snapped him off rather shortly, whereupon Cat, slightly miffed, muttered something to the effect that " She must think I'm some sort of a bum."

It was the wrong thing to say. Air flight crews' nerves being in the state they were as a result of hijackings, the stewardess heard "bum" loud and clear as "bomb," and the far-flung anti-hijacking machinery of the U.S. government went into action.

The pilot put the plane down in an emergency landing in Moultrie, slightly less than halfway to Valdosta, and when it rolled to a stop it was swarmed over by literally dozens of lawmen, from the FBI down to local police. The blissfully unaware Catfish was seized, clapped in irons, and whisked away before he could gather any idea of what was happening.

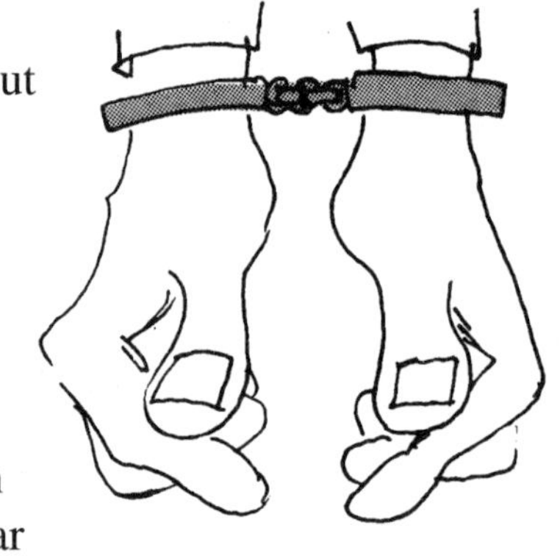

It was all straightened out eventually, but it took a couple of hours for the gendarmes to decide that Catfish was harmless and had no bomb or any intention of ever having one aboard an airplane or anyplace else. He was let off with a stern lecture or two and was darn near sobered by the whole thing.

Catfish was quite a character in those days. He probably never weighed much, if any, over 100 pounds, was a very sharp dresser, played one of the meanest games of pool in the territory, and could handle a deck of cards with true professionalism. He was a talented man, taking it all around.

One of Catfish's credos to live by was, "Never own up to anything."

"If I had stole a sawmill," he has said on many occasions, "had it in my back pocket and the whistle was blowing like hell, I'd swear I didn't know a dang thing about it."

His idea was that if you never admitted to anything it put the burden of proof on the other side, and more than half the time the other side couldn't prove anything. The Cat knew the percentages and played them to the limit, whatever the competition.

Once the Cat was involved in a court proceeding of some sort concerning minor infractions of the law (Cat was probably there as a witness) and the judge at one point asked Cat what exactly did he do with his time, meaning what did he do for a living. "Judge, your honor, sir," replied the Cat. "I don't do anything, for fear I'll do something wrong."

Never admit anything, as he always said.

Considering all these hijackers, I think they ought to fix a trapdoor in every plane and when some thug tries the hijack, maneuver him over the trapdoor, push a button and drop him 30,000 feet into the nearest cesspool.

Did you hear the story about the plane on route to Miami when a man entered the cockpit, put a pistol to the pilots head and said "Take me to Miami!"

"You don't need the gun, friend," the pilot said. "We're already going to Miami."

"Yeah, I know," said the man. "Three times, yet, I been going to Miami before, now this time take me to Miami!"

*(Columnist Poke McHenry says that if he was a judge he'd give every airline hijacker 30 days in the electric chair.)*

# The High Cost of Ego

*This mostly true story (embellished only a little, in keeping with the author's reputation as an accomplished practitioner of hyperbole) was written nearly half a century ago, many years before its author, Vic Smith, became "Poke McHenry." Officially, that is. Poke has always lurked inside Vic's unique brain. Poke escaped, to the public's delight, only after Vic took a copy-editing job in 1974 with the Florida Times-Union newspaper of Jacksonville.*

With the passing of the linotype machine from the newspaper scene went some of the truly unsung heroes of this business — the legion of walking legends known as "operators." The designation referred to their "trade," but in truth many of them were operators in the more sophisticated sense of the word. Sophisticated in this case meaning the natural ability and fine-honed talent for cadging a drink with remarkable tact and finesse. And for spotting naive targets to practice on.

I have known a great many of these colorful characters over the years, and almost to a man they had enough idiosyncrasies and eccentricities to float the psychiatry wing of a major hospital. Many of them were heavy boozers, and the one I shall remember longest was old Herman, who probably, over the years, guzzled more beer for less cost than any of them.

In those days I was a young reporter convinced beyond any shadow of a doubt that I was the greatest writer the world had ever known.

I had, admittedly, had very little success in having anyone share this opinion, due largely to a succession of unfeeling, cynical clods who were obtaining money under false pretenses by calling themselves editors. I was undaunted, however, realizing that these ignoramuses lacked even the basic intelligence to recognize real talent.

Some day, surely, my day would come — and after my

fourth or fifth Pulitzer Prize and when Collier's and Saturday Evening Post and all the other big dealers were tossing millions into the kitty in frantic bidding for my exclusive services, these two-bit editors would blush with shame. Inwardly, of course. Outwardly they'd go around bragging to everybody that I'd never have amounted to anything without the benefit of their judicious training

It was shortly after I had gone to work on a small afternoon daily in the Deep South when I met old Herman.

About quitting time one afternoon, this amiable chap hesitantly walked up to my desk and held out a gnarled hand. He had a friendly, cherubic face, with eyes that sort of crinkled at you from beneath a mop of mostly gray hair, and a beguiling smile that twinkled around his mouth corners like a flickering neon light. He was short of stature, a bit stocky of build and could have been anything from 40 to 60 years old.

"You don't know me, Mr. Smith, and I reckon I shouldn't bother you — I'm just old Herman the linotype operator — but I just had to come up and tell you that I read the stories you've been writing and you certainly have a great deal of exceptional talent," he said. "I say without hesitation that you are the finest young writer this paper has had in the 20 years I've been here. Just wanted you to know, they aren't going to be able to keep you down here very long."

Ah, I thought, here at last is one of God's noblemen. A menial creature, perhaps, but endowed with true appreciation of the finer things. A man with couth and culture. Low though his station in life might be, he clearly was a man of keen discernment and high intelligence.

"Why, I'm happy to meet you, Mr. Herman," I said, springing up to shake his hand. "You are indeed a gentleman. May I buy you a beer, while we discuss this further?"

"Well, I'd be proud and honored to join you, Mr. Smith, if...er...you don't feel it would be demeaning to you," said Herman.

"Nonsense!" I cried, "Come on, let's go!"

Well into the night, Herman plied me with flattery and I plied both of us with beer. And this went on almost on a daily basis for a month or so — and by that time I had already

galloped past such hacks as Kipling, London, Fitzgerald, Hemingway, Faulkner, Dickens and Poe, and was hard on the heels of Shakespeare. And Herman had gulped huge chunks of my never-too-robust paycheck.

Then one day, about a week after the paper had hired another novice by name of Tyro Greenhorn (or something equally suitable) the city editor, several grizzled reporters and I were sitting about the newsroom aimlessly gabbing when the subject of old Herman came up.

"Now there," I said, "is a really remarkable man, a man of unusual brilliance and acumen, a man…"

Somebody snickered. Somebody else giggled. Somebody else laughed out loud, and soon the place was rocking with wall-to-wall guffaws.

"What's so infernal funny?" I demanded. "What…"

"Smith," said the city editor, tears rolling down his oafish cheeks, "we've been watching old Herman milk you for a month now, and I must say you're dumber than most of your predecessors, who caught on a lot quicker."

"What!" I roared, "you mean…"

"Wait!" said the city editor, pointing across the room, where old Herman was hesitantly approaching Greenhorn's desk.

"You don't know me, Mr. Greenhorn, and I reckon I shouldn't bother you — I'm just old Herman the…" Herman was saying, hand outstretched

Yessir, Old Herman was truly an operator. In the cadgingest sense of the word. And I was a sucker, as usual.

# On Divorce

*When Poke was still on the copy desk as an editor for the Florida Times-Union of Jacksonville, he started his "Poke McHenry" columns as a refreshing diversion. His boss at that time, and his close friend, was T-U night editor Mark Wren, long since retired. When this column reached the news desk, Mark put this headline on it: "Woe unto he whose wife readeth this." You'll understand why when you read it.*

ST. MARYS RIVER

Reading about Senator Herman Talmadge's recent troubles, including his divorce settlement with wife Betty, got me to thinking about how much trouble married couples seem to be having trying to get along these days. I note where it cost old Herman $150,000 and his Lovejoy farm, plus an additional 100 acres, to rid himself of that marriage. Pretty costly, but it could have been worse — he could have been married to Jackie O.

When I was a boy growing up there was very little of that divorce business going on, but now it seems to run in a lot of families. I remember one of my daddy's brothers had some trouble with his wife of 20 years, and she wouldn't let him come to the house. He protested rather vigorously, and she actually had him thrown into jail. It was the most scandalous thing that had ever happened in the family. Relatives on both sides of the squabble pitched in and quickly patched up the thing, and the couple went back together. Now in their 80s, they are still together and apparently living happily.

Back in the early days of my marriage, things didn't always go so well, either. Once, in a fit of frustration, I composed the following little Biblical-language-style piece:

Woe unto he who goeth into marriage, for great is the misery thereof.

Yea, verily, he becometh enslaved forever and haveth no freedom, yea, none forevermore. He becometh the bedeviled tool of the whim of the woman, a vicious and vindictive creature without understanding and lacking charity and tolerance in her innermost heart.

Yea, no more shall he enjoy the carefree pleasure of a glass of beer or a game of pool or a joust at poker, lest he be subject to the wrath to come. Yea, even though he cometh home sober day after day and night after night, and although he spilleth the full contents of his purse faithfully into her clutching hands, and although he behaveth himself well at all times and his conduct remaineth forever above reproach (or at least above a roach), yet even then will she suffer him not to have peace.

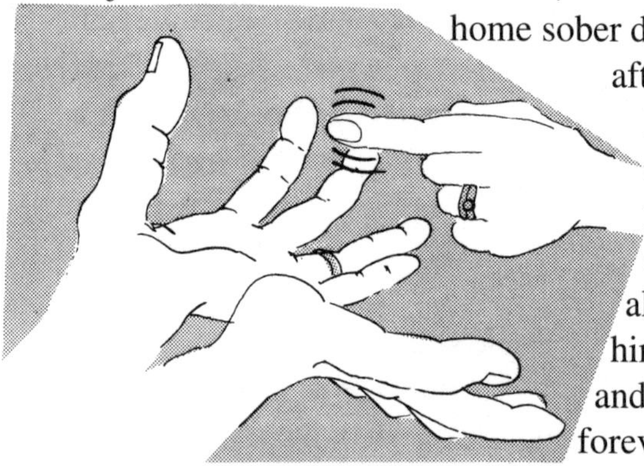

Verily I say unto you, she will drive him without surcease and without end. His "spare time" shall be filled to the uttermost with the mowing of the lawn, the trimming of the shrubbery, the raking of the leaves, the washing of the windows, the painting of the woodwork, the repairing of the plumbing, the digging of the flower bed, the weeding of the garden plot, and lo untold other demeaning drudgery, days without end.

And if he perchance seek diversion and desireth to play golf, or go fishing, or stroll the fields with dog and gun, or otherwise relax from the debilitating rigors imposed upon him by his tortuous existence, doth she have sympathy with him and understandeth his needs and cooperateth in his restorative pursuits?

Nay, verily, I say unto you she hath no compassion in her heart; nay, on the contrary, great are the lamentations from his goodwife.

She berateth him as a sluggard and a drone, and chargeth him with the grievous offense of deserting hearth and home and children for the folly of idleness and nonsense; yea, she accuseth him of having no love for her, she bursteth into tears, and waileth loud and long, and cannot be comforted — yea, even though he ceaseth and desisteth in the pursuit of his plans, and doth offer the most humble and abject apologies, and even though he grovel at her feet, yet will she lift her nose into the air, and walk about with the air of a mortally injured martyr. She will not permit him to touch her, neither will she offer kind words, nor any kind of solace, until she bewildereth him beyond measure, and causeth him to go mad with frustration.

She driveth him to an early grave, and then bemoaneth him with grief inconsolable. Yea, when he is dead and turned to dust, then doth she extol his virtues to her neighbors, and praise his memory, and say all manner of good things about him, and speak how fine a helpmate was he, and how much she did love, cherish, honor and obey him, and make him comfortable in his lifetime.

Yea, verily, woe unto he who goeth into marriage.

*(Poke McHenry has always contended that the chief cause of divorce is marriage.)**

**Editor's note: Poke himself was married to Sarah Katherine Biggers Smith for over 50 years, and would remain her loving husband were she still alive.*

# WOULD YOU BE MY VALENTINE? OR YOU OR YOU OR YOU?

*The misery of many unrequited loves in the life of a small boy are recalled at Valentine's Day time. And how he always sneaked a valentine to himself in the box, so he'd never be skunked.*

ST. MARYS RIVER

It has been so long since I thought about any such thing that I never had any idea today was Valentine's Day until I was asked by the editors if I could write something about the special day for sweethearts.

Well, if I could I'd send a valentine to every one of my women readers, for they are certainly all sweethearts. So happy Valentine's Day, girls, one and all!

Valentine's Day was a big thing at grammar school in Fitzgerald, Georgia, in the distant past when I was a little lad. It was a measure of popularity in each elementary class, with the boys and girls who got the most valentines considered a cut above the rest of us. On a good year I might get three, including the one I sneaked in to myself just to ensure that I didn't get skunked.

I'd always manage to scrounge up enough valentines to send to the prettiest girls in the class, although it never seemed to get me anywhere. Usually some rich punk kid would gain their favor with some elaborate production from the drugstore costing as much as 15 cents, even. Most of us made our own, or bought the three-for-a-penny kind. Of course, it was hard to part with a penny for a valentine when you could get a sizable stick of peanut-butter candy with it. Those girls never knew what sacrifices I made, in vain, For them.

Once I remember I sent a valentine to a girl named Mozelle Pigford, and in it I wrote this verse I had read somewhere:

"If you're as sweet as you're good-looking,
"I'll do the plowing if you'll do the cooking."

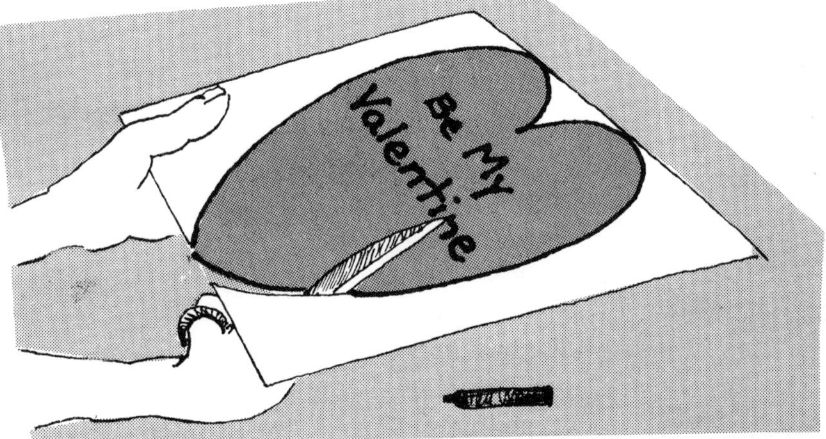


She considered it a proposal of marriage, which I guess in fact it was, and was so tickled with the thing she showed it to the everybody in school and I took an unmerciful riding for months afterward. Got into three or four rousing good fights over the thing, though, which was some compensation. And now that I think of it, I wonder whatever happened to Mozelle?

In those days I was constantly falling in and out of love, and the strangest situation kept prevailing to keep me constantly confounded and frustrated and all my great loves unrequited. What would happen is, I would fall for some little gal like a drunk missing the top doorstep. Invariably, she would also be madly in love, but with some freckle-faced jerk or other not worthy of kissing her shoe heels, particularly while she was wearing them.

Gradually I would survive the agony and my passion would cool, and just as sure as it did my former love would develop a most ardent desire for me. By that time, however, I was off at a gallop after some other little skirt who was just as busy chasing some other freckle-faced jerk.

That happened to me with Gussie Beall, Geraldine Lester, Elizabeth Channel, and Leoress Haskins, four lovelies I can remember offhand, and there were probably others. Each of those gals fell in love with me after I had suffered through an undying love for them while they snubbed me for less worthy fellows. Cads they were, actually. The fellows, not the girls.

So when Gussie would finally decide she loved me I would be panting mightily and futilely after Geraldine, and so forth on and on. I don't recall I ever had a grammar school sweetheart at the same time she had me.

I'll never forget that in the deepest midst of my love for Leoress, who held me at all times in utmost contempt, there came about an incident that brightened the whole world for me.

This was at a Halloween carnival at the school, and a crowd of us was jammed in front of some steps outside the building. Leoress was about two rows of sardines behind me, when somebody up ahead began pushing.

When the domino effect reached her, she stretched forth her heavenly little hand and delivered herself of a slap against my cheek that would have rocked Jack Dempsey.

"Stop pushing!" she snarled.

"Hallelujah!" I said, rolling my teary eyes skyward. "Hallelujah! She noticed me!"

But alas, it didn't mean a thing. She still wouldn't look at me until long after I had lost all interest in her. The course of true love certainly never ran true for me in those days, forsooth.

But things worked out for the best, I'm sure. Probably all those gals grew up and married millionaires, or made millions on their own — and just look what would have happened to any one of them if she'd hooked her life to old Poke's.

And so, a happy Valentine's Day not only to my lady readers, but to all who hold to sentimental things.

# Three Long Lost Loves are Located by Poke

*Poke discovers the joys, along with some sadness, of renewing old acquaintances with sweethearts of bygone days.* He remembers how delighted he was when one of the girls finally noticed him by belting him on the jaw.*

ST. MARYS RIVER

This might be entitled "childhood revisited," or what happened to those five lost loves of my Fitzgerald, Georgia, boyhood that I wrote about in a Valentine's Day column.

I recalled with what ardor I panted (not at the same time, of course) after Geraldine Lester, Gussie Beall, Leoress Haskins, Elizabeth Channell and Mozelle Pigford, never imagining that I would run across any of them again — especially since the last time I had any contact with any of them was in about 1940.

But to my amazement, on the day the column came out, Leoress called me from her home on Jekyll Island, Georgia. Hers was a most welcome voice from the past, and we had a pleasant reunion via telephone.

This prompted me to try to locate the others and,

** Editor's note: This is a follow up column to the one you just read; that is, if you are reading this book in sequential page number order. If not, go back one and then read this.*

although it took about six months, I am happy to report that I have had great reminiscing sessions with the three that are still among us. Mozelle and Elizabeth both died of cancer, I was told, several years ago.

Geraldine lives in Quanty Hill, California,* about 70 miles northeast of Los Angeles, where her husband, John F. Butler, is an engineer with United Technologies. He commutes daily by car.

Leoress married Billy Brewer,** a member of the 1931 graduating class at Fitzgerald High School, the school's championship football team of 1930, and a successful druggist.

Gussie is married to John Pace, and they have a gorgeous home on a portion of the thousand or so acres they own at Doctor's Lake at Orange Park, Florida, a bedroom community 15 miles south of Jacksonville.

I wrote in the Valentine's Day column that the girls probably grew up to become or marry millionaires. Now, while that may not necessarily be true, it is not too far off the mark. Certainly they did better than old Poke, who when referred to as a "poor newspaperman" tells folks not to be redundant, that "newspaperman" is sufficient.

I can also say that, while the girls do not look exactly as they did 45 years ago, all three are still considerably better looking than old Poke. I would even go so far as to say the appearance gap is indeed a great deal wider than it used to be.

When one of my daughters asked her mother if she wasn't upset about me chasing around trying to revive old friendships with these lovely lasses of long ago, my wife said she wasn't the least bit concerned.

"Hah!" she said. "I'll bet they don't even know he eats tripe."

Leoress, who so long ago made me deliriously happy (hooray! she finally recognized me!) by taking first notice of me through the means of a wallop to the jawbone, married Billy in 1938 and he worked a year or so at Central Pharmacy in Fitzgerald before World War II, when he went into the

**Editor's note: Geraldine has since also died of cancer.*
*** Leoress and Billy are both deceased.*

Navy. After the war they settled in Atlanta, where at one time they owned five neighborhood drugstores.

They have been living right next to Millionaire Row on Jekyll for seven years, and Billy spends a lot of his time now on the golf course. Leoress, when the spirit moves her, works a tad in a gift shop, but mostly they take life easy.

Her grandfather, L.M. McDuffie, and uncle, R.M. McDuffie, used to operate the Pig Trail Inn in Fitzgerald, and they served up some of the finest 5¢ hamburgers in the world, along with probably the first pit barbecue offered in that area.

The nickel hamburger was one of the greatest things about the good old days.

I first knew Gussie in the sixth grade at Fitzgerald's Second Ward School, when her mother came from neighboring Wilcox County to teach that grade. I remember her mother fondly as one of the best and sweetest teachers I had. She lived into her 90s.

Gussie's husband was born in Pensacola, Florida, and was a third- or fourth-generation turpentine maker. He was hauling down all of $75 a month when he and Gussie married in 1942, so obviously he has come a long way since then. He first became a sort of self-made chemist, with considerable success, and later got into silver and gold mining in Santo Domingo and Honduras.

(While chatting with Gussie in her living room, I furtively checked out the carpets in case there were any stray nuggets scattered about, but had no luck.)

Gussie and John have four boys and four girls, pretty widely scattered. The youngest two boys, Worth and Hardy, are students in the University of Capetown, South Africa, and plan to make South Africa their home, Gussie said. One of the girls, Susan, who looks a great deal like her mother did as a girl, is living with her parents temporarily.**

Gussie is active in garden club circles, and her pet project this year is acquainting people with wildflowers. Their

**Editor's note: Susan still ives at Pace Island. Worth and Hardy and brother Chris now live in Hawaii. Brother John lives in Georgia. Sisters Ann and Elizabeth now live in Texas and Augusta resides in Fort Lauderdale.*

place abounds with natural floral beauty, along with countless birds and small animals. A visit to that area makes a fellow want to pitch a tent and hang around for a few years or so.

Geraldine once had strong ties to Jacksonville. She went there in 1940 and worked throughout the war years, for a spell with the King Edward cigar folks and for a long time with the Duval County (Jacksonville) Tuberculosis Association. She used to write press releases for the association and deliver them to the major Jacksonville newspaper, the Florida Times-Union, where she struck up an acquaintance with former T-U golf writer Frank Matey, who occasionally would whisk her to St. Augustine on his motorcycle for some sort of sports event.

I talked with her at length in Fitzgerald, where she spent the month of June with her semi-invalid mother, the fine lady who made me a professional fighter a half-century ago by paying me 15 cents to beat up a boy who was pestering her daughters.

Geraldine has two daughters, Scarlett, 24, and Shannon, 20.* Both work at a hospital in Palmdale, California, quite near their parents, and are frequent visitors. Scarlett got her name when Geraldine, still in high school, saw the Atlanta premiere of Gone with the Wind and vowed right then that if she ever had a daughter her name would be "Scarlett."*

Renewing these old friendships and reminiscing about the old school days was a real pleasure. Folks ought to do more of that sort of thing.

** Editor's note: Scarlett now lives in Tennessee and younger sister Shannon lives in the Quality Hill, California, home where Geraldine died.*

# HAPPY BIRTHDAY

*In this column, Poke reprints a birthday greeting from his daughter Vicki on the observance of the 58th anniversary of his date of birth, which was October 29, 1919. Incidentally, 1919 was the Chinese Year of the Sheep, whatever that means. At any rate, we think you'll appreciate the effort that went into this brilliant piece of poetry.*

ST. MARYS RIVER

A few days ago I had another birthday, and I'll tell you what: considering the alternative, I'm downright happy to be 59 years old.

But what it did was make me remember a birthday card I got a year ago from one of my daughters, who now lives in Kansas City, Missouri.

She still is trustworthy because she won't be 30 until next April.*

What she did, she explained, was dream up 58 reasons in the form of a poem (at least I think its a form of poetry, although I am something short of an expert in that field.)

I thought it was so good I've been trying to think of an excuse to share it with other folks. I got the thing not long after I started writing this column, and I hope you enjoy it as much as I did:

"You are:

Handsome, charming, debonair
Toothless, ruthless, without much hair
Hard-working, lazy, full of life
Delightful, crazy, and have a fine wife

***Editor's note: The "brilliant" poet here referred to is the editor of this book, and no longer lives in KC, although it was a great place. As you might imagine, I'm no longer 30 years old, either, but you'd never be able to tell it!***

Intelligent, irreverent, not too bright
Nifty, thrifty, full of fight
Old-fangled, dangled, a card-playing sharpy
Redundant, abundant, the male of the harpy

A swearer, peace-bearer, joyful and smart
A big wheel, a real heel with a pretty soft heart
Good for a laugh or a shoulder to cry on
Always come up with enough to get by on

Neglecting, inspecting, sometimes quite nice
Always around with a word of advice
Clean, mean, loving and true
Dirty, flirty and built like a gnu

Spunky, flunky, a renegade
The leader of the Light Brigade
Cultured and dependable
Vital (not expendable)

A sparker, remarker, uncommon (thank God)
My father, my friend, the salt of the sod!"

Now dreaming all that up must have taken quite a bit of time and mental effort, since there are 57 or 58 descriptive words or phrases in it (one for each year of my life) all talking about me. I thought it was just about the nicest birthday greeting I've ever had from anybody.

Actually, I'd rather just ignore these birthdays, but when they get to coming around about three times a year — or so it seems — they get here so often one can't ignore them.

The birthday of one of my old newspaper buddies of years ago was on December 25, Christmas Day.

He was always complaining that he never got any birthday presents, since people just let one gift suffice for both days.

So one Christmas I bought him a pair of socks and had them gift wrapped in separate boxes, labeling one sock "Happy Birthday" and the other "Merry Christmas."

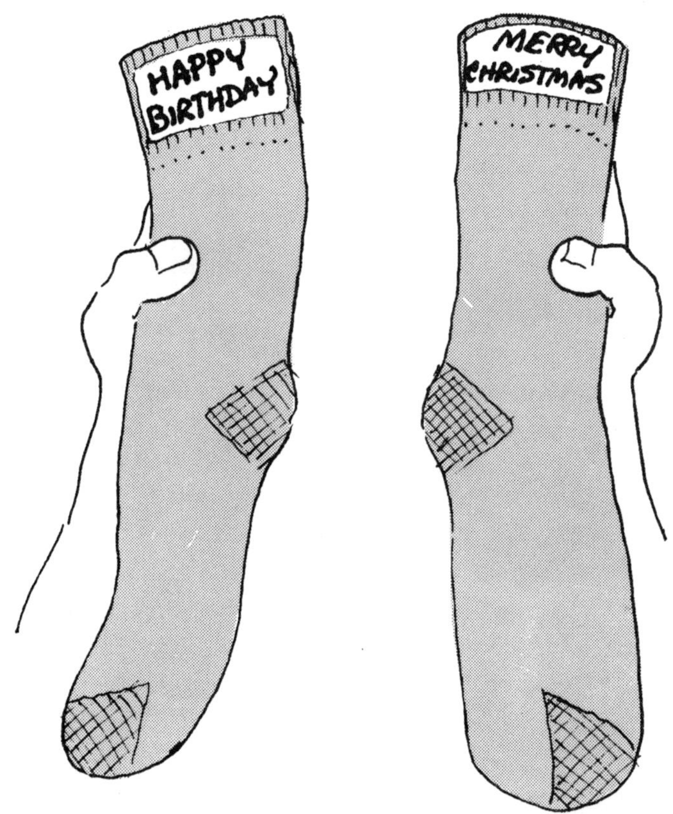


He didn't think it was so funny, but he didn't spurn the socks, either.

*(Poke says for everybody to cheer up — remember, if you weren't as old as you are you'd be dead. Everybody would like to stay at age 18, of course, but unfortunately the only way to do that is die at age 18. If you do that, you're guaranteed never to get any older. And you'll probably miss a lot of fun, too.)*

# A Lost Love...

*This 1978 column is a faithful recording of the shortest-lived romance in the annals of old Poke's many escapades with the fair sex, and the reason this great romance was beheaded so quickly and this great love unrequited, on both sides, so abruptly. Ah, it was indeed a tragedy of unparalleled magnitude. A magnificent example of the adage that the course of true love never runs smoothly, or something like that. But sometimes it does run quite fast, as you'll see here.*

FOLKSTON, Georgia

I used to come through this town every time I went on one of those fish-truck trips with my late uncle, the one I told you about in a recent column wherein I promised another tale or two from those memorable days.* This is another of those experiences from 40-odd years ago, when Folkston was different (but not by much) from what it is today.

This is a tale of lost love, or unfound-in-the-first-place love or something on that order — or disorder.

That uncle of mine was a great one to play jokes on people. Nothing harmful, but he'd rather get a laugh on somebody than make a profit selling mullet. It might be added that usually he got more laughs than he made money on mullet, too.

On this particular trip, we'd been all the way down the east coast of Florida to Vero Beach and Sebastian, had our load of mullet, croakers, trout and various other species and had gotten back to the vicinity of Jacksonville, where we were going to eat supper and possibly spend the night, since it had been a weary day.

Jacksonville, incidentally, had some good eating places

**Editor's note: Okay, you caught us. You haven't read about Poke's uncle and the first "truck trip" yet, at least not in this book. Keep looking for it though, I can't remember if we axed it or left it in. If you don't find it on later pages, buy the next book.*

in those days — good being defined broadly as cheap. For instance, at National Lunch you could get a breakfast of two eggs, bacon, grits, toast and coffee for 15¢. That made National Lunch a mighty good eating place.

Coming back, my uncle told me of a place he liked very much. It was somewhere along U.S. 1 in the Jacksonville vicinity, and he called it "Phillips Camp," as best I remember. Maybe some of you old-timers can recall it and tell me just where it was.

Anyway, it was a truck stop with a restaurant and some cabins in the back, where a fellow could get good sleeping (and probably other) accommodations. Good in this case also being interpreted as cheap.

En route to Phillips, my uncle told me of a beautiful young girl who was a waitress there, and hinted strongly that she might be more than a little interested in me, since he had been telling her what a sterling character I was and all that rot. He had me rearing at the reins to get there and have a look at this peach.

"But there's only one thing wrong," he said. "She was married to a big and mean fellow, and although they are separated, he comes in once in awhile, and he is still awfully jealous of her. Always beating up on anybody he catches looking slantwise at her."

"He's of no consequence to me," I assured my uncle. "Bring him on. No way he's gonna scare me off."

"All right," said the uncle. "But if he does come in while we're there, I'll try to warn you."

"No sweat," I said, exuding bravado. "I can handle him."

Well, we got into the place, and I met the girl, and she was indeed even more than he had said. Perfectly gorgeous pink complexion, raven hair, shining green-blue eyes, lips that would have turned vinegar into nectar, teeth that should have been in a Colgate ad, and a figure half of Hollywood's most glamorous would have envied.

In three seconds flat (the time it took me to size her up from hair to toenail), I was desperately in love with her, and she seemed every bit as sweet as she was beautiful. We were sitting in a booth doing some billing and cooing and getting along famously when suddenly my uncle was jabbing me in the ribs and hissing "There he is! Coming through the front door now! See him?"

Well sir, if you've ever seen a nightmare walking, it was that guy. He was about 6-3, must have weighed 250 pounds, had eyebrows like John L. Lewis, a shock of thick black hair, and a set of whiskers that would have made a boar hog feel like a cashmere sweater. He was wearing bib overalls and what looked to be a dirty BVD undershirt and was as barefoot, as grandma used to say, as a yard dog.

I took one look at him and decided I'd rather tangle with a pack of werewolves in a dark alley full of broken Coke bottles than to give him any lip, let alone trouble. All of a sudden I was completely out of love and nerve, and was ready to sneak out the nearest exit and tear out for the Georgia side.

"Let's get out of here," I said, frantically grabbing my uncle's arm and dragging him out of the booth. "Come on, hurry! Let's go!"

I barely said good-by to the little girl, who looked completely bewildered and more than a little lost at my sudden change of attitude and hurry to scram.

"What… what's wrong?" she said, "why are you…"

"Got to go," I said. "Maybe I'll see you later sometime…"

Back in the truck and rolling homeward, nothing was said for a few miles, then that dastardly uncle began to giggle. Then chuckle. Finally guffaw.

"What's so ding-danged funny?" I growled.

"Hoo hoo… HAW HAW… oooh, oh me… Whaw whaw haw…You know…har har hoo hoo HAW HAW…what?" That little girl ain't never BEEN married! I just told you that and waited…oh, hoo hoo hoo…until the ugliest character I could expect walked in, then…HAW HAW…"

Why I let him live, I'll never know.

Anyway, that was my uncle for you. Always playing a joke on somebody, and I'll admit I was pretty gullible in those days. Still am, mostly. Also, that was the end of my romance with the little girl at Phillips Camp. I went back there several times afterward, but never saw her again.

And that's why, as said at the beginning, this is a tale of lost love, or something akin to it.

*(Poke McHenry has always had exceptional success with the ladies. He arouses their motherly instinct.)*

# "Clark" McHenry Grows a Mustache

*Away from the office for a couple of weeks, Poke grows what he thinks, with modest pride, makes him a spittin' image of Clark Gable, the famous mustachioed movie actor. Alas, one of his contemporaries cruelly tells Poke he looks like the back end of a rat. Had no couth at all, that boorish clod.*

ST. MARYS RIVER

In the post-Christmas and early January doldrums, when the fish weren't biting and there was nothing much to do, I took a few days off from almost everything and, just to be different, I guess, decided to grow myself a mustache. I think I figured that the more of my mug I covered up, the better I'd look. Or rather, the less ugly I'd be.

It created quite a stir the first time I showed up in the Jacksonville, Florida, Times-Union newsroom with the brushy upper lip. Some of the comments were caustic, some clever and some unprintable.

Reporter Pat Yack took a gaze at the thing in its embryonic stages and said it reminded him of what he said was a true story concerning a very young preacher and his first sermon at his first church. The young man was so immature-appearing he decided that a mustache would make him look older, so he attempted to sprout one. Well, after his first sermon, which was a rousing success, he was accepting congratulations from parishioners when an elderly member, leaning heavily on a cane, came up and complimented the young man.

"Thank you, sir," said the preacher, "By the by, what do you think of my mustache?"

Peering closely at the young man's face, the old man muttered: "Confidentially, it looks like the back end of a rat."

So much for what Yack thinks.

Judy Wells Martin, who puts all those funny stories in her Jacksonville *Florida Times-Union* column, allowed as how I looked a mite like Adolf Hitler at first, but got a bit more respectable after another week or so of growth.

Columnist Ken Cruickshank strolled by, did a double take, then mumbled something about the unfairness of life.

"You turkey," he growled. "You get a better mustache accidentally in two weeks than I can with years of cultivation and tender loving care."

Women's editor Wini Rider didn't like it, saying she loved Poke just the way he was. Political editor Hank Drane took one look at it and shaved his off, as did editorial assistant Bobby Smith. Other comments on the new look of Poke ran the gamut from "distinguished" to "disgusting," and just about all intermediate stops between.

Drew Brunson of the layout desk (a man of exceptionally good taste, incidentally) said it looks very good, greatly enhancing Poke's naturally dignified and intelligent appearance. Drew wants (besides a raise) me to go all the way and grow a beard, too — possibly because Drew is the most hirsute character around the paper, with a beard and mustache that would make Blackbeard look like a fuzzy-cheeked lad, and wants some company.

I might just do that, too, especially if Drew insists, in view of the fact that he not only is big enough to arm-wrestle grizzly bears but is a karate expert, too. I seldom dispute anything with fellows like that.

If I did grow a beard I'd probably be the spittin' image of Rutherford B. Hayes, one of my favorite presidents.

This is not my first mustache. A few years back (about 40-odd, come to think of it) I grew one as an indirect result of a bird hunt. While stomping around busting quail out of thickets,

I acquired a horrendous case of poison oak.

It got all over my face, swelled one of my eyes completely shut and reduced the other to a mere slit, and for about three weeks my map was too tender to shave, although the condition had done nothing to deter the whisker proliferation.

One day I strolled by old Charlie Ivemeyer's barber shop in Fitzgerald, Georgia, and when Charlie got a look at my face he collared me and plunked me in a barber chair.

"I'm gonna shave you for nothin' to keep from having to look at that ugly mess," he said. He did, and between us we decided to keep the mustache, which Charlie trimmed up right neat-like, and through judicious use of lampblack in the bare spots I managed to come off looking really sharp.

With my $2 sport coat from Bryant's Secondhand Store, open-throated sports shirt and hair slicked down with Vaseline hair tonic, I was sure I was a dead ringer for Clark Gable.

Oddly enough, however, I could never make any of the local belles cognizant of that obvious fact. One of them (a vapor-headed goose destined to become a slattern, if I ever saw one) did go so far as to say that "Yes, you do look like what some guy said about Clark Gable's ears — you look like a Model A roadster coming down the road with both doors wide open."

Uncouth female clods, the lot of them. If I could have gotten to Hollywood I would have been appreciated.

After a few weeks, my scraggly appurtenance seemingly would grow in only the areas directly beneath my nostrils, where the long hairs swung outward and then back together near the bottom lip in an almost-perfect parenthesis, giving me the general appearance of going around with a ring of hair coming out of my nose.

This sad fact, coupled with my inability to convince those tasteless girls I was Clark Gable, led me to abandon my teen-age mustache project. The lip stayed mostly bare or stubbly until a few weeks ago, and I don't know how long I'm going to put up with this one.*

**Editor's note: Poke still has his mustache. He says the ladies think that kissing a man without a mustache is like trying to eat an egg without salt.*

# Stomp-Down Sensation or 'A No-No'?

*A sampling of what readers thought about Poke's venture into the realm of mustache-growers. Some thought it befitting the occupant of palace or penthouse, while others considered it more proper for a pig-sty or an outhouse. Poke liked it because it covered at least a little bit of his mug.*

ST. MARYS RIVER

Sufficient time having elapsed since our announcement of Poke's mustache, it is now appropriate to take note of what reader reaction has been. So far as I can tell it is running about 3-1 in favor of my keeping the brush, although those opposed are rather vehemently so, for the most part.

Let's look at some of the comments:

"Dear Distinguished or Disgusting:

We good ole boys up here in Brunswick have taken a vote and think that Poke looks like a Pekingese. We believe that Gable 'touch' was much more attractive and find it hard to fathom how one of our South Georgia damsels could reject such a stunning countenance. Poke should at least let the folks know what his secret for prolific hair growth on the upper lip is. It should be noted that three dozen oysters a day were unavailable in Fitzgerald, Georgia, in his Gable Era. I am anxiously awaiting a follow-up story concerning this juicy item."

Bill

That one is from Dr. Bill Disque, an old oyster-eating buddy of mine, and he's certainly right about there being no oysters in Fitzgerald in my "Gable Era." I don't know the secret of growing a healthy mustache, unless perhaps a good grade of hops and malt in sufficient quantities and appropriate measures, applied judicially and with the right regularity, may be the best fertilizer.

Here's one from Jo Ann Dunaway of Jacksonville:

"Why, Poke, that new mustache is a stomp-down sensation! Never let a razor sully its gloriously hirsute grandeur!... You see, the new face foliage not only gives you an aura of masculine beauty, it bespeaks trustworthiness, a fine and rare commodity which we all admire. But now let's don't go for 'overkill' by growing a beard. For one thing, it would definitely hide two of your finest attributes — those dimples! Don't you know that legions of ladies are weak-kneed pushovers when it comes to dimples?"

Well, Jo Ann, my reaction to that is simply "Wow!"

On the other hand, look at this one, from a reader who simply clipped the "Clark Gable" Poke and the recent mustachioed photo and mailed them in with the stern admonition, in red ink and capital letters, "TAKE IT OFF!"

Mrs. Jack Whitney of Hawthorne also sent clippings, one of the regular Poke picture that runs with the column and the other with the new mustache. "Couldn't be handsomer" was her comment on the regular picture and "a no-no" for the mustache.

"Take it off, Poke," Mrs. Whitney wrote. "Now honestly, which do you think looks the best? You know it is the one without, and please, no beard! Why cover up that handsome face?"

Ahem, a most convincing argument for shaving the mustache, that. Creates a regular standoff with Jo Ann, what?

Read on:

"Poke, I really like your new look! Keep the mustache!"

Dottie Clark, Jacksonville.

"Keep the mustache — skip the beard."

Pearl D. Jochum, Jacksonville.

"Please use the photo you have been using and shave off that mustache. You do not look like Poke with it anymore than you looked like Clark Gable with one as a youth."

George L. Pope, Jacksonville.

"I would like you to put the new picture in the paper, as you do look very much like Mr. Gable, and he has always been my 'idol' since I was a young girl."

Joyce Rochester, Jacksonville.

That is about all I have room for. I'll recognize the others in future columns, before deciding whether to keep the "new growth" and use the photo of the new Poke with this column.*

**Editor's note: Poke did, indeed, recognize some of the other comments he received. His new look (with 'stache) was made official when he changed the photo on his newspaper column in 1981. Today, there are few (not even me) who can remember what he looked liked without one. It's sort of like I used to believe my grandmother's dresses came with aprons already on them.*

# The Uglies

*This piece appeared in The Florida Times Union sometime in 1978, and the incident with which it deals took place in the late 1950s. It tells how a former Broadway producer spotted Poke as having perfect qualifications for making vast fortunes in the entertainment field. Poke's fishing companions at the time, disgusting oafs that they were, thought the whole thing the hilarious.*

ST. MARY'S RIVER

One of these days, I guess, I'm going to have to get the *Florida Times-Union* of Jacksonville to run a big picture of me, and maybe folks will get satisfied about just how ugly old Poke is. They keep writing letters and calling up, since the word got out, somehow, about Poke being a regular champion in the uglies department.

But I'm not so sure about that. My friends used to say I looked a lot like Clark Gable. Well, actually they said my ears looked a lot like Clark Gable's, since they looked like a convertible coming down the road with both doors wide open. I even had a mustache once, but shaved it off when I was mistaken for the illegitimate son of Adolf Hitler.*

Ah, well — beauty is only skin deep, and is in the eye of the beholder; handsome is as handsome does, and all that sort of thing. I guess old Poke is in the class of people the late Herb Shriner was referring to when he said, "We had a beauty contest in my hometown and nobody won."

Certainly I and most of the fellows I run around with could ugly up a flower bed, to say nothing of the average beer joint.

**Editor's note: Some folks need review, you know, to keep up. If you think you've read this before, congratulations! You passed the test, now keep reading, there's new stuff coming.*

Which reminds me of a really funny true story — at least it was very funny to the pair of oafs I was with at the time.

It was about 20 years ago and the three of us — brother-in-law James Gresham of Orlando, Florida, great-uncle-by-marriage Leon Lancaster of Austell, Georgia, and myself — were bass fishing at Lake Carlton, a little-known small body of water close to Mt. Dora, down in Florida.

After a hard morning of beating the waters with plugs, we adjourned at noon to a tavern for some hamburgers and beverages. While waiting for the food, I noticed that down at the end of the counter an elderly gentleman was staring at me with uncomfortable intensity.

I would look away, then cut my eyes back toward him, and every time I looked in his direction it was the same: A hard, unyielding, nerve-grating glare, right at me.

Finally he had me squirming like a worm in an ant bed. Unable to stand it any longer, I turned to the man and demanded to know what he meant by constantly staring at me.

"Son," he said, " I don't know what your business is, but you missed your calling. You could make a million dollars. You would be an instant, overwhelming success."

"Well now," I said. "That sounds pretty good. What would I have to do?"

"Nothing," he said. "You wouldn't have to do nothing, you wouldn't have to know nothing, you wouldn't have to say nothing. All you'd have to do would be show up, and you'd be instantly rich and famous."

"Show up where?" I asked, beginning to get really interested.

"In the nightclubs of New York. Las Vegas. In the movies. On television. Anywhere people pay for entertainment. You'd be the biggest hit ever. I know. I'm an old Broadway producer. I know what I'm talking about."

"Well, well now! Tell me more," I beamed, casting a supercilious glance at my two fishing companions, who were taking in all this in flap-jawed amazement. "Why are you so sure I'd be such a big success? My looks? My voice? Personality?"

"You'd be an instant success," said the old man, his voice rising to a roar as he shook a bony finger in my face, "because you are without doubt, question or qualification, the ugliest s.o.b. I have ever seen in my life!"

Well sir, there was a moment of stunned silence, then those kinfolks Jim and Leon literally rent the air with howls and roars of insufferable laughter. They whooped and hollered until it was obscenely disgusting, generally behaving embarrassingly like uncouth louts. Jim sprained his ankle (served him right) when he fell off his bar stool in his unbridled glee.

It was small consolation when, a few moments after the old man lowered the boom on old Poke, a nice little old lady came in, told him he'd had his quota for the day and herded him out of the place.

It was years before those guys let up on me about my short-lived career in show biz.

*(If columnist Poke McHenry's face would stop a clock, the mugs of some of his South Georgia acquaintances would shatter concrete sundials.)*

# Psychic Says Future is Rosy

*Poke visits a psychic for a "reading;" and discovers a seer so intelligent and so acutely discerning that she immediately tags the old columnist a "genius," which proves beyond doubt that she really knows whereof she speaks. "Smart gal, indeed," said Poke. "There's definitely something to this psychic business."*

ST. MARYS RIVER

Back when we had that thing stirred up about Poke's new mustache, one of the readers of this column (and a vigorous proponent of the hirsute upper lip) was Jacksonville, Florida psychic Jo Ann Dunaway. Well, one thing led to another, as the old folks say, and I finally got up the nerve to do something I've had a hankering to do for years.

I went to Jo Ann and got myself a "reading," and I don't know when I've had such an enjoyable time. That may have been due to Jo Ann's having such a high opinion of what the stars and cards and hands and stuff showed for me, and having so many nice things to say to and about me.

Of course, you must understand that she not only is a psychic but has great intelligence, wit, charm and discernment otherwise. Right at the outset she labeled me a "genius," and it takes ordinary folks a mite longer, conservatively speaking, to discover that. Fact is, I have found that it is practically impossible to convince most of them, particularly my editors, of that obvious truth.

Anyway, it was somewhat of a break for me to get to know Jo Ann, even if only by letter and telephone, because I at last got my curiosity about that sort of thing satisfied. I had long been doubtful about going to one of those "madams" you see advertised by roadside signs all over the place, since I had heard some less than complimentary things about some of them.

Incidentally, I do sort of dimly recall some interesting experiences (purely in the interest of academics and scientific research, you understand) involving certain other "madams," but that was a long time ago and in no way germane to this tale.

Jo Ann's astrology computer disclosed, among other things, that Poke is sensitive to criticism, clever with written and spoken word (get that, editors), demands mental and artistic freedom (that, too), loves harmony and beauty — probably a nature lover, is an original thinker who inspires others, can think ahead to the point of being psychic, a perfectionist, demanding more of self than others, has a healthy ego and fights injustice with a biting wit.

Now who couldn't enjoy a session of being told such nice things? It's all strikingly true, of course. Many a stuffed shirt has had the starch bitten out of it by my biting wit. I got some other kinds, too.

Further, Jo Ann said, the planets showed that Poke had some rugged beginnings, but his planetary configuration assured him a "native determination that made him decide that he would compensate for his early beginnings and become 'famous' in some form."

Well, I did have some tough beginnings, at least financially. My folks called dollars "williams," not being familiar enough with them to call them "bills." When I was growing up if freight trains had been selling for a nickel apiece I couldn't have bought the hiss of the air brakes.

Yes I was poor but proud in those days, but things have changed now. I'm not a bit proud anymore.

One of the mystifying things Jo Ann's deductions revealed is that somewhere out there is a relative who is jealous of my "success." Well, if success is synonymous with money, that must be the poorest of all poor relations in the annals of poverty if he/she is jealous of me.

But things will get better. Jo Ann foresees a book in my immediate future, a book that will be a smashing success financially and otherwise, and this will be followed by several

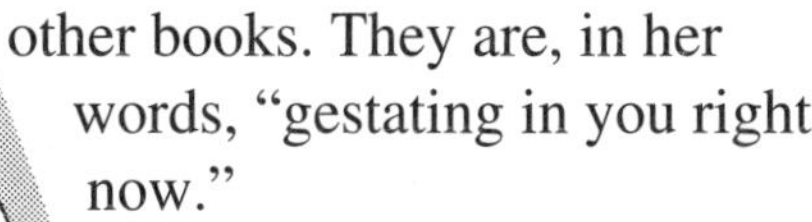

other books. They are, in her words, "gestating in you right now."

There is much more, but that's enough for the moment.

She's still, she explains, in the learning process, and sometimes her prophecies are wide of the mark. On other occasions, they are stunningly close to being exact.*

For instance, she predicted in November 1980 that the Americans held hostage by Iran would be freed on or about the same time Ronald Reagan was sworn in as president. They were.

She forecast that Reagan would survive an assassination attempt during his first year in office. He did.

She is a weekly guest on the Allen Moore Off the Wall Florida Network radio show, does about 12 to 15 personal readings a week, in addition to a bunch by mail and telephone, makes numerous public appearances before civic clubs and the like, and otherwise manages to keep her thumbs untwiddled.**

Moore probably put her best in perspective when he said, "Jo Ann, besides being remarkably psychic, is also extremely entertaining."

Certainly, I found her so at our reading session. I didn't even have to exercise my genius capabilities to figure that out.

**Editor's note: And on some, she's a few years premature, as this first book did not materialize "immediately." We all hope she's right about the financial success of it, but I guess that's up to you readers. Prove Jo Ann right — tell your friends to buy this book!*

***Jo Ann still does psychic readings and makes guest appearances, many of them on cruise ships.*

# Tall Fish Tales

*Here's how Speedy Braswell managed to bring home a 10-pound bass even if the old booger (the fish, not Speedy) did spit out the plug and send it halfway back to the boat. Also, how a world-record largemouth foiled Speedy in a jug-fishing set-to.*

ST. MARYS RIVER

Once I showed up in the *Florida Times-Union* newsroom in Jacksonville wearing a monogrammed shirt (the initials weren't mine, but nobody noticed) and one of the copy boys saw the shirt and jeered: "Look at that! Poke McHenry wearing a monogrammed shirt! I bet the phony don't even know how to fish!"

He's probably right, but I'll tell you one thing: if experience had anything to do with it I'd be a 24-carat expert, for I've sure given those finny fickleheads plenty of opportunities for many years and in many places. But a lot of good things come out of fishing, whether you can put them in the frying pan or not. Like fish stories, and the immortal adage, "The only time a fisherman tells the truth is when he calls another fisherman a liar."

I've got a few of my favorite stories to share with you today, and if you're a fisherman you've probably heard some of them, but bear with me anyway.

First, there was this little boy on a dock, fishing by threading his line down through a crack between boards. A man came along and said:

"Stupid kid! Don't you know you can't pull a fish up through that tiny crack?"

"Silly man," replied the lad. "Don't you know he can't pull me down through it, either?"

Then there was another little boy who had been sitting patiently on a creek bank for hours, and a man came along and stood by watching for a long time while nothing at all happened. No bites, no action, no fish.

At long last, the man said:

"Kid, you about the dumbest thing I ever saw. I been here four hours watching you try to catch a fish, and you haven't even had a bite. How silly can you get, to waste all that time for nothing?"

"Well," replied the kid. "At least I have a chance to get something out of the deal. That can't be as dumb as you just standing here watching me for four hours."

I used to fish a lot down on Lake Seminole, which is located sort of in the fence-corner of Georgia, Florida and Alabama. There was a guide down there by the name of Crawford Braswell, who operated out of Jack Wingate's fishing camp south of Bainbridge, Georgia, and who was universally known as "Speedy."

He was one of the most colorful characters I've ever known. One particularly noteworthy thing about Speedy was, he always drank the same amount of alcoholic beverages, what-ever kind they might be. Speedy's capacity consisted solely of whatever amount happened to be available.

Here is one of his better bass-fishing stories, told around a campfire as a convivial jug was passed around steadily among half a dozen or so of us loafers:

"I was plugging for bass around some old cypress knees in one of my favorite isolated areas of the lake (Seminole) when this 10-pounder hit my Lucky 13 like a sledgehammer smacking an anvil.

"He hung hisself pretty good, but then he leaped high out of the water, shook his head harder than a priest fighting temptation, and flang (sic) that plug halfway back to the boat.

"But I put that bass in the live well, just the same."

"You got him, Speedy?" someone asked incredulously. "After he flung the plug, you still caught him?"

"You betcha," said Speedy. "You see, after he flang the plug, he came back straight down toward the water, with his mouth still wide open. Well, sir, he fell smack straight-on head-first and just impaled hisself on one of them cypress knees that stick up outa the water around a bug cypress tree. All I had to do was pull the boat over and pluck him off like sliding a withered blossom off a young okra pod."

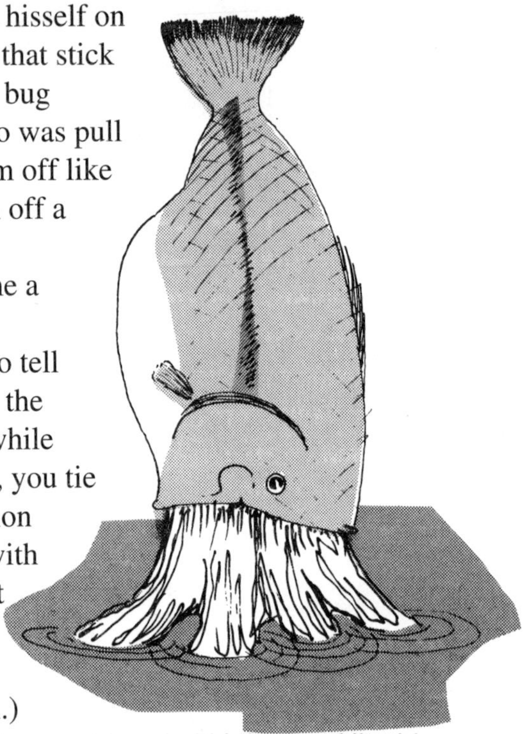

"Pass the jug," came a chorus from the rest of us.

Speedy also liked to tell the uninitiated how he lost the world record largemouth while jug fishing. (In jug fishing, you tie a line to an empty one-gallon plastic jug, bait the hook with a big live shiner and turn it loose to the mercy of the breezes and currents, letting it drift where it will.)

"Well, this day I had several jugs bobbin' around," said Speedy, "when all of a sudden one of them just went plumb crazy. I knew it was a big 'un, so I taken out after him with the boat.

"I chased that jug all over the lake, and got several looks at that monster bass, and I tell you it give me the shakes. He'd a' weighed 25 pounds if he weighed an ounce.

"Finally he got pretty wore down and I eased the boat up close and had my net down and was just ready to scoop it under that feller and go home rich with a new world record bass, when you know what that sneakin' skeester done?

"With one final mighty leap, he came straight up out of the water, swallowed the jug and tuck off for parts unknown."

Well, don't say I didn't warn you that Speedy was a real character.

*(Poke McHenry probably could catch the world record bass, but finds it a lot less trouble and a lot better eating just to catch catfish.)*

# THOSE TALL TALES KEEP ON COMING

*Wild tales abound in this 1980 Poke column. You can find out what happened to an old-timer when his boat ran out of gas and he substituted moonshine whiskey; and what to do with knotholes created by chickens on a diet of sawdust. And, also, fram head fishing, anyone?*

ST. MARYS RIVER

It does seem that our Poke McHenry Liars Club will be a howling (as in gale-force hot-air winds) success when we get it going. Already, more and more readers are sharing tall tales with me through letters, phone calls and personal contacts.*

My old friend Sam Sawyer of Jacksonville, Florida, who calls and chats occasionally, had a pretty good one the other day. Here's Sam's story:

"This fellow was participating in a liars' contest and said that he had got lost in deep woods and it grew dark and colder and as he began to despair, he stumbled upon a snug cave. He built himself a fire and just as he was beginning to get warm and settled in, a fierce, huge, lean and hungry mountain lion burst through the cave opening.

"With a terrifying roar, the fellow said, the lion leaped for the man's throat, fangs bared and needle-sharp talons flashing in the fire light.

"At this point the fellow paused, and one of his breathless listeners asked, 'And just how did you get out of that fix?'

"'Well,'" the liar replied, "'I didn't. That lion killed me.'"

Sam's yarn reminds me once again of my long-ago friend old Frazier. Here's a gem from Frazier:

* *Editor's note: You, too, can be in the liars' club. Just write Poke in care of the publisher.*

"This time I was way up above Abbeville, Georgia, on the Ocmulgee River checking some of my catfish baskets when I went to crank my old kicker and discovered I was out of gas. It was a long way to paddle back to Camp Brooklyn, a popular Ocmulgee River landing, even if it was downstream, and then I bethought that I did have a jug of pretty pow'ful moonshine along, to keep off that chill in the mid-afternoon July air.

"So I poured the tank full of shine just to see if it would work, and when I pulled the rope that old motor coughed a couple of times, cleared its throat and let out a beller like a hungry corpse coming to life.

"Well sir, we took off down that river so fast it was all I could do to hang in the boat and kinda halfway steer the thing. In a matter of minutes we were already past my campsite and tearing along faster and faster. Along about where the Ocmulgee joins with the Oconee to form the Altamaha River, we broke the sound barrier with such a sonic-boom thunderclap of noise that thousands of shell-shocked squirrels instantly dropped dead out of trees along the river banks and as far back in the swamps as three or four miles.

"We went under the U.S. 17 bridge at Darien so fast a Holiness preacher declared the end of the world was at hand and 14 shrimpers swore off beer for a full 30 minutes. Folks around Altamaha Sound thought Halley's Comet had come down to earth as we roared out into the Atlantic.

"We kept getting faster and faster until finally the friction between the boat bottom and the water developed such a heat that the boat caught fire and burnt plumb up. Luckily, I just managed to climb on top of the motor and cling on for dear life, only slightly scorched by the flames.

"So here we went, me and the motor, at such a rate that I figgered we'd hit the coast of Africa before sundown, but all of a sudden the moonshine ran out and that old motor sunk like a load of bricks 6,000 feet straight down to the bottom of the ocean about 500 miles off the coast of Georgia.

"Now you woulda thunk under normal circumstances that a feller in such a predicament as that woulda drownded, but I didn't.

"No sir. Fact is, I wuz et up by sharks."

And now comes Mr. Walter S. "Wally" Hackford, of Jacksonville, Florida, who introduces us to the novel sport of "fram head fishing."

Fram head fishing, says Wally, is a relatively simple form of fishing that most people have never heard of (which probably is a good thing). Anyway, here, according to Wally, is how one goes about fram fishing:

"First, get a loaf of bread; second, get a nice small pine tree; third, get a small boat.

"Take the bread and wet down with water, then squeeze until doughy and roll into small balls.

"Then take the pine tree, cut down to a fairly good-sized club. Take your boat out on the water to a good fishing place, then take your dough balls and throw upon the water.

"When the fish come up to eat, fram them on the head. Very simple, huh?"

Indeed it is, Wally, indeed it is. I wonder why I never thought of it myself.

And to wind up is Mr. John H. Kent Sr., who recalls that times were so hard during the Depression he got so skinny that when he turned sideways he couldn't be seen at all. (Almost as bad as my case: I had to walk twice in the same place to make a shadow.)

John says his family was so poor they couldn't feed both themselves and the chickens, so they started feeding the chickens sawdust, whereupon the hens started laying knotholes, which the family dried out and used for firewood, there being no way they could figure out how to eat a knothole.

# The Season of the Party

*There are times, sad to say, when fellows tend to forget that they have long-suffering wives awaiting somewhere out there for their return from evenings in places they really shouldn't be. Such a tale is this one, a true story of some Yuletide shenanigans of a couple of Poke's friends from bygone days. Most husbands can relate, rather painfully, to the antics of Buck and Howard while a wee bit under the influence.*

ST. MARYS RIVER

Well, this is the season of the Christmas party, or the year-end party, New Year's party, or almost any other old excuse to have a party, and many of the funny old "drunk stories" are being revived and told of the misadventures of the well-meaning souls who have a few too many occasionally.

Almost every time we get together, my grandchildren beg me to "tell us some drunk jokes, Papa." And usually I have a few to tell. One of my favorites is one I heard the first time, believe it or not, from a preacher in a pulpit. (Yes, another believe it or not, old Poke has upon occasion been in a church here and there.) Here is the preacher's joke:

A carload of half a dozen drunks was whizzing down the road and the driver missed a curve. The car went off the road, jumped a ditch, climbed an embankment, knocked down a fence and rolled over in a field, scattering drunks all over the premises.

They gathered themselves together, brushed off the dirt and trash, and discovered to their amazement nobody was hurt.

"Well," said one. "I guess the Lord was with us that time."

"I reckon He was," agreed another dryly. "But I'll bet He won't be caught with this bunch again."

Then there was the one about the preacher who was driving along and came up behind this drunk in a car which was weaving all over the road.

"Dear me," thought the preacher, "that poor fellow is in bad shape. I'd better follow along so that I can help if he gets into trouble."

But while concentrating on shepherding the drunk, the preacher forgot to watch his own driving and ran his car off into the ditch.

Noting this in his rear-view mirror, the drunk stopped and staggered back to the preacher's car to see if he could be of assistance.

"Are you hurt, friend?" asked the drunk of the half-dazed preacher.

"No," said the reverend gentleman. "I'm not hurt. I have the Lord with me."

"Well," said the drunk. "Maybe you better let Him ride up here with me. Way you drive, you're liable to kill Him."

I haven't heard much about it of late, but it used to be that eggnog was a popular Christmas season libation. I never could stand the stuff. It is in the same class as a shrimp omelet, which is a capital way to mess up both shrimp and eggs. Eggnog is a prime way to ruin both eggs and whiskey.

The last time I tried that stuff was at least 25 years ago at a Christmas party, where a dozen or so otherwise normal men and women were sitting around oohing and aahing over how delicious the eggnog was. I was struggling as gentlemanly as possible to spoon down some of the horrid concoction, but having little success and, apparently, turning a bit green in the process for the hostess hastily summoned me into the kitchen, away from the others.

"Here, Poke," she said with a twinkle in her eye as she plopped a bottle of bourbon down before me. "Pour yourself a real drink. I can't stand to see a grown man dry."

She was one grand lady, that one.

Another in my list of better "drunk jokes" is the one about the guy who was negotiating a dark sidewalk in none too steady a manner when he bonked head-on into a huge utility pole. Putting his hands up before his face and on the rough

surface of the pole, he felt his way carefully all the way around it.

When he got back to the starting point, he dropped his hands helplessly and said:

"It's no use. I'm walled in."

Now I'm going to tell you a true story of a Christmas party with a hilarious, although not exactly happy-for-everyone ending:

These two friends of mine, Buck and Howard, got together with their wives over at Howard's house for a sort of cozy little two-family affair. After several drinks, dinner, and several more drinks, it got along about 10 o'clock in the evening and Buck and Howard, as fellows in their cups will do, got the notion they wanted to go out to a pizza place and have some more food and a drop or two of wine.

So they went, assuring their wives they would be back in an hour or so.

But the best-laid plans, etc. as you know…

About 2 a.m. they closed the pizza place and Buck and Howard, having just enough sense left not to try to drive home, called a cab. Buck, having forgotten he even had a wife, let alone where she was, had the cab drop him off at his house, where he went in and passed out across a bed.

Meanwhile, Howard gets home by cab, having left his car at the pizza joint. Buck's car is at Howard's, but Buck has the keys, as well as the house keys.

Before Howard passes out, Mrs. Buck is able to extract

from him that Buck is at home. By this time, as you may have guessed, Mrs. Buck is not in the most jovial of moods.

So Mrs. Buck takes the cab and arrives at her house shortly after 3 a.m. She practically has to tear the door down to arouse Buck enough to investigate what the commotion on the front porch is all about. Finally, however, he staggers to the front door, flings it open and beholds Mrs. Buck standing there.

"Why, Honey!" roared Buck. "Wot in th' hell you doing out at this time of night?"

There are several versions, none printable, of what Mrs. Buck said next. Also, there are several versions of exactly what she did next.

Suffice it to say that it was several days before Buck recovered sufficiently to reappear in public, and then he explained the casts and bandages by telling everybody he had been the victim of a hit-and-run truck driver.

# Drink Cadgers

*Some of the best all-time con men could be numbered among the old-time drink-cadgers, who would come up with some amazing gimmicks with which to bamboozle victims out of a few beers or shots of booze, or the monetary costs of keeping alcoholism alive for another day. Poke here recalls some of the better schemes he saw in divers places.*

ST. MARYS RIVER

A few of us were sitting around having tea the other day when the subject of cadging drinks came up, and everybody's got a favorite story in this field. Some of them actually are true, but for the most part they are jokes like the many variations of the "talking dog" escapades.

Probably the best of the dog stories is that one where the cadger goes in with this nondescript mutt and swears to the bartender that for a free drink he'll make his dog talk.

"Get out of here," the bartender tells him. "I've heard all that sort of stuff too many times."

But eventually the barkeep is persuaded (drink cadgers are most persuasive fellows), but he warns the guy that if the dog doesn't actually talk, both cadger and dog are going to get heaved out.

"Okay," said the dog owner to the pooch, "What's on top of a house?"

"Roof!" barked the dog.

"That does it!" roared the bartender. "Out you go, both of you..."

"No, no! Wait! Give him another chance," cried the drunk.

"Okay," said the bartender grimly. "One more chance, and it better be good."

"Okay, pooch," said the cadger. "Who was the greatest baseball player there ever was?"

"Ruth!" woofed the dog.

Instantly the bartender seized drunk and dog, banged their heads together and kicked them end-over-end out the front door and into a gutter.

The dog staggered to his feet, shook himself thoroughly and said:

"Dang! I guess I should have said 'Ty Cobb'."

One of my favorite con men was a guy we used to call "Carburetor Clarence." Old Carburetor would slip into a pool room, seat himself beside a spectator and strike up a conversation.

Soon he would ask the fellow what sort of car he was driving. He might say Chevrolet, Ford, Chrysler, Plymouth, Rambler — anything, it was all the same to Carburetor.

"What kind of mileage you getting?" would be Carburetor's next question.

Whatever the answer, Carburetor would express genuine amazement.

"Man," he'd say, "with that automobile you should be getting at least five or six more miles to the gallon. Undoubtedly your carburetor needs a simple adjustment. I can fix that thing for you in five minutes, and save you a ton of money on gas costs."

Carburetor would explain that he was a retired (Chrysler, General Motors, Ford, American Motors, depending upon the kind of car he was to work on) engineer and factory maintenance expert.

Nine times out of 10, the guy would wind up letting old Carburetor "adjust" the car's carburetor, at a cost of from $2 up, depending upon what old Carburetor thought the traffic would bear. On Cadillacs and Lincolns and the like, he never got less than $5. For poor folks like me who usually had a battered old used car, he'd charge $2.

I've seen that guy on several occasions operate for one day around a pool hall and come up with enough folding money to keep him in booze for two weeks. I watched him pick up $72, by my actual count, in about three hours one afternoon, in a time when nobody visiting the place from which the con man was operating that day made more than $5 an hour at legitimate employment. Crime does pay, sometimes.

Carburetor's only tools were a greasy screwdriver and a sharp set of wits.

Another great cadger was a fisherman who operated around fish camps down in the Florida. This guy must have had some way of raising huge bream, because he kept half a dozen or so in the live well of his old bateau. He'd pull into a fish camp, where there were always a few transients (mostly folks from Georgia) hanging around looking for somebody with inside information on where the big ones were hiding.

Somebody would ask him if he'd had any luck, and he'd reluctantly hold up a couple of those 2 1/2 pound bluegills and say something like "Well, I did find a few little fellers this morning..."

One look by the anglers at the size of those fish and the canny cadger was assured of a full day's free beers while greenhorn fishermen tried to pry out of him the secret of where he caught them. Finally he would break down and send them off to where they would fish furiously and vainly while the cadger burped his way to wherever he spent his nights, keeping his big bream intact for another sucker-entrapping some different place the next day.

They say he kept those fish around for years and never failed to cash in wherever he showed them.

*(Poke McHenry says that the only time a drink cadger tells the truth is when he calls another drink cadger an unprincipled sot.)*

# Is there a king of mosquitoes?

*Poke says he's been around over most of the world and has been eaten by mosquitoes in many faraway places, but he still vows that those skeeters that inhabit the Ocmulgee River swamp in South Georgia are the fiercest in the world. He has several stories to prove it, too, and here are a couple of them.*

ST. MARYS RIVER

Since I mentioned a while back that the Ocmulgee River mosquitoes are the world champions, a scattered few dissidents have claimed the dubious honor for other areas such as some South Pacific Islands, South American jungles, the Okefenokee Swamp and the Everglades, but I'm telling you none of them is in it with the Ocmulgee critters.

I'm a pretty fair authority on mosquitoes, having furnished innumerable blood transfusions for untold numbers of them of various species and locales over a big chunk of the world. And I've never seen the match of the Ocmulgee toughies.

No doubt it was the Ocmulgee type that inspired the old tale of the two mosquitoes who tiptoed into a tent and found a sleeping fisherman.

"He's a nice one, ain't he?" said the first mosquito. "Must go close to 200 pounds. Think we oughta eat him here or take him down into the swamp?"

"Let's eat him here," replied the second bug. "If we take him back into the swamp, them big mosquitoes'll take him away from us."

I had a brother-in-law, Lyle D. Nichols, who spent 20 years in the Marine Corps and during that stretch he had occasion to encounter some of the world's meanest skeeters, and when he first heard about the Ocmulgee brand he scoffed at our claims for their terrorism and general viciousness.

‘Nothing,” declared old Nick with solemn authority, “can compare with the mosquitoes on Okinawa.”

So some of the boys took him on an overnight outing in the Ocmulgee swamp, and long before daylight the hideously tormented ex-Marine had yelled surrender, and to the day he died, he backed my point of view 100%. I could cite dozens of others, and I’ll lay odds that anyone who doubts the peerless and persistent ferocity of the Ocmulgee stingers will change his mind if he ever spends a night fighting them.

On one occasion years ago, a moonshine-loving friend of mine we’ll call Chester was squirrel hunting in the Ocmulgee swamp with a buddy. Now, about the only way a fellow could keep halfway alive with those skeeters, even in the daytime, was to chain-smoke cigarettes, since the smoke sort of slowed them down.

Well, old Chester became separated from his friend and ran out of matches. He finished off his flat pint of shine, vainly thinking that perhaps he could drink himself into a condition where he could ignore the swarming hordes of hungry bloodsuckers.

After an hour or so, Chester’s companion came back to where Chester was and found him sitting on a stump, stripped to the waist, and his torso, arms, face and neck completely hidden by a blanket of mosquitoes.

“What in the name of the saints are you doing, Chester?” asked the horrified companion.

“Well, I run out of matches and couldn’t smoke, and the booze didn’t help any, so I just decided to set here and let the *&%$#&@#$!!! get a bait!” said old Chester, who must have given up enough blood on that stump to make alcoholics out of the next 17 generations of Ocmulgee mosquitoes.

Many are the tales, true and otherwise, that have been birthed by the Ocmulgee mosquito, and my old friend Frazier, to whom I have referred from time to time, could spin some of the best, such as this one:

“I was setting under a hickory tree minding my business, which at the moment was potting a squirrel for supper, when I got hit by a blitzkrieg of them skeeters. They was just about tearing me apart when I spied an abandoned 80-gallon syrup kettle nearby and grabbed it and turned it upside down over me.

(An 80-gallon syrup kettle is a flanged, quarter-to-half-inch-thick cast-iron bowl big enough to stew down 80 gallons of cane juice into syrup at one cooking.)

"Well sir, I hardly got settled under the kettle 'til I heard something sounded like a high-speed drill, and pretty soon here comes a skeeter beak boring through that iron kettle. I flattened it with my gun butt, but here come another and another and another, dozens, hundreds of skeeters drilling through that iron. I tell you, I wore myself to a frazzle braddin' them bills on the inside of that kettle.

"Finally, they got to be so many skeeters pinned to that kettle that they just up and flew off with the thing, and the rest of the skeeters proceeded to eat me right down to my bones.

"Them is some tough mosquitoes down there in that Ocmulgee swamp."

Right he was, and the situation hasn't changed to this day. If you don't believe it, come along with me some night and see for yourself.

# The Truth Behind Some of the Nation's Great Lies

*This bit was written about 1980, or a little earlier. It deplores the waning interest in the grand old practice of tall-tale-telling, and offers up a few choice Poke-coined examples of the art. Poke has always contended that it is easy to tell the truth, but to spin a really intriguing and spellbinding lie is an achievement worthy of any man's admiration and heartiest approbation.*

ST. MARYS RIVER

Alas, it seems that another bit of Americana may soon be no more, and that is a real pity. I refer here to the Burlington Liars Club, a quaint organization originated in 1929 by a newspaperman (who else could have been better qualified?) by name of Otis Hulett.* Otis, now 82, apparently has decided that 50 years at the helm of that sort of thing was enough.

I learned the latest development on the club through some clippings somebody sent me from the current issue of the magazine 50 Plus.** It has a fine piece about the club and its history from the time of its hatching in the small community of Burlington, Wisconsin, until the present time. Hulett and his friends had a lot of fun with the thing for half a century and it got Burlington more publicity, probably, than any other thing could have.

Through the Depression years everybody got a chuckle out of the yearly champion lie, and eagerly awaited an announcement of the winner's name and the story he told.

** Editor's note: Mr. Hulett died in the early 1980s.*
*** 50 Plus is still in publication, under the new title "New Choices."*

Here are some of the biggest whoppers, as reprinted by the magazine:

"My wife is so lazy she feeds the chickens popcorn so the eggs will turn themselves when she fries them." (1937)

"The strongest wind I ever heard of blew our cast-iron kettle out of the country. It was moving so fast that lightning struck at it five times and missed." (1953)

"The food at this school is so bad that if it weren't for the salt and pepper we'd starve to death." (1974)

I used to submit an occasional piece to the Burlington Liars Club competition, but they threw all mine out on the grounds that anything told by a man of such impeccable veracity as old Poke couldn't possibly be a lie. (Now that one right there should get me first prize in any liars' contest.)

That sort of reminds me of that first year when Hulett and his pals were trying to decide from among scores of fine lies which was the biggest, the town police chief strolled up and somebody asked him why he hadn't entered the contest.

"Who, me?" asked the chief in a wounded tone. "Why, I never told a lie in my life."

Whereupon, the committee instantly tossed out all formal entries and declared the chief the champion for the year.

With a bunch of friends, I used to hang around many of those old-fashioned country stores in South Georgia and swap tall tales with some real pros. Probably the champion of them all, at least in my experience, was old Frazier, an intrepid hunter, fisherman, scrounger and generally loved good old boy. Frazier was particularly fond of stories about the size and ingenuity of the Ocmulgee River swamp mosquitoes. The following is typical of the yarns he used to spin:

One time old Frazier was down in the swamp, seated near the edge of a high bluff, his back resting against a huge old oak tree about three feet in diameter at the point where it was supporting him. Frazier was still-hunting with his .22 rifle, hoping to plink a few squirrels for supper, and while he was sitting there he dozed off.

He was awakened abruptly by a noise that sounded like a high-carbon steel drill whining through tough material, and in a moment felt a sharp pain as something stabbed through his hunting coat and into his back.

Leaping up, the startled Frazier saw that a monstrous mosquito had slipped up behind him and bored right through that oak with his bill and was preparing to siphon our hunter's lifeblood right from his veins. Quickly, Frazier seized his gun and with the butt hammered about four inches of the beak flat against the tree, thus effectively riveting the monster to the spot, then stepped around the tree and dispatched it with his rifle.

Next spring, Frazier revisited the place and saw that the weather and varmints had thoroughly flensed the mosquito, leaving the towering backbone and rib cage standing stark and white. Being a man of quick wit and improvisation, Frazier covered the skeleton with tarpaper and galvanized roofing tin, thus creating a sturdy, weatherproof shelter from the elements. It was a mighty cozy campsite cabin, but for being a mite drafty due to the lofty ceiling.

Frazier was always having his friends down for some trotline fishing and moonshine drinking, and once he had an old Army general as a guest, and the general was so struck with the design he took a sketch of it back to the Army, and that's how the military Quonset hut, made famous in World War II, was born.

I could take you down to the very place where Frazier's mosquito cabin stood except that, unfortunately, the river changed channels years ago and cut under the bluff until it toppled into the water — cabin, oak tree and all — and was carried away to sea.

The last I heard of the mosquito bones, some Icelandic seafarers had salvaged the framework, still intact, from the ocean and converted it into the keel and side ribs of a mighty whaling vessel which, for all I know, still is plying the seven seas.

So much for old Frazier. If the Burlington club really has given up the ghost (story) perhaps we might take up the torch and organize a Poke McHenry Liars Club. Anybody interested?

# THIS TALL TALE IS ABOUT A TEENSY-WEENSY LITTLE SQUIRREL

*This 1980 column is about a few tall tales, an oyster that should have been listed among the wonders of the world, and how come a catch of 58 king mackerel averaging 10 pounds apiece weighed a total of only 300 pounds? Anyway Poke can figure it, 58 fish weighing an average of 10 pounds each would weigh 580 pounds, total. Wouldn't they?*

FERNANDINA BEACH, Florida

At the request of W.I. "Pop" DuBose, one of the fine gentlemen of this area, I was up here this week to tell a few stories to the local Rotary Club.

I told the members first that I was sure that the only reason Pop asked me to come (it was a request made just a few days before the meeting) was that he must have run out of possibilities for good speakers, since calling on Poke for that was something akin to what I used to think about girls basketball — a thing to go to when you had absolutely nothing else to do or any other special place to go.

(I wrote something to that effect several years ago, and was instantly beset by a veritable army of players, coaches, mothers, fathers, brothers, aunts, uncles, cousins, and miscellaneous characters who just disagreed in general. Every one of them threatened individually to inflict so many knots on my noggin I'd look like a five-pound cluster of grapes. I immediately developed an immense fondness for girls basketball, a feeling that is with me even unto this day. Hell indeed hath no fury like a scorned girls basketball player and her backers.)

But to get back to the subject — while awaiting the meeting start Pop told me a few tall tales, mostly about Texas, and then really rang a bell with a story of a fellow hunting squirrels with black powder gunshot shells.

Spotting a squirrel's head peering out of a hole in a tree, he blasted away, and when the smoke cleared the squirrel apparently was still there, untouched. He repeated this 25 times, using up every one of the lone box of shells he had, and there was still a squirrel peeking out of the hole.

Mystified, he walked to the foot of the tree, where he found 25 dead squirrels. He then realized what had happened and quickly plugged the hole in the tree with a "lighterd knot" to keep the rest of the squirrels penned in until he could return the next day with more ammunition.

"Well sir," said the fellow later "when I got back there the next morning, there was so many squirrels packed inside that tree that the sides of the trunk wuz "breathing" in and out as them squirrels breathed. Never seen anything like it."

The Texas stories reminded me of one of my favorites. Seems this Texas guy was bragging away (as I have heard that a few of them do in rare cases) and there happened to be an Alaskan in the crowd.

"If you don't shut up," the Alaskan said, "we are just liable to cut Alaska in half, and then Texas would be the third-largest state in the union."

Anyhow, part of what the Rotarians were doing this week, as was most everybody else in Fernandina Beach, was getting ready for the annual shrimp festival.

I came up once sometime back to one of Fernandina Beach's shrimp festivals, thinking to get some really extraordinary seafood, which I hanker for chronically and get kind of wild about when I get near the ocean. Well, there were lots of places whereat to sample goodies, and I guess I must have chosen the less-than-extraordinary one. I tried some steamed (or roasted, I can't remember now what they called them) oysters, as a starter.

I opened one of those oysters and it was a sight to awaken the adrenaline of an archeologist. That oyster was the most wizened, bedizened, bewrinkled, withered specimen of an oyster it had ever been my displeasure to evaluate. That oyster looked as if a tribe of aboriginal head shrinkers, man and boy, had practiced on it for 300 years. That oyster must have been the model for Dick Tracy's Pruneface. It was an oyster that should have been in a museum, for the scrutiny of worldwide scientists and the writing of scholarly papers.

Come to think of it, that was an extraordinary eating place, although not in the sense I had in mind. So I gently laid aside my steamed (or roasted) oysters and sought sustenance elsewhere.

But I'm sure that that was a rare aberration among the dispensers of food for the shrimp festival, and the festival goers today and tomorrow will fare much better than I did in that isolated incident.

Also while in town I went by the Fernandina Beach News-Leader newspaper office and picked up a paper fresh off the press, and among the other interesting things I found in it was a report of some fishermen who had gone out and scored a magnificent catch of king mackerel.

The thing kind of puzzled me, though. It said that they caught a total of 58 kings that had an average weight of 10 pounds, and that the total weight of the catch was 300 pounds.

Now what I can't figure out is, if they caught 58 fish that weighed an average of 10 pounds each, why didn't they have 580 pounds of fish? Is that some of this new math?

# "A TRUCK BACKED THROUGH THE WINDSHIELD INTO MY WIFE'S FACE."

*This collection is an example of how funny things have a way of finding old Poke's notice and winding up in a column such as this one, which appeared circa 1980 in the Jacksonville, Florida Times-Union newspaper.*

ST. MARYS RIVER

Somehow funny things just seem to gravitate to me, and that's a blessing, seeing as how I like to laugh so much and always can use a little levity to share with you readers.

Today I have something that was picked up by Jacksonville, *Florida Times-Times-Union* police reporter Steve Garnaas* and shared with me. It is from the North Florida Area Safety Staff, and I made an unsuccessful effort to find out who that is, or they are, in order to give the proper credit as the source for what I think is some extraordinarily funny stuff. It probably is old, but it is new to me and I hope will be to you.

To begin with, the last sentence of the lead-in paragraph of the 'report' qualifies incontestably for the understatement-of-the-year award. Here is the paragraph:

"Following are actual statements found on insurance forms where car drivers attempted to summarize the details of an accident in the fewest words possible. The instances of faulty writing serve to confirm that even incompetent writing may be highly entertaining."

That last sentence is what I mean about the understatement, as I think you'll agree when you read this:

"Coming home, I drove into the wrong house, and

**Editor's note: Garnaas is now a reporter for the Denver, Colorado, Post, and has been for several years.*

collided with a tree I don't have."

"The other car collided with mine without giving warning of its intentions."

"I thought my window was down, but I found out it was up when I put my head through it."

"I collided with a stationary truck coming the other way."

"A truck backed through the windshield into my wife's face."

"The guy was all over the road. I had to swerve a number of times before I hit him."

"I pulled away from the side of the road, glanced at my mother-in-law and headed over the embankment."

"In my attempt to kill a fly, I drove into a telephone pole."

"I had been shopping for plants all day and was on my way home. As I reached an intersection, a hedge sprang up, obscuring my vision and I did not see the other car."

"I was on my way to the doctor with rear end trouble when my universal joint gave way causing me to have an accident."

"My car was legally parked when it backed into the other vehicle."

"The pedestrian hit me and went under my car."

"As I approached the intersection a stop sign suddenly appeared in a place where no stop sign ever appeared before. I was unable to stop in time to avoid the accident."

"I was sure the old fellow would never make it to the other side of the road when I struck him."

"I saw a slow moving, sad faced old gentleman as he bounced off the roof of my car."

"I told the police that I was not injured, but on removing my hat, found that I had a fractured skull."

"The indirect cause of the accident was a little guy in a small car with a big mouth."

"I was thrown from my car as it left the road. I was later found in a ditch by some stray cows."

"The telephone pole was approaching, I was attempting to swerve out of its way, when it struck the front end."

"To avoid hitting the bumper of the car in front, I struck the pedestrian."

"An invisible car came out of nowhere, struck my car and vanished."

There you have it, and if you can go through that list without a chuckle you either have a severe toothache or need to be embalmed, especially now that the weather has turned off so warm.

This is the sort of thing that reminds me from time to time just how wonderful people really are, now aren't they?

While trying to locate the North Florida Area Safety Staff, I chatted a bit with Mike Gould, the Jacksonville Sheriff's Office information officer,* and he passed on a tale good enough to qualify for the liars' club.

Mike said his grandfather penned in with a board fence some hogs that were so skinny he had to tie knots in their tails to keep them from escaping through the knotholes in the boards.

See? I told you funny things just gravitate to me.

**Editor's note: Gould is still an information specialist with the City of Jacksonville.*

# TALL TALES

*This 1978 column contains a few samples of what could have been expected if Poke's liars club had ever been organized and gotten off the ground. Unfortunately, Poke, being too busy with important things like fishing, hunting and crap-shooting, plus inventing a few tall tales himself, never got around to it. Or maybe the other tall-tale tellers became discouraged upon getting a look at their competition from old Poke himself.*

ST. MARYS RIVER

Since I mentioned that we might organize a Poke McHenry Liars Club, readers have shown an increasing interest in a revival of tall-tale telling, and several have sent me examples already. I'm happy about this, for no one loves a good yarn better than I do, and I believe about 90% of the rest of the people feel the same way. I guess maybe the other 10% either have no sense of humor or feel there's something immoral or worse about outlandish stories. I think they are missing a lot of life's pleasures, but that's their business.

One story, another variation of an old and oft-told tale, came to me from Bob Ross of Brunswick, Georgia. Bob writes:

"Twenty-five years ago I was operating a small hog and corn farm in some bottom land in West Tennessee. One June day while chopping cockleburs out of a corn field down near the river, I was attacked by a big cottonmouth moccasin. I defended myself with the hoe and chased the snake back to the river. The hoe handle, however, started to swell from the bites of the snake. That hoe handle swelled until I had a 70-foot-long, 5-foot-diameter log down there in that corn field.

"Well, needing a new pigpen, I took my mule team and another borrowed from a neighbor and drug that log up to the barn where I had a sawmill. I sawed that log into enough planks to make a pen into which I put 300 hogs.

"That night the swelling went out of those hoe handle planks and squoze my 300 hogs to death. That ended my farming. I just gave up and became a politician."

Well, if old Bob had stayed on the farm he could have run his own windmill with that kind of hot air, so becoming a politician seems an eminently fitting career for him.*

Mel Newton of Orange Park, Florida,** also wrote a nice letter and included his favorite fish story. It also is a variation of an old one, but still good:

"Tom and Bill were fishing a river and Tom told Bill that, about a year previously, he had dropped his kerosene lantern overboard while landing a catfish, then almost a year later near the same spot he snagged the lantern, pulled it up and it was still burning.

"This was a mite much for Bill, who responded that Tom's yarn reminded him that while cane-pole fishing for bream, he had caught a 34-pound bass a week before.

"'Now Bill,'" said Tom, "'I hate to call you a liar, but they just ain't never been no such thing as a 34-pound bass.'

"'Well, Tom," said Bill, 'I will take off about 20 pounds of bass if you will blow out that lantern.'"

Egad, that reminds me of the fellow who caught an 18-pound bluegill on a three-pound cricket.

Mel said he enjoys the column and wishes I'd "work a little harder and give us more than one column a week." Careful with that work stuff, Mel — you know that puts a crimp in a feller's fishing time.

Continuing with another excerpt from Mel's letter: "I was raised in the South and can relate to everything you write about, especially the Depression years. I have been there. Like you, I am a pretty fair country cook, and love good things to eat, which my ample waist line will attest to.

**Editor's note: Bob Ross and Poke still spend time together. Bob is retired and living in Brunswick, Georgia.*

*** Mel Newton is retired and still lives in Orange Park.*

"I used to do all the barbecuing for my Masonic and Shriner outdoor activities, and was known far and wide for my 'secret' barbecue sauce. Of course, the reason it was secret was that I always had a few snorts before I made it and I never could remember what I put in the stuff. Then, too, a bunch of hungry Shriners will brag on boiled tennis shoes if someone else will cook it for them.

"I cut out the recipe for the cake you had in the paper, and it sounds delicious, but for heaven's sake send me the recipe on how to start the starter or print it in the paper."

Since that column on the brandied fruit and how good it is when used in a cake, I have received a score or more of starter recipes, and as soon as I can get them sort of sorted out I'll grind out another column on the subject. Maybe by next week I can have that done, since Mel's is only one of many requests for the starter recipe.*

One lady wrote all the way from Battle Creek, Michigan, to get the recipe. She said, "In December as we came home from Florida we passed through Tifton, Georgia, and bought The Florida Times-Union/Jacksonville Journal, Georgia edition… there was an article about brandied fruit cake. I cut out all the information hoping I might be able to find someone who would have a recipe for the starter. No luck yet. So now I wonder if you happened to have any luck with anyone sending in the recipe, and if you did would you please let me know how I could get it."

Glad to hear from the lady, and I'll send her a copy of the column on starter recipes just as soon as it's written.

**Editor's note: Poke tried to get the recipe and print it, but his wife, from whom he stole the cake recipe, refused to let her secret for the starter go.*

# "FOOTBALL PLAYERS ALL FALL DOWN."

*"Football players all fall down." And that, from the mouth of a female child, tells it all.*

ST. MARYS RIVER

A fellow named Paul Galloway, who wrote a clever piece about teaching women all about football, had to be just funning, for if he's smart enough to write he knows he's tackled an impossible project.

Meaning no disrespect for the ladies, it remains that teaching them all about football is about as easy as teaching a catfish to play bridge.

Now hold on, there, gals — this is not what you think. The fact that women don't learn football does not connote a lack of intelligence. On the contrary, it again proves they are smarter than us menfolks, and are far too practical-minded ever to see any logic at all in the game, and rightfully so.

They see it as a bunch of generally desirable young men doing their dangdest, with unbounded élan and the most reckless of abandon, to knock one another out from between their respective ears. Being generally sensible, most women figure that these young men could be engaged in much more pleasurable activities than practicing legalized mayhem upon one another under the guise of good clean fun.

Having concluded that there is absolutely no sense in the whole thing, the womenfolks are no more interested in learning the intricate details of the game than the catfish is in learning how to play bridge. Which, in the final analysis, may be the only sane way to consider the game of football.

But who is sane, when the big game gets under way? Certainly not the college fans such as those of Georgia, Florida,

Alabama, Auburn, Tennessee and other SEC schools. They go crazy a few weeks before the start of every season, have several recurring relapses and never fully recover.

But getting back to women and football — I do believe that the tersest and most fitting and all-encompassing description of the game came from my now teen-age granddaughter* when she was all of a year and a half old.

It happened once when I was watching some game on the tube, and she came careening around my chair to an abrupt halt before the screen. She studied the situation somberly for maybe 20 seconds, then turned to me with this classic:

"Football players," she intoned, "all fall down." Then she resumed her normal romping through the house.

Well, now just think about that for a minute. Doesn't it just about cover the field? Football players do indeed all fall down, again and again, and sometimes some of them don't get up again for awhile, and a few never do. I guess that tot said it for most womenfolks — so far as they are concerned the whole thing all falls down, and can stay there.

It is really hard to say what the fascination of the game

** Editor's note: The granddaughter, Kitti, is now 27 years old and has presented Poke with three great-grandchildren.*

is, but whatever it is, I have been ensnared by it, man and boy, for about half a century. I loved to play it, back about the time Pudge Heffelfinger was starring for Yale, and have watched it as spectator and reporter upon hundreds of occasions, on both the high school and college levels. I've even done a little officiating and a little coaching. And it never ceases to give me a thrill, although one cannot really watch a football game if he has to keep track of the action closely enough to report it accurately and clearly to the readers of next day's newspaper.

Back when I first got married, I tried, like Galloway, to teach my bride the finer points of the game. She never even learned the rougher points, and I realized then that it wasn't because she was dumb, but that she just didn't see any justifiable reason for the existence of the game.

My sisters, all of whom are smarter than I am, no doubt, never did learn the game either, although all their brothers and boyfriends either played it or were crazy about it in some other way. It is a hopeless waste of time to try to interest women in football; and besides, there are better things to try to get them interested in.

Still, I love the game personally, and am particularly gratified when something happens like the great Georgia Bulldogs' comeback last Saturday to beat Tennessee up there in Knoxville. After that one, I feel the Dogs have finally got revenge for that time in 1968 when Tennessee "stole" a 17-17 tie in the fading moments of the game by "completing" a dropped pass for a touchdown and then hitting on a two point play.

That's paying them back, fellows.

So go ahead, Mr. Galloway and all the rest of the young bucks who think they can convert their womenfolks, and waste your time. I'll use mine in what I always hope will be to a much better advantage with the gals.

# Football 'Brains' are Stranger than Fiction

*Poke thought things were bad in college football 15 years ago, from the standpoint of academic achievement, as this column reveals. It gets everything but better, every year that rolls by.*

ST. MARYS RIVER

That time of the annual fall madness, as some wag dubbed the game of football many moons ago, is upon us again. And that brings to mind a column *Florida Times-Union* sports editor Bill Kastelz of Jacksonville* had on the sad state of college academics/athletics, or how many "jocks" get by and get out of college with virtually no education, not to mention no diplomas. I note by reading the column that nothing has changed over the past 40 years, unless possibly for the worse.

Since the column was written, college authorities on the West Coast have reduced the PAC-10 to the PAC-5 conference, for post-season play, by finding all sorts of things wrong with the way some of the biggest names in college athletics, such as the University of Southern California and the University of California at Los Angeles, have been misconducting their sports business. But that's been gone over thoroughly elsewhere, so we won't bother much with it here.

But because of the ridiculous lengths necessary to go to in keeping star football players eligible for the weekly mayhem necessary to keep the big boys in the wire services' Top 25 and in running for lucrative bowl bids, many good stories have arisen to be told and retold by after-dinner speakers. And some

*Editor's note: Kastelz retired from the T-U in 1982 after 35 years with the paper, the last 27 as sports editor.*

of these stories are "more truth than poetry," as the saying goes.

During World War II, for instance, freshmen could play college football, and if a kid went into the military service whatever playing he did there didn't count against his eligibility when he returned to his college after his service stint. This led to some strange situations, indeed, such as Barney Poole, the great Ole Miss end, playing about seven years of college football at Mississippi and West Point. Shorty McWilliams of Mississippi State also played with Army and his college team, I don't know for how many years, and there were many others.

An outstanding example of college "crip courses" for athletes prompted the Atlanta Journal, about 35 years ago, to turn out a short, piquant editorial that went something like this:

"From a college press release, we note with interest that Mr. — (a great triple-threat back for the University of —) has successfully completed two semester hours of theory of coaching, two semester hours of advanced tennis, and two semester hours of fundamentals of swimming.

"This is fine, and all well and good.

"But in the interest of the all-around education of the man, what we'd like to know is what is his percentage at drawing to an inside straight and how does he do at Kelly pool?"

Even further back than that player's day, players could become eligible and ineligible on a week-to-week basis, depending upon their ongoing grades. There is a well-known businessman in South Georgia who once played a mean game of tackle for an SEC school, and he was conspicuous by his absence one game.

"John, what happened to you Saturday?" a fan asked later.

"Aw, they said I was illegitimate," growled John.

And then there was the tale of the Kentucky player who got in such a bind with his grades there seemed no way to keep him in school, let alone on the football squad. But the coach cried so hard that the dean finally agreed that if the player could answer one simple question he would declare him eligible to play.

So he asked the player, "What is the capital of Kentucky?"

"Duh-h-h... Lexington!" said the goon, triumphantly.

Shaking his head sadly, the dean said, "See there, coach, how can we keep a guy in the University of Kentucky who doesn't even know what the capital of the state is? Out he must go."

"Wait, wait!" cried the desperate coach. "Lexington is just 30 miles from Frankfort, the capital, and 30 from 100 leaves 70, and 70 is a passing grade anywhere!"

Then there was then one about Gorilla Jones, the terrific tackle who couldn't have gotten out of the first grade in a school for retarded apes. The dean called the coach and told him he was going to have to kick Gorilla out of school for cheating on an exam.

"How do you know he cheated?" asked the coach.

"Look at these papers," said the dean. "All 10 questions on the first page are answered identically by Student A and Gorilla."

"That don't mean nothin'!" snapped the coach. "Maybe the other guy was copying Gorilla's paper."

"We considered that possibility," replied the dean. "But look over here on Page 2, at question No. 11. Student A's answer is 'I don't know.' Gorilla's answer is 'I don't know, either!'"

There are dozens of other tales similar in nature, and more will develop as time goes on because it seems that, like the poor, the "dumb jock" athlete will be with us always. Too many of them are like what old Connie Mack is supposed to have said about one of his pitchers of yore: "A guy with a million-dollar arm and a ten-cent head."

Sad to say, in sports these days a lot of guys with ten-cent heads are getting millions of dollars for ten-cent abilities.

# It's a Shame That One Team Had to Lose

*Poke confesses that he left the Georgia-Florida football game in 1980 only moments before Georgia uncorked the most significant play in the school's long and golden history: a 93-yard pass play for a touchdown with only a minute left to play to pull out a 26-21 victory. It was a play that vaulted Georgia to the top of the national ranking and the one play of the year ultimately responsible for Georgia's first and thus far only national championship.*

Leave it to old Poke to miss the greatest play in University of Georgia football history

When Lindsay Scott caught that pass from Buck Belue and went through Florida's south forty like a runaway mule through a corn patch, guess where I was?

Where I was, was flagging a cab driver to deliver me to the front door of the Times-Union/ Journal building, just after the Florida punter had, I was convinced, patted down the last shovelful of dirt on Georgia's undefeated season by laying one out inside the 10-yard line. With just over a minute left and Florida leading 21-20, Georgia was second and 11 on its seven-yard line and apparently had no chance to win.

Smart old Poke tiptoed out to beat the crowd and quickly caught the passing cab.

"There go the pore old Bulldogs," I thought. "Done in again, in spite of all those heroics by Herschel Walker. Nothing to be ashamed of, though, 'cause Charlie Pell's Gators had taken control and turned what had seemed a routine loss for them into what seemed a sensational, certain and certainly well-deserved victory. It ain't any disgrace to get beat by a team playing as tough and skillfully as the Gators did."

Seldom have I ever made such a bad guess.

I have been watching these Georgia-Florida battles for many years, and so nothing either team does can surprise me anymore. But I do believe that comeback yesterday by the Bulldogs had to surpass anything I can remember. And now I can't tell my grandchildren that I saw it. Unless I lie a little bit.

Well, for the sake of Georgia's Southeastern Conference and national championship ambitions, I'm glad the Dogs pulled it out, but I do hate to see a bunch of kids lose a game where they put as much effort into it as the Gators did. It is too bad that in a titanic struggle like this one, somebody has to lose. They both earned wins, for I cannot see how Florida could have done any more and Georgia was fortunate enough not to have to do any more.

I got my first in-person look at that Herschel Walker character, and he is frightening. Being a Georgia fan from a long time back, I'm certainly glad he's a Bulldog. It would give a man a case of the weak knees and blind staggers just to contemplate having to face that feller from any position on the defensive team.

There is no doubt in my mind that if Walker stays healthy, the wordsmiths are going to have to invent a whole new set of superlatives to describe his efficiency and accomplishments on the football field. None of the clichés I know can do the job.

My old friend Harley Bowers of the *Macon Telegraph*, to whom everything he's ever seen about Georgia football has been, play after play, game after game and year after year, the best he's ever seen, finally has a subject in Herschel Walker upon which he cannot exaggerate.

I saw Harley in the press box yesterday, before the game, and of course he said, "Walker is the best I've ever seen." This time there was no hyperbole in the evaluation.

Walker, said Harley, was favoring a bad ankle yesterday. It slowed him down, I noted, to the tune of a measly 258 yards on the ground — including a 73-yard touchdown sprint in the opening moments of the superthriller. This sort of leads me to believe he might have really done the Gators some damage if he'd had two good legs.

Herschel did what he did despite being the prime target of as fierce a defense as Florida's Gators have produced in many seasons. Before these lads of Pell's are through they might well be the best ever to protect Gatorland. And that freshman quarterback Wayne Peace is as good as any first-year man in the country at his position and a great deal better than most.

There just isn't any way to defend against a back like Walker, though. Give him the ball 25-30 times a game and he is as certain to produce a touchdown or two as the sun is to come up in the east. Walker is big and he is fast. Lots of boys are big and fast. But when you say "fast" concerning Walker, you are talking about a guy who weighs 220 pounds and has about eight forward speeds, the first of which makes an ordinarily fast defensive back resemble a hen settin' eggs.

And even that isn't the secret of Walker. He has that sense of timing so rare that it approaches uniqueness and that indefinable instinct that all great running backs are blessed with. Like a superbly tuned heavyweight boxer, he reacts to an opening and kills you instantaneously with no more conscious effort than it takes to breathe. And he has the balance of a guy running across the Grand Canyon on a piano wire.

He is a joy to watch, as was that whole grand affair at the Gator Bowl yesterday. They just don't make football games any better than that one. It had everything a spectator could want even before that fire-and-brimstone thunderbolt finish, I keep telling myself — in consolation for not hanging around for a moment in Georgia football history comparable to all the great moments the Bulldogs have enjoyed through the years.

Indeed, this might have been the moment that Georgia won a national football championship. Certainly it was a moment that saved the Bulldogs from being removed from any consideration therefor.

Long live Walker, Scott, Buck Belue, Vince Dooley and Co., and may their tribe finish with a perfect year.

And genuine condolences to the Gators, who, as said, deserved better.

# Bulldogs Never Had to Fold 'Em

*A look back at the fantastic football season the University of Georgia put in the record books for the season of 1980 and the January 1, 1981, victory over Notre Dame that gave the Bulldogs the national championship. The season, the first for the incomparable Herschel Walker, had many thrilling and unforgettable moments, beginning with an opening squeaker over Tennessee and including an unbelievable last-minute win over Florida.*

ST. MARYS RIVER

Everybody said it couldn't be done, but nobody convinced Vince Dooley's "lucky" Georgia Bulldogs that they couldn't do it, and so now Georgia owns incontestable possession of the collegiate football championship of the United States of America and possibly the universe.

All of us owe the Dogs our finest accolades for an absolutely stupendous season, from the opening win over Tennessee, 16-15, to the unending drama of the Sugar Bowl battle to the death with mighty Notre Dame and the subsequent 17-10 triumph.

Many observers of the game of football had told me personally, and I had read it repeatedly in the newspapers, that Georgia was just a lucky team, that the Dogs hadn't played anybody, and that they were in serious danger of being completely blown out of the bowl game, their No. 1 ranking and the national title by the brute power and matchless gridiron tradition, strength and savvy of the Irish.

I never did buy that. I told anybody who'd listen that the Georgia team was reminiscent of some poker players I have contended with (unsuccessfully, I might add) over the years.

When these guys hit their hole card once in a while, you can call it luck. When it happens time after time on every big pot, you got to figure something else is going for the fellows who keep raking in the chips. They just got you whipped, and the best thing you can do is fold 'em and go home.

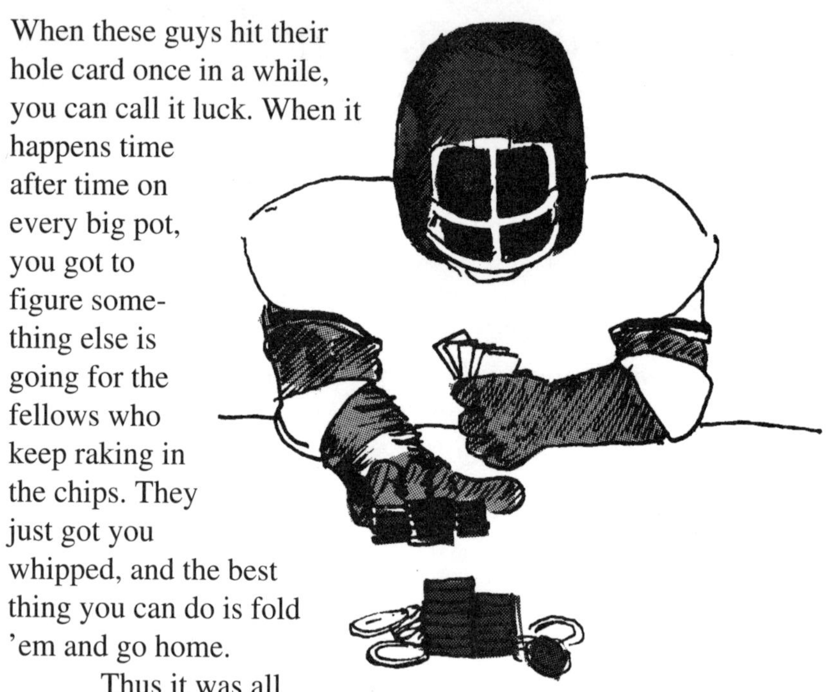

Thus it was all through the year with the Bulldogs. They did just whatever they had to do in order to keep the wolf away from the door, rescue the fair maiden, find the buried treasure, marry the boss's daughter and live happily ever after.

Against Clemson, it was a 69-yard punt return and a 99-yard pass interception return by Scott Woerner and a last-gasp 25-yard run by Herschel Walker to take the pressure off in an adrenalin boiler. Against South Carolina it was knocking Heisman Trophy winner George Rogers loose from the ball to stop a practically assured Gamecock winning score and preserve a 13-10 Georgia victory. Against Florida it took a 93-yard pass-run by Buck Belue and Lindsay Scott to prevail over Florida in the final minute of what appeared a certain defeat.

Mississippi was another hard-to-tame tiger, Auburn roared back to make it a ball game after trailing 31-7 and Georgia Tech even made it close after being on the verge of a rout. Things never seemed to come easy for these Bulldogs, and that makes their accomplishments even sweeter to contemplate.

Notre Dame's players, along with their gracious coach, Dan Devine, were most generous in their appraisal of the Georgia team, saying without dissent that the Dogs were the best team they had faced during the year, and this included, of course, Southern California's Trojans, who thumped the Irish by 20-3.

I wonder now, in light of comparing what happened to his Gamecocks against Pittsburgh in the Gator Bowl fiasco (it was 37-9 Pittsburgh), what South Carolina Coach Jim Carlen has to say. He never overlooked an opportunity, it seemed, to belittle the Bulldogs after they had beaten his team. He kept intimating, if not saying outright, that Georgia was not in the class with Michigan, beaten in Ann Arbor by South Carolina, or Southern Cal, a 23-13 winner over the Gamecocks.

I guess that if old Jim has a vote on the No. 1 team to be announced tomorrow, it will go to Pittsburgh or Southern Cal.

Pittsburgh did look mighty good in the Gator Bowl. But then, Pittsburgh wasn't going up against anything like the caliber of team that Georgia was against Notre Dame. Watching the Gamecocks against Pitt and then watching Notre Dame against Georgia leads me to believe Notre Dame would have treated the Gamecocks equally as badly as did the Panthers.

The fact remains that of all the great, near great, good, bad and indifferent major college teams in the country for the 1980 season, only Georgia escaped unscathed — unbeaten and untied through the regular 11-0 season and the only team of the many during the year ranked No. 1 able to hold that ranking through its bowl game against one of the nation's annual powers.

If you can remember that far back, Ohio State started the year as No. 1. Then it was one after another, including Alabama for a spell and even Notre Dame until the Irish barely managed a 3-3 tie with Georgia Tech. They tied Tech, too, mind you — Tech didn't tie them.

It was after that week that the Bulldogs took over the top spot and they never looked back.

There are many great heroes on this Georgia squad —

Woerner, Chris Welton, Jeff Hipp, Eddie Weaver, Jimmy Payne, Rex Robinson, Jimmy Womack, Belue, Scott, Amp Arnold, Nat Hudson, Nate Taylor, just everybody you can think of — but without doubt the individual who meant the most was the best freshman football player Georgia ever put on a field: Herschel Walker.

He may be the best freshman player anybody ever put on any field. He took the most terrible pounding Notre Dame's multimuscled monsters could put on him, including a separated shoulder, and always jumped up ready for more. And did he put it on those defenders, too! The constant primary target of a defense that had shut out Alabama and held every other back it faced to 86 yards or less, he smashed and crunched it for 150 yards and two touchdowns.

The guys who did the Heisman voting must be suffering considerable pangs of conscience when they look at what Walker did compared to what Rogers did when all the chips were on the table.

Thanks, Vince, Herschel, Buck and all you others. You have made all Georgians mighty proud of you.

# Sports Writers and Fantail Bass

*After the fantail bass, will the fantail quarterback be next? Poke might just invent him, as he did the fantail bass many years ago. He brings the piscatorial wonder back in this 1978 column, to illustrate the overall naivete of sports writers. Naivete is a refined word for ignorance, in most cases.*

ST. MARYS RIVER

University of Georgia football coach Vince Dooley got some adverse print on Georgia sports pages for electing to kick the tying point late in a game with Auburn, rather than try for two points and a victory. But that bad press was because the only thing more naive than the average sports writer is a below the average sports writer. And the naivete of even an above the average sports writer, an exceedingly rare few, is extremely high.

But that's the way sports writers are. I doubt very much that the great majority of them could analyze the game and come up with the proper decision that the Bulldogs were extremely lucky to get out with a tie, since the Auburns made a shambles out of their defenses all day and should have won the game easily. The Auburns, you remember, missed four field goal tries and lost a touchdown to an official's opinion after a 50-yard run to the Georgia goal line as the first half ended.

It would have been great if the Bulldogs could have won, and it is yet possible that they may go to the Sugar Bowl, since it is no lock that Alabama will beat the Auburns. But whatever happens, Dooley should not be criticized for gaining a tie. He should be congratulated that he didn't take a royal shellacking on the scoreboard, as he did otherwise.

Now all that is a long preamble to what I started out to

write about, which is the naivete of sports writers in general. Sports writers are the most gullible people, by far, in the newspaper business. They'll believe anything, and consequently are the easiest to hoodwink.

There is a child-like innocence about sports writers, which probably is a direct outgrowth of their child-like mentalities. So don't be too hard on them when they exercise all that poetic license. Just remember that they need all the help they can get.

Of course, this doesn't apply to all sports writers; occasionally one will come along with genuine intelligence (after all, old Poke once was a sports writer) but that is the rare exception. Most of them are as naive as one I knew on a South Georgia paper years ago.

This guy was an all-out gung-ho eager beaver on sports, but he knew very little about anything beyond a smattering of understanding of baseball and football. It was particularly irksome that he never wrote anything about fishing, probably because he knew absolutely nothing about the subject. For example, he got all excited and was ready to run a picture in the paper of a 12-pound carp some trot-liner had brought by.

Well, the city editor and I, being fishing buddies, cooked up a little thing for the sports editor. We sent him a cleanly typed and very official-looking letter from a fictitious fisherman. The "fisherman" complained that he had, a few days before, caught an extremely rare "fantail bass" in the Flint River near Albany, Georgia, where our newspaper was published, and there hadn't been a word about it in the paper.

Now this sports editor had a habit of trash-canning any letters of criticism, but we got around that by indicating on the bottom that a carbon copy had been sent to the publisher, who got highly upset at even the hint of anything critical of the paper. We knew the sports editor couldn't ignore the thing if he thought the publisher had a copy.

Meanwhile, the city editor and I had alerted all the leading fishermen in the organization, knowing that the sports man would question them. (This is another illustration of the naivete of sports writers. A simple bit of elementary research would have shown him that no such thing as a "fantail bass" had ever existed, but it never occurred to him to "look it up" —

just to ask a few fisherman.)

He started with me, and I assured him, in bug-eyed wonder, that if indeed a fantail bass had been caught in the Flint River, it was a story of worldwide import, since the fantail bass was thought to have been extinct since the last recorded catch in Australia in 1896.

By the time he had interviewed the chief photographer, the composing room foreman, a couple of printers and a reporter or two, all of whom were in on the joke, the sports editor was convinced he had one of the scoops of the century. He began making frantic (but of course futile) efforts to get in touch with the letter-writer for more details on the catch. As for the fantail bass itself, the guys on the paper supplied him with a wealth of fantastic descriptions and lurid historic detail. He accepted, of course, what we told him as gospel.

Well, he sat down and wrote a beautiful column about the thing and was all set to print it. We might have let him do it, too, except for the fact that he got in touch with the wire services, whose people didn't know any more about fishing then he did, and was fixing to have the "scoop" spread all over the world. We decided to call a halt before the thing got completely out of hand.

I just thought I'd tell you the story of the fantail bass, so that maybe you'd have a better understanding of sports writers in general, and thus know just how little the national rankings of football teams by sports writers really are worth. One day one of them might come up with a fantail quarterback; who knows?

*(Poke says the best thing about sports writing is that it beats working for a living.)*

# First Gator Bowl Game

*Reminiscing on the birth of the Gator Bowl football game, and some classic tales from Wake Forest's Peahead Walker, legendary and long-time coach. How a wooden leg was kidnapped and held for ransom.*

Wandering around in Jacksonville, Florida, on the eve of the annual Gator Bowl contest always sets me to remembering about when the whole thing started back in 1946. By some quirk of fate, as erudite cliché-spouters would say, I attended what they called the "First Annual Meeting of the Gator Bowl Association."

What I remember best about it was that the Wake Forest coach, Peahead Walker, was one of the speakers. (Wake Forest and South Carolina were the opponents in the first Gator Bowl contest.) Peahead's subject was listed on the program as "Phlegmatic Platitudes."

Peahead got up and said he didn't know what a phlegmatic platitude was, whether it was something good to eat, suitable for wearing or played tackle for the Green Bay Packers. So, he said, being totally unfamiliar with phlegmatic platitudes, he'd just discard the things and just talk about football.

He then proceeded to reel off a number of stories that had all of us roaring with laughter. I thought he was one of the most entertaining speakers I'd ever heard, and I heard him several times afterwards, and he never failed to leave me laughing.

One of the stories he told was about the time when he was playing semi-pro baseball, at $5 a game, while he was going to school at the University of Alabama. The manager, owner, business manager and promoter of the team was a gentleman with a wooden leg.

Well, the manager got seven games behind in paying Peahead for his efforts on the diamond. That amounted to $35, which was no mean bundle in those days.

Try as he might, Peahead couldn't collect from the man. All he could get was evasion and promises.

So one dark night Peahead sneaked into the two-bit hotel where the man had a room, eased into his room and tip-toed away with the manager's wooden leg.

Great was the uproar next morning, when old Peg-Leg found himself rendered immobile by loss of his leg. Peahead called him up and told him he was holding the leg for the "ransom" of the $35.

Peahead got the money, and that probably is the only case in history of the kidnapping of a wooden leg.

Out of the $35, Peahead said, he bought himself a handsome new suit of clothes and took it back to his dorm, arriving just as his roommate, a theology student, was getting ready to go on a heavy date.

"Peahead," said the roommate, "that is one more fine-looking suit. How 'bout letting me borrow it tonight?"

"Well," Peahead said he thought to himself, "this guy being a student to become a preacher, surely I reckon it'll be all right to let him borrow the suit."

So the preacher-to-be went out wearing the suit, and that was the last the University of Alabama saw of the preacher-to-be, and almost the last Peahead ever saw of the worthy gentleman.

"About 20 years later, however," Peahead recalled, "I was down in Miami and happened to stroll by a great big old church, and on a sign in front of the church was the name of the preacher, and it was the same name as my college chum.

"I wondered if it could be the same guy, so I strolled in

and quietly took a seat in the rear, and sure enough, it was him.

"He preached a slam-bang whiz of a sermon, and when it was over he stood in front of the pulpit while a great crowd of folks who attended the services filed by and shook his hand and told him what a wonderful preacher he was.

"I waited patiently until the last one had gone by, then I started down the aisle toward him.

"Well sir, he was positively beaming at me, all aglow with the spirit, but the closer I got the more his expression changed. By the time I got nearly to him he had recognized me, and his expression had changed from glowing benevolence to consternation, concern, and downright fear.

"'Walker!' he said to me. 'What in the world are you doing here, Walker?'

"I come to get my suit," Peahead said he informed the gentleman firmly.

At that, Peahead said, the preacher threw up both hands as if to ward off his tormentor, and uttered the following classic:

"Get out of here, Walker! Walker, you don't dare touch me! You can't mess with me! I'm saving souls for Jesus Christ!"

There was more to Peahead's talk, but those are the stories I have remembered vividly all these years and I guess I'll never forget.

South Carolina's coach at that time, Rex Enright, also made a talk during the program, as did Peahead's old buddy and longtime coaching rival, Frank Howard of Clemson.

The funniest story Enright told had to do with a halfback from the Purple Hurricane of my old high school at Fitzgerald, Georgia, named Tommy Attaway. The coach said his Gamecocks were trailing Clemson by six points and he wanted desperately to get out at the half no further behind, but Clemson had unleashed a killing passing attack of McFadden-to-Blalock. It clicked once for 20 yards, again for 20 and yet again for 20 and by this time the Clemsons were inside the Gamecock 20 with time for but one more play.

Enright called time, grabbed Attaway, and told him: "Tommy, get in there on defense in the backfield and don't pay any attention to anything except Blalock! Stay with him at any and all costs! Don't let him get a hair away from you! Watch Blalock! Watch Blalock! Got that?"

"Yes sir, coach," said Attaway, dashing into the fray.

On the next play, McFadden passed to Blalock for a touchdown as the half ended, and an enraged Enright made a bee-line for Attaway.

"I thought I told you to watch Blalock!" he screamed at Attaway.

"I did, coach," replied Attaway brightly. "And I want to tell you right now, he is one of the finest pass receivers I've ever seen!"

*(And with that, Poke wishes the Gator Bowl people and everybody else the happiest of new years.)*

# WATERMELONS AND DOVES

*No matter how many experiences an outdoorsman has throughout his years as a hunter and fisherman, there's always something new to be learned. This 1979 column was written about such an experience that occurred in the late 1950s or early 1960s on a farm in Seminole County, Georgia, near Donalsonville and Iron City. To date, the watermelon-loving dove phenomenon has remained unique in Poke's life and times.*

ST. MARYS RIVER

Lately there has been a lot of trouble with truck drivers striking and farmers losing a lot of watermelons and other crops in the fields because they didn't have any way to get the stuff to market.

It reminds me of some halcyon days of years back when my Albany, Georgia, friend Ace Adams, the old New York Giants pitcher, had a farm down around Donalsonville.

Every year at the start of the early dove season in September a bunch of us would gather down at Ace's farm for the opening day shoot. We never were sure just where the doves were, or even if there were any around, but always we managed to find them flying around someplace.

This farm was a dream place to get away to. There were no television sets, and not even any books or newspapers. Once I went looking for some bathroom reading matter and couldn't find anything but a 12-year-old copy of a Popular Mechanics magazine.

The acreage was right on Spring Creek, which is one of the prettiest streams in Georgia or anywhere else. It is full of fine fish, too, and the hardwoods lining its banks harbored countless squirrels.

In short, this was a place you could settle into and just let it all hang out, as the saying goes. And believe you me we did, too, about a dozen or two of us who used to make it an annual event.

The particular year of this story was one ( I believe the only one) when the state raised the daily bag limit for doves from 12 to 18. This prompted old Ace to grumble, "Confound it, I had enough trouble killing 12. Now the so-and-sos expect me to kill 18!"

That year Ace rented 125 acres of his farm to a nephew who planted the whole 125 acres in watermelons. He had contracted with various markets to deliver the melons to them at an agreed-upon price and an early date, and he went about raising watermelons as methodically as a carpenter builds a house. He irrigated the place, fertilized it copiously, and did whatever else it is you do to make watermelons.

And pardners, he made watermelons. I don't know if you have any idea of how many watermelons you can grow on 125 acres, but it is an astounding number. I didn't know there were that many watermelons in the world when I took a look at that field about the time it was ready for harvesting.

The grower had 18-wheel-semi rigs coming in in relays to haul those melons out of there. They were gathered in the field by hand and hauled by pickup truck to a collection center and loaded on the trucks by conveyor belt. It was a regular assembly line business that sent those melons rolling to the markets of the north.

When the grower got all he needed to fill his contracts, he just quit harvesting. He explained that by this time everybody else's melons were coming in and that he could do no better than break even, if that well, by gathering the rest of the mammoth crop. So he left at least half — and maybe two-thirds — of those melons to rot in the field.

Well, the dove season opened a few months after the grower abandoned the watermelon field with those thousands of melons decayed there.

Ace and I went touring the place trying to spot doves, and we found them in that watermelon field literally by the thousands. I guess they were eating the seeds of those watermelons, but whatever it was they were truly there in plenty, and they stuck around as if it were a baited field.

On opening day about 15 of us spread out around that huge patch and anybody who didn't get his limit of birds (and there were some who did not, by any stretch of law-abidement, stop at 18) just couldn't hit them. We all got limits on Saturday, Sunday, and Monday, the first three days of the early season, and when we left Monday afternoon you couldn't tell that the population of birds had been depleted in any manner. There were still countless doves gobbling watermelon seeds.

Now, I don't know if that was just a freak thing or whether doves really go for abandoned watermelon patches, since I had never seen anything like it before and haven't since. But it might be something for the farmers to watch out for, if they have to leave melon crops in the fields. Just don't bother the things till dove season gets here, which won't be long, and there just might be better shooting than anyone expects.

# REMEMBER WHEN GASOLINE WAS 20 CENTS PER GALLON?

*Here's a 1979 column of reminiscences about buying a Cadillac in the good old Depression days of the 1930s, when they made 16-cylinder V-type automobile engines that vigorously gulped 20-cents-a-gallon gasoline and, in at least one case, burned five quarts of oil per 18 miles. And of taking pretty girls out to look at the moon, and other things. Read on:*

ST. MARYS RIVER

I see in the news now that the government is going to set 15.4 cents per gallon as the maximum retailers can profit per gallon of gasoline they sell. It is being said that this means mostly another increase in the price at the pump for the juice America lives by, but that in some areas it will mean a rollback of prices.

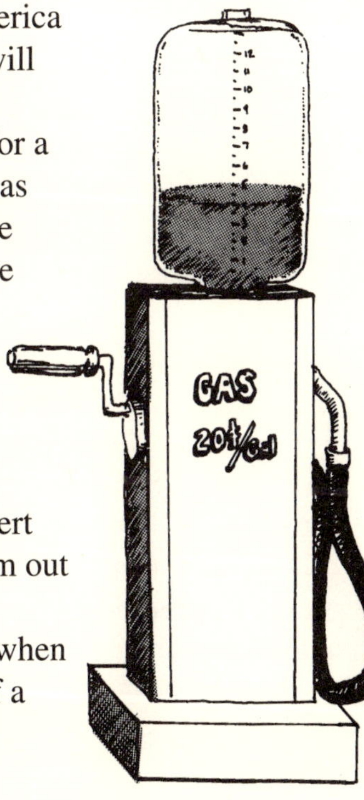

Personally I have thought for a long time that the retailers are just as much involved in the gasoline price ripoff of the American public as are the oil barons of the United States and the sheiks of OPEC. But I'll leave most of the comment on that to the big-time columnists and editors, most of whom are in the class of what I consider an expert to be. An expert is a so-and-so from out of town with a briefcase.

Some of us can remember when the long-standing standard price of a gallon of gas was 20 cents, and on occasion during gas wars I have bought the stuff for less per gallon than what the retailer is allowed as profit margin these days. Young folks today find it hard to believe that there were really days when you could put five gallons of gas in your car and change the oil (five quarts) for a buck and a half.

In those days you also could buy a stomp-down, genuine, juicy, fresh, all-beef, good-sized, all-the-way hamburger for a dime. Cokes were a nickel, and the price of the swankiest movie in town was a dime. Shucks, a fellow in those days could take a couple of dollars and treat his date to a really fine evening. Nowadays two bucks won't pay the tip at a fast-food stop.

At one time during those memorable experiences, a friend of mine by name of Lee Luke and I pooled our resources and bought us a Cadillac. It was a vehicle that had been worn out as a bootlegger's car, and was some dilly of an automobile. It was seven or eight years old, I guess, and was a sport roadster with rumble seat, a dashboard that probably was the forerunner of the instrument panels of a four-engine jetliner, a V-16 (that's right, believe it or not, 16 cylinders) engine under a hood roughly as long as a bowling lane.

Lee and I promised one of the Honest John used car dealers in our town $60 for the Cadillac, paying $15 down and agreeing to pay off the balance at $15 a month.

Well, we got it on a Saturday and had dates that night with a couple of the local belles, and they were some kind of impressed when we called for them after washing and shining our new car, putting five gallons of gas in the empty tank and pouring in five quarts of oil necessary to bring the stick up to what we considered a safe driving level.

Off we went to Bowen's Mill — a popular parking spot for teen-agers in those times — to look at the moon, among other things. It was nine miles from our hometown of Fitzgerald, Georgia, to Bowen's Mill. Lee was driving, with his girl in the front seat, and my girl was in the rumble seat with me when we tooled out of town.

Lee got the old Caddie accelerating pretty good,

although the engine was making some strange grunts and gurgles, along with an occasional whomp and blamp. But, when the speedometer needle hit 55, that old car began to shudder so hard I swear I thought the front wheels had turned sideways. It was all Lee could do to keep it in the road until he could slack back on the speed. It never wobbled until reaching the 55 mark, and then you couldn't hold it.

In the general shakeup, something (it definitely wasn't me) put a bad bruise on my date's knee and also put her out of sorts for the rest of the evening, but that's another story.

When we rolled back homeward about midnight, the engine seemed to be getting fearfully warm, doing a lot of smelly smoking and emitting an alarmingly louder and more frequent series of blomps, blangs and barrumphs. Then it quit, just inside the city limits, before we even got the girls safely back home. We figured it was done for altogether, but actually we were simply out of gas. A check of the stick showed we also were out of oil, too.

It was hard to believe, but painfully true. To drive our "new" Cadillac an 18-mile roundtrip had taken five gallons of gasoline and five quarts of oil.

As a natural consequence of this, Lee and I figured we couldn't afford that chariot even with gasoline at 20¢ a gallon and oil at 10¢ a quart, and so on Monday we dispossessed ourselves of one badly used Cadillac by returning it to old Honest John. He squawked mightily and of course wouldn't hear of returning any portion of our $15; indeed, he threatened to have the law on us for something or other, but we simply threw him the keys, walked off and left the Cadillac-owning business to people a mite more affluent than we were.

Years later I did own one more Cadillac and that surely is another complete story, which I'll try to remember to write down in the next week or two, between fishing trips.

*(Columnist Poke McHenry says he told everybody they'd be sorry when they junked their Hoover buggies and took up automobiles.)*

# Foiled Ranger

*Almost every man, at some crucial point in his life, faces a situation where he either has to back down or choose some foolish action that will get him uselessly killed, or at least badly maimed. Today's story, written in 1978, is one such example. What would you have done?*

BRUNSWICK, Georgia

The controversy keeps raging around here about whether or not to put a crimp in the Florida boys' hunting in Georgia, and this keeps talk of poaching alive, and that keeps reminding me of tales of poachers I have heard of over the years.

One of the best stories concerns an eager young game warden who'd just gotten his uniform, badge and gun and sallied forth to bring the law down upon all those villainous characters out there busily breaking Georgia's game and fish restrictions and requirements. It was right after Georgia had put in the law requiring fishing licenses, which has been a good while ago.

This Ben Hill County, Georgia, warden had parked his pickup truck about as far into the Ocmulgee River swamp as he could drive, then set out on foot "patrolling" the river bank looking for law-breaking fisherman. He found three, about a mile from his truck.

The trio consisted of a huge man in his early 40s and two grown sons, both nearly as big as the old man, who'd stretch the scales near the 300-pound mark and wasn't fat, either — just a big, tough hombre.

"Howdy," said the warden. "Having any luck?"

"Some," replied the old man.

"What are you catching mostly?"

"Fish."

"Hey, fellow, now you just don't talk too much, do you?"

"Nawp."

"Well, I guess you fellows have your fishing licenses, don't you?"

"What's a fishin' license?"

"You mean you don't even know? Well, you see the state has just passed a law and now everybody's got to have a license to fish."

"Never heerd of sich a thing. We ain't got none."

"In that case, I'm going to have to make cases against you. I'll have to take you in."

"Take us in whar?"

"To the courthouse. You'll have to post bail if you want to go to trial, or pay fines otherwise."

"How you propose to take us in, dead or alive?"

"Well, ha ha, that is, of course I wouldn't shoot you, or anything like that…"

"Naw, I don't figger you will, sonny. Shoot a pore old

man and his two boys, who ain't even fighting you, jest because we ain't got no fishing license? You'd sure git into a lotta trouble that way. Besides, you don't even know who we are, or how important. Why, I might be the governor's brother, for all you know."

"Who are you anyway?" asked the now nettled game warden.

"Ain't gonna tell you, sonny," the old man said slyly. "And neither one of my boys can talk." At this point he bestowed a look upon the boys designed, successfully, to keep them as mum as King Tut.

"Now," said the old man. "You don't know who we are, and you ain't gonna find out. And we ain't goin' no place with you, 'less you carry us. We ain't gonna fight, we jest gonna set down right here and let you tote us to your truck. I heerd you come in, and I know about how fur it is to yore pickup. You gonna git pretty tired time you tote all three of us all that ways.

"You gonna have to tote us one at the time, and by the time you git the second one toted the first un'll be long gone from the truck.

"Fact o' the matter is, podner, they jest ain't much of a damn thing you can do, is they?"

The warden had gone from frustration to irritation to a burning anger, but the fact of the matter was, there wasn't a thing he could do about the situation. At least nothing he could think of in reaching back into his limited training and experience.

He thought of trying a bluff with his gun, but the old man seemed to read his mind.

"I said we weren't gonna fight, sonny," he said. "But you start pulling that gun and you could come to a bad accident right quick. You standin' too close to me to ever git it out, and by the time you did, me and the boys would have it away from you and we got some pretty drastic ideas what we'd do with it, asides from shooting you. We don't take kindly to folks pullin' guns on us."

So the ranger did what any sensible man would have done — he backed out of a bad situation with as much grace as he could muster, but he could not refrain from leaving them without saying "I'll see you again — there'll be another time."

"Any ol' time sonny, any ol' time," said the old man jovially as the defeated warden beat his bitter way back to his vehicle.

# Lawyer Gets the Last Laugh on a Game Warden and a Deer Head

*In this 1979 column appearing in the Jacksonville, Florida Times-Union daily newspaper, Poke recalls an actual case where the brow-beating skills of a clever lawyer cleared a man accused of illegally killing a deer. It was a typical outcome in many such cases in the Great Depression years of the 1930s.*

ST. MARYS RIVER

It is odd how telling a story will remind someone of a similar tale — such as did the "barroom lawyer" I wrote about a few weeks back. The lawyer was old Francis, and he routed a farmer from a tavern by tearing apart the farmer's action in confiscating a horse and bicycle from a pair of youthful watermelon snatchers.

It reminded me of a game-poaching arrest and charge story that unfolded in New Smyrna Beach, Florida, back in the 1930s, when my uncle was operating a fish truck up and down the east coast of the Florida.

This tale also concerned a sharp-shooting lawyer (possibly old Francis's grandfather) and it actually took place in a courtroom.

The prosecution put a game ranger on the stand and introduced a deer head as evidence, Exhibit No. 1, or something like that. The ranger identified the head as the one he had taken off of a poached (illegally killed) deer.

But then came the cross-examination, and the fun began.

"What did you say that object was?" the defendant's lawyer asked the witness.

"A deer head, of course," replied the ranger.

"How do you know it is a deer head?" asked the lawyer.

"Why, of course it's a deer head! Anybody can see that! What do you mean 'How do I know?'"

"Who made you an authority on deer heads? Have you been to college and got a degree in identification of deer heads? Can you prove you are qualified to state positively and

irrevocably and beyond a shadow of a doubt, at the risk of perjuring yourself, that that is a deer head?"

This line of questioning went on and on, with the lawyer continuing to skillfully lead the witness deeper and deeper into confusion as the jury members found it harder and harder to keep from laughing out loud. Finally the poor game warden was so befuddled he admitted that he had no idea what that deer head was and that as a matter of fact (this educed by the lawyer) it could have been a piece of flotsam that just came drifting down the river.

This, of course, ruined the state's case and the poacher went free. But I suspect the fact that most of the jurors probably were in sympathy with the defendant had as much to do with his escaping punishment as did the cleverness of the attorney. You see, back in those days just about everybody was scrabbling for a living and many a man badly bent a few game and fish laws to help feed his wife and children.

There is no doubt, however, that a good lawyer has helped many a defendant who stood before the court hoping not for justice but mercy.

Many funny jokes have been created about lawyers of the Francis type, but most lawyers I know (and I know a lot of them) are good sports and can laugh at themselves, as all folks with balanced senses of humor can. So I don't think they'll mind if I pass along this oldie:

Seems a doctor, architect and lawyer were having a friendly discussion about whose profession was the oldest.

"Mine is, of course," argued the doctor. "When God made woman he took a rib from Adam, and that was a surgical procedure, which means medicine is the oldest profession."

"Oh, no," the architect claimed. "God created the world out of chaos, and that was the greatest architectural achievement of all time. That means my profession is the oldest."

"Ha!" snorted the lawyer. "And who do you think created the chaos?"

# Jogging for Office

*This 1978 column will tell you, among many other things, how an affable and likeable politician got re-elected while in prison, and how this same fellow earlier took charge of a blackjack game high above the earth and cornered the money market, even though he "knew nothing" about the game and was only playing to be "sociable."*

ST. MARYS RIVER

This year is getting away like doves winging downwind, and another election season approaches. So the political bug already is busy biting hither and yon, not to mention the likes of Dawson Mathis.* Hither and yon may survive and shrug it off, but once a guy like Dawson is smitten he is lost forever.

The other day I was poking about Albany, Georgia, and bumped into a Mathis aide. "Is he running for what I hear he is?" I asked.

"He's walking," said the aide, a bit on the smirky side. In fact, as smirks go, his was pretty close to 100 proof. "He's walking."

Since then, obviously, old Dawson has stepped up his walk to a jog and is warming up to take off in a full-fledged gallop at the United States Senate seat of the Hon. Herman E. Talmadge. Old Herman being in a mite of trouble, maybe, everybody seems to think this may be the year he's ripe for the bagging.

Dawson believes that he can, with his pretty face and charming manner, woo enough voters over the state to make him a U.S. senator. And he might do it. I never thought he had a chance to get elected U.S. representative, but he made that in a walk. And now he's been in Washington for five terms, and

*Editor's note: Dawson Mathis was a Georgia politician who served 10 years as a U. S. representative from Georgia's 2nd District.*

to the best of my knowledge and remembrance he has never done anything constructive.

This, of course, places him exactly on the level with his 434 contemporaries. None of them has done anything constructive.

On the other hand, old Dawson hasn't done anything destructive, either, which places him a cut above some of the other such mental giants in the House who go about taking actions that always make the country anything from a mite to a mountain worse off than if they'd done nothing.

I imagine Dawson will, if he does take on old Herman, find that despite all his woes Herman is not going to be an easy nut to crack. One of my buddies remarked the other day that if they caught old Herman in the act of robbing a bank, the people of Georgia would still re-elect him.

I don't know if that is true or not, but I do know people have some odd outlooks concerning their elected officials. For instance, about five years ago the late Jewell Futch was sheriff in Lowndes County, Georgia, and was under all sorts of prosecutions for various charges. I was in a service station at Twin Lakes, a small community in Jewell's domain, and asked the station operator if he reckoned old Jewell was guilty.

"I don't know," he replied. "He probably is. But I don't care. If he was running I'd still vote for him."

Then there was the case of the middle Georgia town that, a few years ago, had a mayor that got into trouble with the feds, was convicted and sent off to a correctional institution. While incarcerated there, he ran for another term and the people of the town re-elected him mayor.

I knew this man, and if he was a crook he was the most jovial and congenial miscreant I have ever had the pleasure of knowing. Once I was on one of those military junkets where they take civilian VIPs and fly them around to various bases for sundry purposes, and the mayor was one of the VIPs on the trip.

We were on an old piston-engine aircraft refitted in a manner befitting the stations, and general lifestyles, of its passengers. In other words, there was a bar, card tables, plush chairs, a galley and other little creature comforts. Somebody suggested a blackjack game, and I was all for joining until someone asked the mayor if he'd play and he replied:

"Well, sure. I don't know the first thing about the game, but I'll play just to be sociable."

I'd had heard the likes of that often enough in my wayward career to know better than to risk my poor stock of capital in that game. Sure enough, after about four hands the mayor hit blackjack, got the deal and proceeded to corner the money market. One Army colonel lost more than $300, a theater manager was whisked out of about $100, and half a dozen or so others lost varying amounts, none less than $85.

As the beaming mayor was sorting and stacking his not inconsiderable additional wealth, I remarked: "Mayor, I thought you said you didn't know anything about that game."

"I don't son," he replied with an outrageous wink. "But it beats hell out of farming, don't it?"

It is no wonder the folks re-elected him.

*(Columnist Poke McHenry gave up poker when he was called by a woman who said she had two pairs. "What are they?" asked Poke. "Two pairs of queens," she replied.)*

# Lo! The Bureaucrats

*Although this column first appeared on June 2, 1979, there has been no change in U. S. government policies and procedures, except for the worse, during the ensuing years. It is far harder to get the attention of the members of Congress than it is the hardheadedest mule that ever ignored a command. This is no doubt because the hardheadedest and dumbest mule that ever lived is smarter and more tractable than the smartest congressman occupying space in Washington today.*

ST. MARYS RIVER

Here's a news item that's downright interesting, and tells pretty clearly how the average little Georgian feels about the Feds today:

"Atlanta (AP) - Government efforts to interest small businesses in Georgia in exporting aren't working — primarily because the businessmen think larger firms will reap the profits, a University of Georgia study shows.

"One is literally flabbergasted by Georgia's small business persons who are unaware of the availability of assistance from state and federal agencies. Small businesses are convinced that none of the schemes the U.S. Government dreams up ever have any teeth and for all practical purposes can be considered paper tigers.

"One often hears, for example, the argument that every time the United States sets up… rules to facilitate exports or activity of a smaller firm, it becomes so complicated that only large companies with the help of a Washington super-lawyer can reap the benefits."

They are so right, those small business "persons." I haven't seen any of Washington's proposals to help small business folks in the exporting business, but I don't have to see

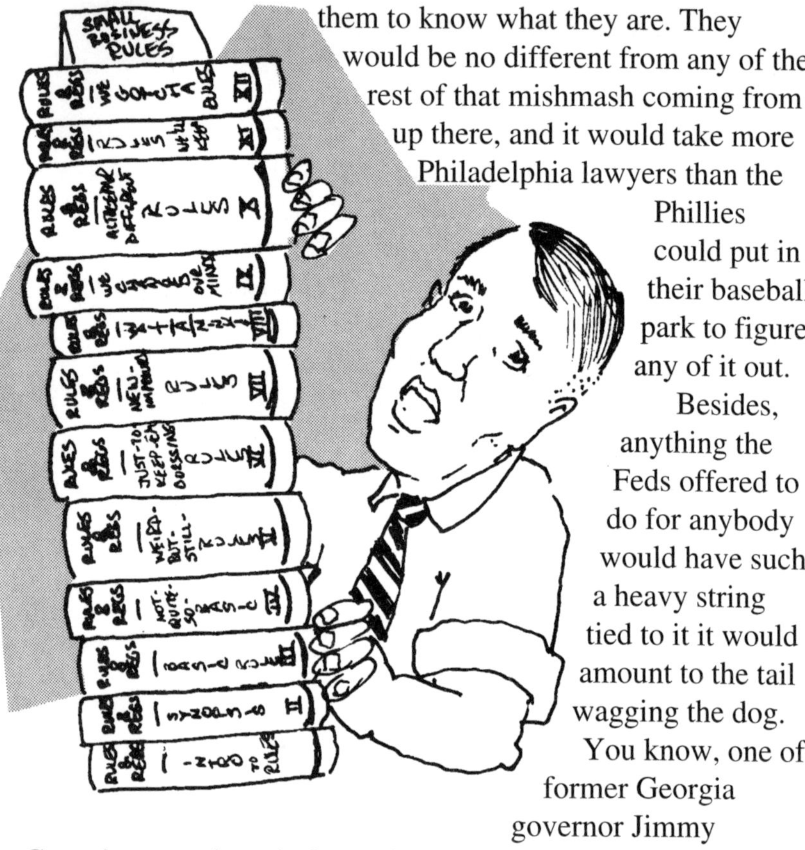


them to know what they are. They would be no different from any of the rest of that mishmash coming from up there, and it would take more Philadelphia lawyers than the Phillies could put in their baseball park to figure any of it out.

Besides, anything the Feds offered to do for anybody would have such a heavy string tied to it it would amount to the tail wagging the dog.

You know, one of former Georgia governor Jimmy Carter's campaign platform planks when he ran for president was that he would "reorganize" the federal government. That was one of the many reasons I did not vote for him, and urged everyone else I could buttonhole not to vote for him. I figured that if Jimmy reorganized the federal government like he did Georgia's, we'd be in a heap more trouble — and aren't we, though?

It all reminds me of an incident several years back involving a couple of girls I knew who worked for the base newspaper at the Marine Corps Supply Center at Albany, Georgia.

One day while at work they smelled something burning, or about to burn. The scent got stronger, and they began to look for the cause. They couldn't find anything, but decided it might be prudent to call the fire department, which they did.

Firemen arrived promptly, fanned out through the place and discovered a short-circuited air conditioning unit, red hot and about ready to set the whole place aflame.

Well, the girls felt pretty proud of themselves, thinking that at least they would be commended for probably saving a valuable building and a batch of expensive contents.

But no! On the contrary, a few days later there came down from headquarters a rather stiff reprimand, pointing out that the girls failed to follow the proper procedure for reporting fires. It seems there were 12 steps, to be taken in strictly regulation manner (and probably in triplicate) in order to properly report a fire. The employees were taken to task rather severely for gross neglect of bureaucracy, or some such thing.

Not only were the girls censured, but headquarters sent around to all departments copies of the 12 steps for reporting fires, to be posted in prominent places and be followed in strict order and with absolute implicitness and undeviation, whether or not your coattail might be ablaze all the while.

I tell you what's the truth, if the government had had anything to do with the Chicago fire, the thing would have eaten its way to Pittsburgh, at least, before the proper authorities had been properly notified.

*(If you think columnist Poke McHenry is in contempt of the federal government, all branches, you are so right.)*

# Maybe Dirty Dan Has the Answer for President Carter

*In this 1979 column is the tale of Dirty Dan, illustrating the woeful ineffectiveness of President Jimmy Carter; and the "security" old Tuck demanded for a $2 loan.*

ST. MARYS RIVER

The country seems to be getting into a worse-and-worse mess, and the administration certainly isn't doing anything positive about it, as far as I can tell. Old Jimmy Carter seems to have about as much clout as that fellow who was the victim of Dirty Dan in the old joke.

It seems this guy was a rancher, and one day he loped home on his horse only to find that his house had been looted, his bunkhouse burned down and all his hired hands chased off, his cattle rustled, his horses stolen, and his wife raped. Stuck down in the front yard was a big sign proclaiming, "Dirty Dan Done This."

Well, the rancher rode into town and went into the saloon and asked the bartender if he knew anybody named Dirty Dan.

"Why shore buddy," said the bartender. "He's that big guy with the black beard back there at the poker table."

The rancher approached the poker game, taking note that Dirty Dan weighed about 300 pounds and was wearing a pair of pistols so big they should have been on wheels.

"Your name Dirty Dan?" the rancher asked the big tough guy.

"Yeah, what about it?"

"Did you go out to my house today and loot the place,

burn down my bunkhouse, chase off my crew, steal my horses, rustle my cattle, and rape my wife?"

"Yeah, what about it?"

"Lemme tell you something buddy," said the rancher sternly. "You better watch that stuff!"

I thought of that joke when I read the other day where the Carter administration had warned the steel companies that they'd better be careful in raising prices lest they be in violation of the president's guide-lines.

In case they should be, they'd better watch that stuff, by golly.

Carter's position generally also is about like that of old Tuck, Who toiled many years in a variety of capacities on one of South Georgia's newspapers.

One day old Tuck marched into the editor's office and, pounding the desk top with his fist, informed the boss that "I'm gonna have a raise or else!"

"Or else what, Tuck?" replied the boss-man rather coolly.

"Oh well then, in that case," said Tuck, "else I'll just keep working for what I'm getting."

Tuck was another of the many great characters I have

been associated with through a lifetime in the crazy newspaper business. I once heard a guy ask Tuck to lend him two dollars.

"What?" yelped Tuck. "I tell you what to do. You bring me a plank from the deck of Noah's Ark. You bring me a rib from the whale that swallowed Jonah. You bring me one of the 30 pieces of silver with what Judas betrayed the Lord. You bring me the rod what Moses parted the waters of the sea with. You bring me the jawbone of the ass with what Samson slew the Philistines. You bring me the rock what David slung down Goliath with. Yeah now, you go and bring me all them things. And when you do, then maybe, jes' maybe, I might let you have that two dollars!"

Tuck wrote a good deal of philosophy and poetry, some of it doggone good, and I have always regretted that I never got around to copying a lot of it and preserving it for posterity. Then one day old Tuck was not with us anymore, and I don't suppose anybody ever saved what he had jotted down.

I wish he was still around. I'd like to hear his opinions of Mr. President Carter and the mess he's in, along with the rest of us.

*(Columnist Poke McHenry thinks every president the country has had in the past 40 years has been worse than the one before him, and Carter is an outstanding example of that belief.)*

# Muley Stories

*Some tales about mules, and how their general demeanor compares to that of certain politically active persons who claim to be of the female persuasion, and other such nonsense.*

News item:

"Sanger, Calif. (AP) — As Mosco pounds down the track, his four legs driving and neck outstretched, he has the unmistakable mark of a champion.

"Equally unmistakable are those mule ears. But Mosco isn't just any mule. He is the champion of the world.

"At Bishop, California, a Mojave Desert town called the Mule Capital of the World, Mosco won a 440-yard race named for former California Assemblyman Larry Chimbole who authored legislation establishing a five-year pilot program of pari-mutuel mule racing.

"In his first year in the infant sport, the 4-year-old has won mule racing's unofficial triple crown. "He was named Running Mule of the Year, the American Mule Association's champion for 1978, and last July won the Larry Chimbole Mule Championship of the World, the first pari-mutuel mule race."

Somehow it seems altogether fitting and proper

that California should be the place where the mule finally gets some respect, seeing as it is so full of jackasses. They may be about ready to elect a mule governor, which would be a distinct improvement over what they've been having.

The mule has been the source of a great many jokes over the years as, considering his origin, temperament and intelligence, he naturally would have been. This humor is typified by the story about the mule trainer who opened classes by whanging the mule between the eyes with a two-by-four scantling, explaining that in order to train a mule you first had to get his attention.

A favorite mule story of mine concerns the farmer whose mule came down sick and he was told that a neighbor, Jed, also had recently experienced the same thing.

Meeting with Jed, who was about as verbose as Cal Coolidge with a toothache, the farmer asked Jed if he hadn't had a sick mule lately.

"Yep," said Jed.

"Well, what did you do fer him?"

"Gi'e 'im a quart o' turpentine."

"Thanks."

"Y'welcome. Giddap."

With that Jed drove his wagon down the road one way, and the farmer his in the other.

A week later they met again as they were driving their wagons down the same road.

"Whoa," said the farmer. "Jed, didn't you tell me you gave your sick a mule a quart of turpentine?"

"Yep."

"Well, I gave mine a quart of turpentine, and it killed him."

"Killed mine, too," said Jed. "Giddap."

Another good mule story concerned a sharecropper who was trying to sell a blind mule and was doing his best to keep the prospective buyer from knowing the animal couldn't see. The mule, sensing a stranger was laying hands on him as the shopper tried to get a close look, panicked and charged headlong into the side of the barn, with a shattering crash.

"Man," said the prospective buyer, glaring hard at the sharecropper, "that mule is blind!"

"Nawsuh! No suh, ain't no sucha thing!" the owner avowed heatedly. "That mule ain't noways blind! That mule just don't give a damn!"

For sure, nothing in the world is as hard-headed as a mule, unless it is a women's lib fanatic. Come to think of it, "Ms" could be an abbreviation of "mules," couldn't it?

Tell 'em you read it here first.

*(Columnist Poke McHenry actually has nothing against women's libbers. And less than that for them.)*

# Cows and Fish

*Reminiscing about the good old days when cows roamed the wilds, and the highways, of Florida, and when Georgia motor vehicles had two tags, and when a Florida tag inspector couldn't arrest a Georgian because if he did, Florida would have been liable for $300 worth of fish — a heap of fish in those days, indeed.*

ST. MARYS RIVER

Seeing a recent newspaper story of the days when tick-infested scrub cows roamed the South Georgia and North Florida woods brought back some memories.

No, contrary to what a lot of folks think, old Poke is not old enough to have ridden the fence line back in the 1920s, but he is old enough to remember the scrub cows of the 1930s. They were so tough you just about had to have diamond edged blades in the machine to grind hamburger and you couldn't, as the old folks used to say, "stick a fork in the gravy."

In those days the cows roamed wherever they so desired, and that included crossing roads or highways whenever it suited their fancy. There was no law forcing folks to fence them in, and if you killed one with a car you were responsible for the animal. Nowadays it is different, and the owner of the animal can be held liable for damages to the vehicle, I understand, if it hits a cow on the highway. And you could buy three brand new Model T automobiles, in the old days, for what the average damage is now to one of these overpowered tin cans they call automobiles when it hits a cow.

I remember a tale about one tenant farmer who had some of those scrub cows and calves, and one of his calves kept getting out and foraging in a neighbor's garden.

The neighbor fastened the calf in his barnyard and told

the owner he was going to charge him 50 cents a month for "keep" for the animal. The tenant agreed to pay, but three months went by and he hadn't anted up anything.

"You owe me $1.50," said the neighbor. "And if you don't pay up I'm just going to keep the calf for the buck-fifty you owe me."

The tenant scratched his head in thought for a few moments, then said. "Let him stay another month, boss, he's worth $2."

I used to ride up and down the east coast of Florida with an uncle in his fish truck, hauling fish back up and wholesaling them to markets in South Georgia. We dodged many a scrub cow on the old U.S. 1 highway in those years, and had some great experiences otherwise.

Once my uncle had lost one of the tags on his truck (they had tags on the front and the back end in those days), and while we were stopped in Deland for some sort of business the old man had there, a state tag inspector, or some such varmint, sniffed around and saw that we didn't have but one tag.

He told my uncle flatly that he was going to have to buy a Florida tag, at a cost of more than $50 (Georgia tags cost $3 then), before he could drive the truck back to Georgia. My uncle showed him a letter from the Georgia vehicle registration folks, acknowledging my uncle's notification to the state of his lost tag, and permitting him to operate with one tag until a replacement could be obtained.

"You can't hand me that stuff," the inspector said. "We know how you Georgia boys buy one set of tags and put 'em on two trucks and claimed you've lost tags. The governor of Georgia already has told us to arrest you guys and make you buy tags."

"Do you take your orders from the governor of Georgia?" my uncle asked him slyly.

"Never mind!" snapped the inspector. "The fact is you are gonna buy a Florida tag."

"No, I'm not," my uncle said.

"Then by golly," the inspector said. "You are gonna sit in jail here till you do."

"Okay," said my uncle, who was a whole lot shrewder than he looked. "I'll go to jail. But I've got about $300 worth of fish on my truck, and they ain't gonna last long in this hot weather (It was in July). And if they spoil, the state of Florida is going to have to pay me for them."

"Nonsense!" growled the inspector. "We won't be responsible for your fish if you're in jail. No way."

"Well, you better check on that," chuckled my uncle. "You might wind up paying for that $300 worth of fish yourself." This started the guy thinking, and upon a bit of investigation, he found that the state indeed would have been responsible for the fish.

This left him in a hole from which the only way out was to let us go, albeit with a long tirade about bums and deadbeats from Georgia, which just made my uncle's chuckles louder and more prolonged. I wanted to kidnap the obnoxious inspector and drop him in the nearest stock dip.

It was just one of many memorable things that happened to me along that old fish-truck route.

*(Poke McHenry was 18 years old before he found out there were other kinds of "bought fish" beside mullet.)*

# Computers Can Scare Air Out of You

*Poke speculates in this early 1980s column about the possibilities that might take place if the day ever comes when commercials airliners are fully controlled in flight by ground-based computers. But, with a computer, you really have nothing to fear...*

ST. MARYS RIVER

I got a tad uneasy when I read a news story disclosing that the Federal Aviation Administration (FAA) plans to replace 12 flight service centers in Florida with three automated stations.

To me, "automated stations" means "computers." And while computers are among the most marvelous things known to mankind, there is a sort of tortoise-and-hare syndrome about them.

When it is working right, a computer leaves mere man as far behind as the swiftest of rabbits would leave an arthritic turtle with four bum legs and inner-ear trouble.

But the computer doesn't always work right. Or even, sometimes, at all. I know this from more than five years of enchantment with the computer system down at my *Florida Times-Union* newspaper office in Jacksonville.

It is pure joy to work with that thing when it is purring along in perfect peace and production. There is nothing to compare with its efficiency writing, editing, amending, revising, polishing, shaping and preparing for print all the news that's fit and all such deathless prose as this.

In fact, I have become so spoiled so far as writing is concerned that I now disdain such mundane contraptions as typewriters. And I'm one of the old-timers who used to snort that it was patently impossible to create a machine that could do things better than I could with paper, pencil, scissors, glue and ruler. And rubber eraser, upon occasion.

I quickly revised my thinking after being introduced to the computer, and even more quickly fell in love with the thing.

But the untempered truth remains that the computer is subject to whim and caprice. It sometimes takes fits of distemper and occasionally comes down with such things as massive coronary occlusion or degenerative galloping neurocirculatory asthenia, or worse.

When this happens, there is great weeping and wailing and gnashing of teeth in newsrooms. Sweet-tempered, soft-voiced editors and reporters have been known to say mildly uncomplimentary things about the tools of their trade.

Other folks have periodic troubles with computers, too. I called one of the Jacksonville, Florida, hospitals the other day to ask about a patient, and the information people couldn't give me any up-to-the-minute data because their computer was "out." Or "down." Or perhaps down and out. I told them I was well aware of the feeling.

So when I got to thinking about flight service and computers, I was reminded of that terrible old joke about the commercial-airliner flight from Chicago to Los Angeles.

It was a beautiful sunshiny day with no wind to speak of, and the takeoff was totally smooth and without incident. The 100 or so passengers had just settled back after the tension of takeoff and were making small talk when they were called to attention by the intercom.

"Ladies and gentlemen, good morning!" came the pleasing tones from a well-modulated professional voice. "We want to inform you that you are a part of a history-making event in aviation.

"For the first time since mankind first lifted heavier-than-air craft into the skies, you are flying on a plane without a crew. There is no captain, no co-pilot, no flight engineer.

"Everything is being done by computers from the ground in Chicago and Los Angeles. We will fly at 19,000 feet, our estimated cruise speed is 373 nautical miles per hour, and our estimated time of arrival is 4:32 p.m. Pacific Standard Time today.

"Now please do not be alarmed because you have no flight crew. We assure you that with our ultramodern system of computer control, nothing can possibly go wrong.

"So you have absolutely nothing to fear… to fear… to fear… to fear…"

Well, anyway, I got over my uneasiness when I called the Flight Service Station at Craig Airport in Jacksonville. A most cooperative and pleasant spokesman there informed me that what the "flight-service stations" do mainly is advise pilots on up-to-the-minute weather conditions. They also process flight patterns, serve as direction finders and otherwise have helpful capabilities.

Actual flight control is handled by people such as controllers at the FAA center in Hilliard and in towers at major airports.

Even after the 12 stations are condensed, as it were, to three, the human element will still play the most important role in flight service, my Craig spokesman said. The three stations will have more automation so that they can handle heavier loads, he said.

So I really have nothing to fear… to fear… to fear…

# Borrowers Are All A-Loan

*This column was written back in the days of Jimmy Carter's presidency, when inflation was running amok and interest rates were skyrocketing to new highs. It tells of some lending pitfalls and some of Poke's personal experiences in the field of high finance, as related to the grand old pastime of pool-playing. Greed will get you in trouble, you know.*

ST. MARY'S RIVER

Everybody's talking about inflation and high interest rates these days, and it certainly does cost a lot to borrow money. But of course it always did, even back in the heyday of Amos and Andy on the radio. I remember once when that old slicker Kingfish went into the short-loan business.

"How much interest you charge, Kingfish?" asked Andy.

"Three per cent," replied Kingfish.

"Why man, dat's cheap!" said a beaming Andy.

"Yeah, uh, well, dat's 3% per hour," explained Kingfish.

It is getting to be about like that these days, too.

Once years ago on the old *Albany* (Georgia) *Herald*, when James Davis was the business manager, one of the employees named Mose had need for some extra funds and applied down at the bank for a loan. After discussing the matter at length with Mr. Haley, one of the great bankers of that day, Mose went into Mr. Davis' office with a loan note in his hand.

"Mr. Davis," said Mose confidently. "Mr. Haley told me to tell you that if you'd sign this paper, he'd let me have a hundred dollars."

Mr. Davis eyed Mose long and hard.

"Mose," he said finally. "You go back and tell Mr. Haley that if he'll sign that paper, I'll let you have the hundred dollars."

I don't know if Mose ever got his $100 or not, but Mr. Davis' reaction to the note-signing request was the safest way to go, as I found out upon several painful occasions when I went on notes with other people.

In another classic story of money-lending in Albany, a rich land-owner had need of $10,000 in cash for an immediate deal of some kind, and went down to the bank to get the money. He was well known and was good for at least 10 times the amount needed just on his signature, but just before he applied a new banking regulation had gone into effect making it mandatory for a loan of that size to have a co-signer.

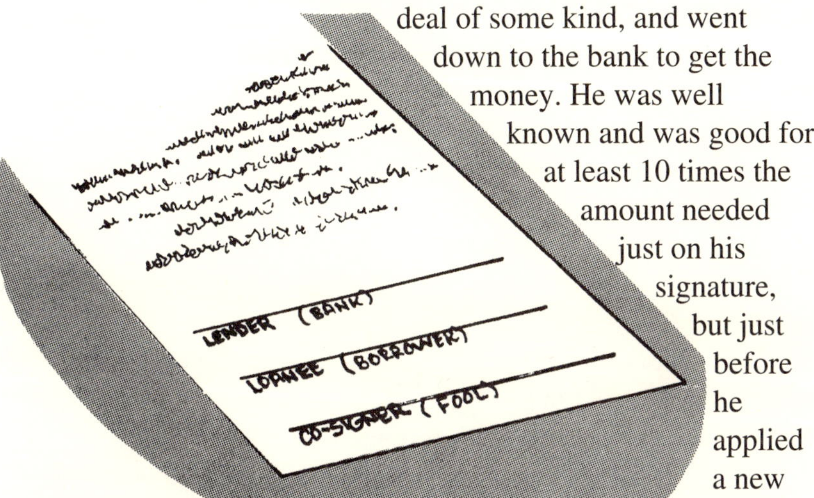


Informed of this, the landowner looked around the bank lobby and spotted old Steve, a town character known to seldom have enough spare change to buy a cup of coffee, let alone a decent meal.

"Steve," commanded the landowner, "come over here and sign this note with me!"

Steve bounded over and without a qualm signed with a flourish the paper that would have made him liable for $10,000 in case the borrower defaulted. It didn't worry Steve; he knew nobody'd ever get $10,000 out of him, no matter what method they tried. It didn't bother the banker either, because he knew the landowner would repay the money within a few days and the whole thing would be forgotten.

And that's what happened, except that old Steve didn't forget it. He went in to the bank and applied for a $200 loan, then took the note to the wealthy landowner and asked him to co-sign it.

"You think I'm crazy?" asked the landowner in

amazement. "You know and you know that I know there is no way you could ever pay back that $200. Of course I won't sign that thing!"

"Fine friend you are," roared old Steve. "I sign a $10,000 note for you and you won't sign a measly $200 note for me! I'll never do you no more favors, you skinflint!"

Once I had a friend named Milton, who was something about the equivalent of a corporal in the Air Force, had a wife and houseful of children, and labored under the delusion he could beat me playing pool. I beat him like a drum regularly, and then started letting him "owe" me for the lost games.

He got $40 in debt to me, then came and said he had an emergency in the family, had to have a loan, and that if I'd co-sign a $200 note at one of the short-loan companies he'd pay me my $40 out of the loan.

I should have known better, but I let visions of $40 dancing in my head override my judgment, signed Milton's note and collected my $40. A couple of months later the finance company was after me to pay the thing, since Milton was two payments behind and, they said, they couldn't find him.

Well, I managed to stall them off until I found the guy, and then discovered that he had borrowed money all over town, was $2,000 in debt and had no way, he said, to pay anybody off. But I kept badgering him and his wife until she admitted that her parents had money, but she said she was too proud to call upon them to bail the family out.

I prevailed upon her, I fear none too gently, to get in touch with her father, who promptly sent them the money to get even with the world and get me off the hook. It gave me a jaundiced outlook on signing people's notes, and in that respect I'm still yellow.

*(Columnist Poke McHenry says he's certain he must be a big wheel, because no ordinary little old catfisherman could get as deep in debt as he is.)*

# Sometimes These Yankees Can Embarrass us Rebels

*This appeared in the Florida Times-Union sometime in 1979, and is a true (for a change) tale. It is about a Pennsylvanian (by marriage) member of the family who managed, inexplicably, to embarrass Poke and his two brothers on a fishing excursion in deep South Georgia. The Yankee caught the most fish, proving beyond question that it doesn't take intelligence to catch fish.*

ST. MARYS RIVER

Sometimes a fishing trip can be downright embarrassing, as was one I went on over in Turner County, Georgia, a couple of weeks ago with two of my brothers and The Yankee. We went to a farm pond full of practically hand-fed channel catfish, where all you're supposed to have to do is throw a hook out anywhere and rake 'em in.

The brothers are Goat and Charlie, and The Yankee is a Pennsylvanian who wormed his way into the family by marrying one of my nieces. I told her that if she married that guy all her children would be half-breeds, but you can't tell these youngsters anything.

Goat is a whole lot younger than I am. In fact, I had already won World War II when Goat was barely out of diapers, so I didn't see too much of him when he was growing up. I don't know why we called him "Goat," unless it was because he looked like a goat and ate old newspapers.

Being the ambitious type, Goat decided to waste some of the best fishing years of his life going to Georgia Tech, where he became an engineer, and I mean one of the kind that don't run freight trains. Now he's got a fat job with a big outfit in Tennessee.

Charlie, on the other hand, for a long time was a good old boy. He's older than Goat but a good bit younger than me, and when he was growing up I taught him to catch fish and shoot doves. I must have done a fine job, since he usually beats me at doing either these days.

In his early 30s, Charlie chucked one of the best jobs around, that of being a game warden, and decided he, too, would join the educated crowd. He went to Mercer University (Macon, Georgia) and now is a successful lawyer, but he hasn't forgotten how it is to loaf on a pond bank.

So the four of us descended on the pond, visions of a fresh catfish fry dancing in our noggins. Now, I expected to catch fish. I always expect to catch fish because, after all, I am old Poke. I expected Charlie to catch fish, because of his training. I figured that Goat might catch fish because of his family heritage. I didn't expect anything out of The Yankee but hot air and loud noises, which is what you usually expect out of any Yankee.

And what happens?

The Yankee catches the first fish. The Yankee catches the second fish. Then the third, and the fourth. By this time, great consternation prevails among the McHenry boys.

"Hey Yankee," I yelled. "You know how many rebels it takes to whip a Yankee?"

"It takes a bunch," he said, smirking like a lip-smacking possum munching persimmons.

"That's right," I said. "It takes 10. Nine to shake him out of the tree and one to stomp him."

"Very clever," said The Yankee, very coldly.

By this time, Goat was siding The Yankee like paint on a board, dropping his bait right into the spot where the fish were being caught. Nothing happened, except The Yankee caught the fifth fish.

"Hey Poke," shouted Goat in a tone somewhere between a sneer and a jeer. "Tell me what I'm doing wrong! You're the expert! Come on, give me some advice, expert!"

Now I ask you, is that any way for an upstart sibling to

treat his esteemed elder statesman brother? Conducting himself like a disgusting brat, no less.

Meanwhile, The Yankee caught the sixth fish.

"Much more of that," muttered Charlie, "and I'm liable to show him it only takes one Rebel to whip a Yankee."

Things didn't get any better. When we finally yielded to the shades of darkness and diamond-point drilling of the mosquitoes, The Yankee had 12 big fat beautiful catfish, Charlie had two little scrawny ones and me and Goat were skunked.

It always has flat beat me how three or four people can fish in the same place, in the same manner, at the same depth, with the same bait and tackle, and only one of them will catch fish. It is a thing as unexplainable as a UFO or the way some women think. But it happens at some time or other to everybody who fishes with any sort of regularity.

When it happens to old Poke and it is done to him by a Yankee, it is particularly embarrassing, to put it unlike the way I put it to The Yankee.

Oh, well. Even blind hogs find acorns once in a while.

*(Poke McHenry says that in the Civil War we could have whipped the Yankees with cornstalks, but the so-and-sos wouldn't fight with cornstalks.)*

# Charlie's Letter

*Poke's brother, Charlie, poses a threat to Poke's security as a columnist. Charlie gave up a good job as game warden to become a lawyer, and also proves to be a better writer than most columnists and any lawyer has any business being.*

OCILLA, GEORGIA

This is the county seat of Irwin County, and it is the place where my brother Charlie bases his law practice, but more important, it probably has more productive fish ponds per capita than any other county in Georgia.

Which latter is mainly the reason I like to poke (pun intended) around up here, hoping somebody will invite me to go fishing.

Most of the time when I come up old Charlie has something lined up for us, and it was on one such occasion recently that we went with brother Goat and The Yankee, that Pennsylvania pretty boy who married one of our nieces and added insult to injury by outfishing us.

This prompted me to write a column about the affair, which prompted Charlie to concoct a literary effort in answer, or something, to the column I wrote. I tell you what's a fact, when you got a writing genius like old Poke in the family, everybody wants to get into the act.

To tell the truth, grudgingly, old Charlie wrote a dang good piece, and I'm kinda afraid to print it, lest the editor fire me and hire Charlie. But I'll take the chance, and let you read what Charlie has to say:

"Dear Poke:

"Our sister up in Fitzgerald (that's sister Baggy — you remember she was the first to get into the writing act right after you started writing that thing) was kind enough to give me a copy of your recent column about the fishing trip that you, Goat, myself and the other fellow went on over in Turner County. Basically, the article was pretty accurate, but there are a couple of items that need clearing up a little.

"Now, I'm not fussing at you, but if you are going to continue to write for one of those big-city newspapers, you ought to try to be as accurate as possible, because there are some people around who still believe what they read in a newspaper unless, of course, it's one of those Yankee-run papers up in Atlanta. Nor am I suggesting that you would (perish the thought) ever stretch the truth. It's just that, apparently, in your advanced years *(my WHAT, you whippersnapper!)* your memory ain't quite what it used to be.

"If you think back, now, you'll remember that we didn't start off calling the kid "Goat," it was "Frog." That was because of all the pretty girls who were always trying to kiss him. We finally figured out that they thought he was a prince in disguise. At least that was the only logical reason we could think of for them preferring him to one of us. We started calling him "Goat" when he got to smelling like one, and not just because he ate old newspapers. Also, when he finally realized what all that kissing was about, we had to pen him up for awhile.

"Now, the real reason I left the job as game warden was not because of my thirst for education (as you are aware, my thirst runs to other things). It was simply because I supported the wrong man for governor one time, and Lester (Maddox, governor of Georgia at that time) was about to ship me off somewhere way up in the northeast part of the state. Any fool knows that if both of your legs are the same length, getting around in those mountains can be tough. Besides, when I decided to go to law school, I plumb misunderstood what it meant to be a member of the Bar.

"Otherwise, the article was OK. I agree with you about Goat's performance. But he does have a pretty good defense. Those boys from (Georgia) Tech all have the same problem:

When they get hold of something that don't work out on a slide rule, or is not completely logical, they go hollering for the calf-rope.

"There is, of course, a logical reason for The Yankee outdoing you and me, Poke. As you recall, if being a Yankee isn't bad enough, that fellow is a teetotaler to boot, and he meandered around the pond all afternoon, while you and me had to stay within a few feet of the tailgate of the wagon. I've told you upon more than one occasion that that dang ole cooler you got is just too big to drag around a pond dam.

Why haven't you invented a cooler that can be attached to your belt and gotten rich so we could retire and spend more time humiliating Yankees on fishing trips?

"Keep up the good work and let me know in a few days if you think we ought to invite Goat on a dove shoot next month. The Yankee is out!"

*"Charlie"*

Well, if old Charlie is as good a lawyer as he is a column-writer, he oughta be making enough money for both of us to retire on in another six months. Of course, retiring is a bit of a problem for me, since I reckon a fellow has to get "tired" before he gets "retired," and I really don't do enough of anything to get very tired.

*(Actually, Poke McHenry has retired many times in his career, generally at the behest of his various employers.)*

# CADDY, PART II

*All about how Poke came into possession of a fabulous road vehicle — a 1939 four-door Cadillac sedan rigged up with all the speed-enhancements and other accessories necessary for the successful transportation of top-quality moonshine whiskey (and how Poke found out about the superb quality of the stuff).*

ST. MARYS RIVER

Since I told the story about a 16-cylinder Cadillac I had co-owned briefly many years ago, and mentioned that I later owned another one of the things, several people have been pestering me for details. So today, here is the story of old Poke's second and final Cadillac:

On a dark wintry night in early 1952, a black four-door sedan cruising into Albany, Georgia from the east aroused the suspicions of two Dougherty County police officers, who attempted to stop the car for investigation.

They didn't have too much luck. The sedan spurted away from their police cruiser with the greatest of ease, led them a frisky and risky chase around and about through town, and then bored into the night out U.S. 82 highway west toward Dawson. For five miles the officers chased the black car in vain, at speeds up to 95 miles an hour (as fast as the police car would run), but each time they would attempt to pull alongside, the car would ease away from them again.

Finally one of the officers started cutting loose a few rounds from his .38-caliber revolver, and when two bullets plowed into the rear of the fleeing car, the driver lost his enthusiasm for the chase, stopped and fled into the woods, to be hounded down at another time.

One of the officers drove the car back to the courthouse and emptied it. The back seat had been removed and where it had been was stacked 120 gallons, packed in two-quart fruit jars in cardboard cartons, of some of the finest moonshine whiskey ever confiscated in Albany or anyplace else. I know that to be a fact, because I came into possession of five gallons of the stuff.

Well sir, the car was a 1939 Cadillac, although it resembled the 1939 model only in outward appearance. It had a 1948 Cadillac big V-8 engine, high-speed rear end, electric fuel pump, over-sized rear springs and dozens of other accoutrements considered essential to the health, well-being and longevity of a quality whiskey-running car. The rear wheels were 16-inchers and the front 15-inchers. It might have been the design that grew into the drag racers of a later day.

In those days, cars seized under those circumstances were sold at public auction in front of the county courthouse to the highest bidders, and the arresting officers got a cut of the proceeds. As you have guessed by now, I just had to have that Cadillac, and I had made the mistake of letting those officers know that I was prepared to bid up to $200 for it. So when the day of the sale came, about six months after the seizure, I was there with $200 borrowed from the place I worked against my future income.

Naturally, they ran the price up to $200 and as soon as they got my bid they knocked it off on me. I thus became the owner of my second Cadillac.

It took about two gallons of gasoline, a lot of tinkering and sweating and the repair of a couple of tires before I got the thing cranked up and driven away for the first time. I drove to a filling station and, in the full glow of proud ownership, instructed the man to “fill ’er up.” In those days a little bell would ring on the gas pump each time a gallon went through the hose, and eventually it dawned on me that a lot of little bells had been dinging and the Cadillac showed no signs of getting filled up. In horror I looked at the pump just as the 21-gallon "ding" sounded and screamed at the man that that was enough. I'd never bought that much gas at one time before in my whole lifetime, and I barely had enough money to pay for the 21 gallons. I never did learn how much gasoline that old car would hold.

I did finally, however, get me a back seat for it. I bought a 1939 LaSalle, which was a "baby Cadillac" and had interchangeable parts with my car. The LaSalle cost me $40.

I got pretty good service out of my Cadillac, but I never could get any dependable lights on the old thing. I tried everything in and out of the books in efforts to rewire the lights, but there were so many relays, fuse boxes, switches, circuits and who knows what else, each one more grimy than the others, that I never could get the things to work right. I even took the LaSalle lights off and replaced the whole things off the old Caddy but it still didn't work. Sometimes I'd have lights that would blind a coon at 500 yards, and the next minute would look like the magneto lights of a Model T Ford. And sometimes right in the middle of tooling down the highway they'd go off altogether.

I guess I would have kept the old car after all, though, except that one night I came in pretty well into my cups, as the saying goes, and as I turned into the backyard the horn started blowing and stuck wide open, as it were. Now if there was one strong point about that Cadillac, it was the horn. Brethren, it had a horn that would arouse a dead yak from here to Tibet.

It was the wee small hours of the night, lights were popping on all over the neighborhood, and above the din of the horn and the shouted cursings of the neighbors I heard "It's that (bleep bleep) McHenry again..."

Needless to say, Mrs. McHenry took a dim view of all the proceedings, also, and shortly thereafter I traded the Cadillac down at the Buick place for a 1947 Dodge, which became a famous car in its own right during the 15 or so years I drove it. But again, that is another story.

*(Columnist Poke McHenry says a rumor that he once lost a car race to Barney Oldfield is not so. "It was Eddie Rickenbacker," Poke maintains.)*

# Royal Tabernacle May Be Empty, But Memories of Gatherings Persist

*This is a column on the history of Uncle Billy Royal and the Royal Singing Convention of Mystic, Georgia. Royal was founder of the convention, which was legendary among followers of gospel music and singing in the South. Poke first wrote about this event for the Fitzgerald, Georgia, Leader, and the Atlanta, Georgia, Constitution, in 1946. The column here was written for the Florida Times-Union, a Jacksonville, Florida, newspaper, in 1981.*

MYSTIC, Georgia

Going through this town recently, I was stunned by the rundown, neglected, thrown-away appearance of the ancient and honorable Royal Singing Convention Tabernacle, an Irwin County landmark for 61 years and the focal point of one of the county's most far-famed traditions.

I was smitten with nostalgia for the good times that I, and countless thousands of others through the years, had enjoyed at the annual Royal Singing Convention the third weekend in every July.

I was smitten with dismay when I learned that with the 85th renewal of the event in 1977, the Royal Convention had faded into oblivion. Now the old tabernacle is literally on its last legs, those being the stout pillars that hold up the venerable roof that for so many years sheltered, at one time or another, most of the South's finest gospel singers — and a whole lot of bunglers like me.

The father of the Royal Singing Convention was William Jackson "Uncle Billy" Royal, the "professor" of many a “singing school,” an institution that was for at least a hundred years a part of practically every rural family in South Georgia — fathers, mothers and children alike. These schools taught people the rudiments of music and the basics of gospel singing, and spawned generations of stompdown good singers throughout most of the Southland in general and South Georgia in particular.

The interest generated in gospel singing by the growing number of participants soon led to the forming of regular conventions such as the South Georgia Singing Convention found by Uncle Billy Royal in 1875. This one became so popular that various counties requested it from year to year, and this prompted Royal to organize a permanent convention in his home county of Irwin.

Thus was born the Royal Singing Convention on July 1, 1893. It mushroomed from its beginning to the point where none of the participating churches was big enough to

accommodate it. As an example, when the convention was held in Frank (a small community near Ocilla, Georgia, the capital city of Irwin County, of which Mystic is a part) the railroad ran an excursion train from Ocilla, Irwinville, Alapaha, Fitzgerald and Nashville, all South Georgia towns and/or county seats of the surrounding area. Attendance was estimated at from 3,000 to 5,000 for that session — and that was a monstrous assemblage for the year 1912.

That was the first year a huge tent, bought by convention members and capable of accommodating 2,000 singers, was used for the event. The tent was the meeting's shelter until a small tornado destroyed it in 1920. Then, through public subscription, funds were raised to erect the tabernacle at Mystic.

It was built, in time for the 1920 Royal Singing Convention, for the staggering sum of $5,279.46 — pews to sit 2,000 and all.

Uncle Billy was first president of the convention and reigned through the 1930 gathering before dying of a heart attack May 24, 1931, at graduation exercises at Mystic's Irwin County High School. In her *The Royal Singing Convention, 1893-1931*, reprinted by *The Georgia Historical Quarterly*, Karen Luke Jackson, great-granddaughter of Uncle Billy Royal, recorded that "Royal had just led the song 'Inside the Gate' in the song services preceding the commencement sermon when he was stricken with a heart attack. E.W. Holland, a Missionary Baptist preacher from Pearson, Georgia, who was to preach the sermon, realized what was happening. He asked that the congregation remain seated and sing *Nearer My God to Thee* while Uncle Billy was being carried down the aisle." Royal died while being taken out of the auditorium.

In 1953, a monument topped with a bronze bust of Uncle Billy was unveiled and dedicated in front of the tabernacle as about 4,000 people looked on.

Uncle Billy was succeeded as convention president by his son, "Uncle Jimmy" Royal, who in turn was succeeded after his death in 1950 by his son, Erston Royal, who presided from then through the last session four years ago.

"It breaks my heart to see it all end," says Mrs. O.L. Luke of Ocilla, a daughter of Uncle Jimmy, the mother of Karen Luke Jackson and for many years one of the key workers in keeping the convention alive. "I had so hoped that we could carry it on for a hundred years. But it just wasn't to be."

She said that officers of the convention still have not determined the final disposition of the old tabernacle and that a decision probably would be made soon.*

Many factors contributed to the fading away of the traditional convention. Old singers were dying out, and few new ones were taking their places. Television had arrived, along with universal air-conditioning, and fewer and fewer people preferred the sweat and gnats of the open-air tabernacle to the living-room comfort of Saturday and Sunday afternoon sports events. More and more people were participating in outdoor activities, and more and more places — such as nearby Crystal Lake in Irwin County and Holiday Beach at Douglas — were attracting folks who once enjoyed the all-day singing and dinner-on-the-grounds good times at the Royal Convention.

On the Sunday of one of the last Royal songfests, for instance, country singer Buck Owens appeared in person at Crystal Lake, drawing an estimated 10,000 people to that spot.

Well, gone for good, I guess, are the days when sleek limousines squatted alongside battered pickup trucks as the high and the mighty mingled happily with the masses to make joyful noises unto the Lord at the Royal Singing Convention.

The heart-warming event was a victim of the changing times, as so many like things have been, and while we might mourn its passing, we can always rejoice in the memories it leaves.

**Editor's note: The deteriorating old tabernacle was eventually dismantled. On its site is now a memorial park. Poke was the main speaker at the park's dedication ceremnoy on July 29, 1991.*

# HOG KILLING TIME AND HOT BISCUITS

*This 1978 piece recalls the earlier days when Marvin Griffin was governor of Georgia, and even earlier and happier times when we ate fresh-stuffed country pork sausage and new ribbon cane syrup, both created by the expert hands of a master at those arts, and the hot biscuits and fresh-churned butter resulting from the equally unparalleled expertise of his farm wife. And then, of course, how we shot doves by the thousands in those halcyon days down on the farm during the 1930s.*

ST. MARYS RIVER

Folks who have regular jobs take vacations, and that is a nice thing to do — get away from it all for a bit. Of course, it is better if one can stay away from it all. What brings these sage observations on is that Thornton Hartley, the Jacksonville, *Florida Times-Union*'s farm editor, is having another one of those vacations and asked me to do another guest column for him. Thornton said his readers seemed to really enjoy it the last time I pinch-hit for him, so I herewith say "thanks" to all of them.

Recently I was over in Albany, Georgia, at a shindig promoted by Sheriff Lamar Stewart, and one of the guests was former Georgia Governor Marvin Griffin, one of the great story-tellers of our time. He had everybody laughing hard with a yarn about his big old 1955 Mercury automobile and its air conditioning, a thing novel in cars in those days. But Marvin had it in his car when he was governor.

He said he was tooling along one day when he spied this old farmer beside the road. It was in July and the temperature was hovering around 100°, as Marvin stopped and offered the old fellow a ride. He got in, sweating profusely from exposure to that broiling Georgia sun, and sat down right in front of the air conditioner, which was going full blast. "Putting out snow," in Marvin's words. The farmer had a tractor part in his hands and explained that he was trying to get to a big town about 15 miles away to get it repaired. Marvin offered to drive a mile or so out of his way in order to take the farmer to his destination.

But in a matter of moments, Marvin looked over at the old fellow and saw that all the sweat had evaporated and he was blue around the lips, shivering like a scared dog with the dysentery, and sporting goose pimples the size of overcoat buttons. After a couple of more miles, the old farmer told Marvin that if he didn't mind to please let him off at the next crossroads.

"Why?" asked the governor. "I thought you wanted to go on into town and get the part for your tractor."

"Well, I wuz goin' to," said the old man through chattering teeth, "but I've changed my mind. The weather's turned off so cold I think I'll go back home and kill hogs."

Every time I think of killing hogs I think of a long-departed friend named Don Freeman, who was a farmer in the very best of the old-time traditions of syrup-making, meat-curing and sausage-creating. He didn't just make sausage. He created masterpieces of gourmet delight.

About 40 years ago, in the days when folks shot doves in the morning (and I mean at the break of day on the bitterest cold mornings man can imagine for our South Georgia part of the world) we used to gather at Don's house long before daylight for one of those shoots.

It would always be during or right after syrup-making and hog-killing time, after all the crops had been gathered, and the farm families had settled in for the winter. We would gather in Don's wife's kitchen, where she would have a roaring fire in a huge old wood range, with those heavenly homemade fresh sausages sizzling in iron skillets on top of the stove and tremendous pans of fluffy biscuits browning in the oven. On the long table, with benches along the sides instead of chairs, would be jugs of new ribbon cane syrup and mounds of freshly churned country butter. There would be gallons of strong coffee, I mean the kind of stuff that would float a horseshoe, and brother, you may live to be a thousand and try food all over the world and you'll never find anything to beat that in Don Freeman's kitchen on a bleak and blustery December daylight.

We would, of course, stuff ourselves to the point we didn't care whether the doves flew or not, but we were well fortified against the weather as we waddled to the dove field.

In those days, too, the sky would be dark with incoming birds on the coming of daylight over the usually baited field. Nobody paid much attention to game laws back then. Enforcement of whatever laws there were was spotty and primitive. Many times the game wardens of the areas would take part in shoots over baited fields. I was on a shoot one time when, believe it or not, more than 14,000 doves were killed in a single day. And then later on folks wondered what happened to all the birds.

Back to farming, one thing a farm or a garden does is give you something to gripe about, which is a necessary thing for all farmers — good-natured grousing about things in general. I remember a story of a farmer who, for 20 years, had one thing or another go wrong with his efforts. He had either too much or too little rain, or it came at the wrong time, or the boll weevils ate up his cotton, the blight soured his peanuts, the worms got his corn, and so on.

Then came one glorious year when everything fell into place. He prospered in every area — the most bountiful yields ever, the highest prices on the market, just nothing in the world went wrong.

And how did he take that?

"I'm getting out of this racket," he grumbled. "It's a helluva note when a feller ain't got nuthin' to gripe about."

So much for another pinch-hit job for Thornton. Hope his farm families like it.

# Moonshining

*A fond look back at how it was in the good old days of the real whiskey runners, and the moonshiners who produced some of the world's best drinking liquor. It was sippin' whiskey long before Jack Daniel ever made the term popular with discriminating drinkers.*

HOMERVILLE, Georgia

The Georgia editor of the Jacksonville, Florida newspaper, the *Florida Times-Union*, asked me recently if I knew any moonshiners or anything about the situation in that line of business as it is, or isn't, at the present time.

You know what moonshining is — the illicit manufacture of distilled spirits, usually corn liquor, out of sight or knowledge of state or federal revenue people.

Well, I've been out of touch with that sort of thing for a long time, and I don't know any of the fellows who are in it nowadays, but I know what they are producing and I wouldn't walk within 10 feet of an uncorked jug of the stuff. The fumes probably would knock a mule down.

In the old days, though, moonshiners were conscientious fellows and really took pride in their work. Too, they had to make excellent stuff, because everybody in the county was in the same business and if your product was inferior it wouldn't sell, not to mention possibly getting you hauled off to the slammer for its tendency to occasionally kill folks who drank it. So the better shine makers created some pure potables that were the best alcoholic drinks in the world.

Not only did real moonshine go down smoothly, it had a kick that would make a swamp rabbit tackle a wild boar, and probably whip him.

I understand that there are still a few folks making it in the old ways, but to my knowledge none of the good stuff is being made outside the mountains of North Georgia and Tennessee and the like. But if I knew where any good stuff was being made I wouldn't tell, because from what I remember about moonshiners they take about as kindly to newspaper reporters as they do "revenoors." Messing with moonshiners can be hazardous to your health in several ways.

I once bought a moonshine-hauling car for $200 at a sheriff's sale. After confiscating the car, the police took 120 gallons of crystal-clear pure sparkling corn whiskey out of the area where the back seat of the sedan had been. It was all in two-quart fruit jars packed in cardboard boxes, and it was some of the finest moonshine ever run off anywhere. I know, because I got five gallons of it. From the sheriff, no less. Free, too. We had some sheriffs with real couth, back then.

I took my five gallons of that good shine and put it in a charred keg, and added a box of dried peaches, and let it sit there and meditate from early in July until about Christmas time. When we opened the keg we really had something "fittin" — nice amber color left after the booze had dissolved the peaches, wonderfully mild and smooth peach brandy flavor, little flecks of charcoal — truly nectar. And with a wallop that would render rubber-legged a charging brindle bull.

On another occasion, when two carloads of us from Albany, Georgia, were coming down U.S. 441 in the Fargo and Homerville, Georgia, area, a funny thing happened concerning some whiskey runners. I was in a car with a fellow named George Gill, who was driving a new Buick, and ahead of us were four other fellows in J.T. Melvin's new Oldsmobile. We were heading for Jacksonville and the Gator Bowl, where Georgia Tech was playing Pittsburgh, best I remember. I think it was 1956.

J.T., being a big Shriner, had a siren on his car for use in parades, etc.

Somewhere on that long flat lonely stretch of road, a green 1949 Plymouth coupe came cruising past us, and we were doing 80. Probably a quarter of a mile behind the Plymouth came a 1950 black four-door Dodge sedan. Both went on past us and right on by J.T. and his crowd.

"J.T. won't put up with them old cars passing him," said George.

Sure enough, in short order the whole crowd was out of sight. Well sir, about 10 miles down the road we spotted J.T.'s car on the side of the road, blowing off steam and looking like a badly exhausted cross-country runner with a hangover. The boys were standing around it cracking up with laughter.

"What happened?" we naturally wanted to know.

"Well," J.T. said. "When that old Dodge passed me, I gradually began picking up speed. But the faster I went, the faster he went. Finally, going about 95 or 100 and right on his bumper, I hit the siren.

"You won't believe what happened then. A big cloud of black smoke belched out of that old Dodge, and he left me like I was settin' eggs. He was just cruising at 95, and he must have hit his afterburner, or something. I never seen anything like it. I done run my Olds ragged and red-hot, and I couldn't even come close."

Well, I knew what the situation was. The Plymouth was the decoy, and the Dodge had the goodies in it, and nobody was about to outrun either one of them. The idea was, get the law officers, if any spotted them, to chase the first car, which wasn't hauling any booze, and would be guilty of no more than speeding, if caught. Meanwhile, the real booze car would be many safe miles away.

That was the way it was, and those old boys just loved the excitement of a chase, and most of them were equipped to leave anything else on the road eating dust.

Moonshining, like everything else, just ain't what it used to be.

*(Georgia columnist Poke McHenry, being a law-abiding sort of fellow, never drinks moonshine anymore. Probably any less, either.)*

# Fourths of Old

*In the good old days back in Fitzgerald, Georgia, Poke's hometown, they really knew how to celebrate the Fourth of July. This column recalls several of the escapades Poke remembers, including a classical one about one of the better-known local heroes Poke calls "Old Slim," who got himself and everybody else in the local jail drunk with the sheriff's cache of whiskey.*

FITZGERALD, Georgia

This being the Fourth of July and the fact being they just don't make Fourths of July like they used to anymore, I am writing this piece from the place where they used to make them like they should be, as in the long-ago days when I was a boy growing up around here.

In those halcyon times The Fourth was truly a fun-filled community event, with practically everybody participating in such activities as water fights, watermelon eatings, fish fries (and I mean flopping-fresh channel catfish right out of the Ocmulgee River), boxing matches, parades, and, during election years, probably the biggest attraction of all — political speeches.

I mean, in those days those fellows would really get down to it in their politicking. Eight or 10 candidates for governor or some other high office would take turns ripping each other into tatters, and you never heard of such a bunch of scalawags as everybody but the candidate currently speaking was.

I remember one Fourth down at the Blue and Gray Park when some fellow from Valdosta, Georgia, by the name of H.B. Edwards was one of the aspirants for governor. Everybody called him "Hell Bent" Edwards, and he was head and shoulders above anything else there that day in consigning his opponents to hell on an express train.

I was about 12 at the time, and old Hell Bent thoroughly convinced me in short order he'd be the greatest and grandest (and certainly the loudest) governor Georgia ever had or could possibly have. Alas, the voters didn't share my fervor for Hell Bent and he quickly faded from the scene.

On another occasion I remember hearing old Gene Talmadge thunder his venom and vituperation at "them lyin' Atlanta newspapers" and a whole bunch of other folks. Coatless, hair down across his eyes, tie loosened, red suspenders twanging, old Gene was an unforgettable sight. And his wool-hat audience, whooping "Give 'em hell, Gene!" between squirts of Brown's Mule tobacco juice and swigs of corn liquor, also made ineradicable impressions on young minds such as mine.

Fitzgerald was filled with zany characters in those days, such as Homer Waters, who had the "funny car" that was the main attraction of every Fourth of July parade; and D.C. Jackson and Drew Hill, the Negro heavyweights who battled each other to bloody pulps (and never to any decision except a draw) every Fourth as the main event on the boxing card until they got too old to crawl into the ring. D.C. and Drew were the greatest of friends, actually, and both of them were heroes and, in later years, great friends of mine.

But the most memorable of them all to me was an astute businessman I'll call Slim, which was not his real name but close to it. Slim celebrated one Fourth of July by sitting underneath a big sycamore tree in a park right in the center of town, a jug of moonshine in one hand and a .38-caliber pistol in the other. He alternately took swigs from the jug and potshots at the sycamore balls, until the gendarmes slipped up on him.

Slim was a guy whose exceptionally keen intellect otherwise was exceeded only by his inordinate fondness for the bottle.

There was another glorious Fourth, which came on a Monday, and found Slim, sober for once but a bunch of his friends in the slammer nursing monstrous hangovers. This came about due to a Saturday night misunderstanding in a back room of Po Boy's Pool Room, Grill and Beverage Emporium.

Slim, at the time, had been on the wagon for a couple of weeks, due to a slight altercation with Mrs. Slim, who had worked his head over with a spike shoe heel at a juke joint — but that is another story.

It seems about half a dozen of Slim's cronies had gotten into a friendly debate over the integrity of some strangers in a crap game, and in their boyish enthusiasm had made pretty much of a shambles of Po Boy's place. They were all in the sheriff's hotel under various charges of drunk and disorderly conduct, assault and battery, destroying private property and a few other things, placed there late Saturday night and with no hope of resurrection until the judge got back from his Fourth of July holiday on Tuesday.

Hearing of their plight, the sober Slim decided on Sunday to visit them at the jail. He was admitted by the sheriff into the "runaround," a sort of hallway girdling the place between the outside walls and the cellblock. About the time the sheriff let Slim into the runaround, he got a call which took him away from the jail.

Thinking he'd be gone for only a few minutes, he told Slim he'd just lock him up in the runaround and let him visit with his friends.

Well, the sheriff didn't get back right away (he was gone about four hours, actually) and Slim was an inquisitive man. He noticed a huge wooden cabinet in the corner, and had a suspicion of what it contained. It was padlocked, but Slim was a man of many talents (given 15 minutes and a hairpin he could have opened the vault at the town bank), so the lock was no trouble.

Sure enough, there in the cabinet was the sheriff's entire stock of confiscated hooch — a veritable treasure trove of gallon jugs, quart fruit jars, flat pints and assorted medicine bottles, filled mostly with sparkling moonshine.

"Well, well!" welled Slim. "I'm sure the sheriff won't miss a wee nip or two of this nectar, it being right nigh onto the Fourth of July. And surely he wouldn't mind if I slipped a shot or two through the bars to my friends, it being a holiday and all."

You can guess the rest. When the sheriff got back he found Slim and every inmate of the place roaring drunk, his phone ringing off the hook with people wanting to know what the heck all that racket in the jail was about, and his choler considerably on the rise. Sighing, he dragged our hero into an empty cell and clanged the door shut on another chapter in the saga of Slim.

Like I say, they don't make Fourths of July like they used to.

*(Georgia columnist Poke McHenry usually celebrates the Fourth of July by having tea with the ladies of the DAR.)*

# 'Gadabout' has Gone Fishing and Never Wanted to do Anything Else

*Poke remembers he interviewed a 71-year-old fisherman in 1967, then heard he was still at it at age 85, and went to see if 'twas true. He found the old fellow was off in Maine for some cooler summer fishing. Here's the latest on the late Gadabout Gaddis, circa 1981.*

WELAKA, Florida

Fourteen years ago I did a piece in another newspaper* about a 71-year-old man and his dedication to and skill in fishing, and after I heard he was living down here in the "Bass Capital of the World" area, I just had to come down and see if he was still at it and if he could still beat me catching fish and wear me out physically in the process.

I was disappointed. He wasn't at home but had gallivanted off to Maine for some cooler-summer fishing. It figures.

Roscoe Vernon "Gadabout" Gaddis, his friend E. Joe Schmidt** and others of these parts tell me, is still at it. I find to my amazement that, according to the folks who know him around here, most of what I wrote about him at 71 still applies at 85. Hear this of June 29, 1967:

"I'll give you a rundown on one R.V. 'Gadabout' Gaddis, the original non-conformist who discovered fishing at an early age, liked it so much he dedicated his life to it and thereby made himself not only a financially independent character but the most happy, chipper, frisky, physically strong,

**Editor's note: Poke refers to the Albany, Georgia, Herald, where he was sports editor for many years.*

*** Both Gaddis and Schmidt are now deceased.*

mentally alert and spiritually satisfied specimen of homo sapiens I have encountered to date.

"Let me give it to you from his highly popular book, *The Flying Fisherman:*

"'I'm doing exactly what I've always wanted to do — fish and gallivant. And I've been doing it most of my life. I hung out the "Gone Fishin'" sign almost 65 years ago and have been gone just about ever since.

"'You can believe me or not, but over the last 55 years I can't remember ever having spent 30 consecutive nights under one roof. I've had the hankering to roam since I could walk; to fish since I was 7.

"'Except for a few remote childhood fancies, I have never really wanted to do anything else. And so I haven't done anything else. It's as simple and confounded as that... What I mean is that I loved fishing from the first time I ever put a line in the water, and it wasn't long after that I made up my mind that I was going to make a living out of it somehow, someday.'

"But you can't quite classify as a bum a guy who owns airplanes, cars, boats, fabulous fishing gear, homes from Maine to Florida, business interests Scrooge would envy, no telling how many more liquid assets and an abundance of other mark-making achievements.

"Not to mention the ability to skip about a bouncing boat like a feeding bluejay, face up to the wind or rain or broiling sun or raging rapids and fling flies or plunk plugs until he wears out even a guy like Jack Wingate, who takes a lot of wearing out."

(Wingate, known all over Georgia as "Mr. Lake Seminole," has operated a fish camp on the lake since the first fingerling catfish wandered into the impoundment, or maybe since the first fingerling catfish was invented, I don't know. Gadabout was at Wingate's place at the time the 1967 column was written, testing the fishing for one of the 26 television shows "The Flying Fisherman" did annually at that time. Wingate was his guide and boat paddler.)

To continue with excerpts from the column:

"This Gadabout Gaddis is a remarkable cuss, to say the least. Makes us youngsters approaching the 50 mark inwardly furious to watch him outdo us with such surprising ease. A regular inspiration, confound the old booger.

"Gaddis is sort of energy personified, or unlimited, or something equally repulsive. He's doing what he wants to do, making a pot of money out of it, having unlimited fun and obviously getting younger all the time.

"Disgusting carryings-on for an old man of 71, wouldn't you say?"

But he's still at it, and he's still rather on the affluent side. Schmidt escorted me out to the lovely spot on the St. Johns River where Gadabout hangs out, when he's in repose long enough. Schmidt also pointed out a massive island containing no telling how many umpteen acres worth more money than the St. Marys River's got bass, and informed me that old Gadabout owns it all, with no obligations due on it to any man. He's not interested in selling it, either.

Schmidt, a former newspaper reporter, editor and publisher, is a fine fisherman in his own right, as is his wife, B.J. She had her picture in the *Putnam Courier-Journal*, which Schmidt used to publish, after she landed a 32 1/2 - pound snook that took top honors in the recent Sanibel-Captiva Islands Fishing Derby.

Ah, well — old Gadabout'll be back from Maine probably sometime in September, and I'm gonna wheedle him into taking me fishing, even if he can still, at 85, beat me. It'll be worth it.

# Poke's a Great Test Taker, But a Bit Short on Aptitude

*If you don't have any negotiable assets lying around, you may not exactly smell like a wet dog, but neither do you have the necessary "aptitude" to suit the requirements of some tests, as Poke unhappily discovered many years ago. He remembers this little experience in the following column, which appeared in the Jacksonville, Florida, Times-Union newspaper in 1978.*

Floridians are having quite a to-do over that functional literacy test they've been making all the school kids take to determine whether or not they know anything that might help them get along when they get out of school and have to make a living.

I don't know what everybody's so upset about. If a kid doesn't know enough to pass on to the next grade, keep him where he is till he does know. This "social promotion" business is another educational exercise in fundamental stupidity and should be expeditiously exorcised from the educational program. How do you like them 50-cent words?

Also, there is much agitation in the Florida legislature to make teachers take tests, to prove they know what they're teaching. That probably is a better idea than testing the kids, because I'll bet a bunch of teachers aren't at all qualified to really impart knowledge, and if they aren't it's high time they were culled out and made to go to work for a living.

But what got me started on this is that I like to take tests. I always have liked to take tests. I never hit the genius level or better on many of them, but I liked to take them. I'd just love to take that Florida functional literacy test. Probably it would show that old Poke is not even functionally illiterate — just plain illiterate.

One of the most unusual tests I ever "took" had to do with an insurance company that had advertised to the effect that "How do you know you are not on your way to fame and fortune in the insurance business? Come in today and take our aptitude test! You may have a great future in insurance! You may find the rich rewards you've always dreamed about! Come take our aptitude test today!"

Well, I'd noticed that insurance peddlers generally wore fancy clothes, had nice automobiles and pockets full of money, and apparently never did any work. So I allowed as to how I could use one or two of them rich rewards, provided there wasn't too much labor involved, and forthwith presented myself at the office to take the aptitude test.

"Welcome, Mr. McHenry!" said the man. "So you've come to take the test! Great! We'll get started right away. First though, I have a few questions to ask you."

"Fine," I said " Shoot."

"Mr. McHenry, what is your net worth?"

"Huh?" I said. "My net worth? Well, I got this old landin' net that's worth maybe a couple of bucks, and a couple of minnow nets and some seines. Which one you..."

"No no no no!" he barked, giving me a look as if I were something a snapping turtle had just spit out. "I'm talking about your financial worth. What in short is your financial condition?"

"In short," I said, "precarious."

"How much money is in your checking account? Do you own a home? How many and what year and what kind of cars do you own? Any rental property or other real estate, land, buildings? Stocks or bonds, cash, paid-up insurance policies with cash or loan value? Savings accounts, U.S. government bonds? Diamonds or other valuables of that nature?"

"Well, now," I said. "I don't have any of those things."

"All right, McHenry. How long could you sustain yourself without regular income?"

"You mean how long could I work for nothing? No time. I couldn't do it because if I didn't have any income I'd starve. And I wouldn't do it for largely the same reason."

"Well, obviously, McHenry, you lack the necessary qualifications to become a success in our business. You do not fit into our scheme of things. Please close the door as you go out."

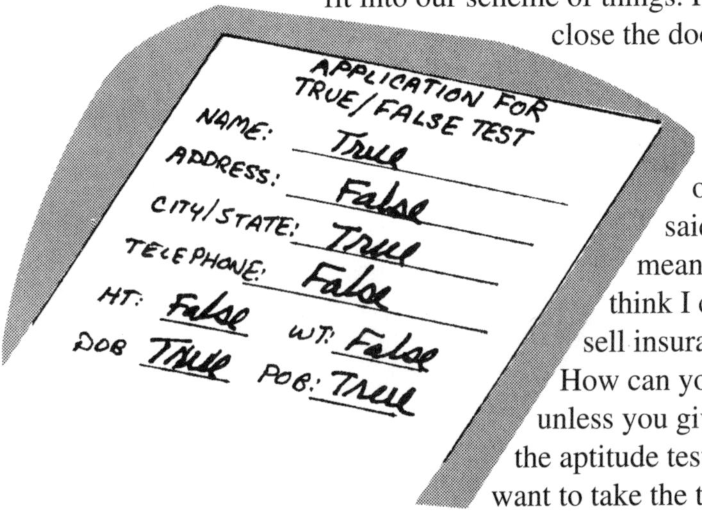

"Hold on!" I said, "You mean you think I couldn't sell insurance? How can you tell, unless you give me the aptitude test? I still want to take the test."

"The test? Oh yes, harrumph, the test. Yes. Well, McHenry, I'm afraid you've just had it. Don't forget to close the door."

And that I'm sure, brought an abortively premature end to a great and brilliant career in the insurance business, not to mention costing me all those rich rewards.

Those aptitude tests can be tough.

*(Poke McHenry found the Army's intelligence test such a snap he deliberately missed several questions, for fear they'd make him a general right off the bat and he'd miss all those poker and crap games with the regular G.I.s.)*

# TEMPTATIONS

*Is it true that everyone has his price? Not everyone did, in this tale Poke remembers from the long-ago days when he was a $60-a-week reporter. It still makes the old boy uncomfortable with himself to think that, for one fleeting instant many years ago, he almost yielded to temptation. Read all about it:*

ST. MARYS RIVER

Nowadays there is a lot of skepticism about the press. Smart people don't put much faith in what they read in the papers and even a lot less in what they hear on the radio and through the "boob tube." Sad to say, much of the news media's recent loss of credibility has been thoroughly deserved, as the few intelligent people left in the business will attest to.

But in all the years I've been associated in various capacities with the news business, I've run across very few news people who were not completely honest. Integrity was, in fact, just about the only asset a reporter had. He certainly never made much money in his chosen field. Probably the only worse-paid professional people were the school teachers, but then on the average school teachers were in much better supply than good reporters, so maybe with the former it was a case of more workers than jobs, which tends to hold down salaries. With good reporters, it was a case of tight newspaper owners and editors, combined with the somewhat weird propensity for good reporters to so love the work they'd do it for peanut shells, which is somewhat less nourishing than peanuts.

All of that has been said to lead up to the following, which leads me to the conclusion, after reading it myself, that the reader has been cheated so far in this column, and deserves a better fate. Anyway, keep trying, and maybe it'll get better as it goes along.

It has often been said that every person has his or her price, and this was aptly illustrated in the old story about the man who approached a beautiful female stranger and abruptly said: "Madam, would you commit adultery for a million dollars?"

She stared at him contemplatively for a moment, then said "Yes, I believe I would."

"Would you then," he continued, "do so for two dollars?"

"Certainly not!" she snapped angrily. "What do you think I am?"

"We've already established that," he answered. "Now we are just trying to arrive at a price."

I'm sure that this "everybody-has-his-price" theory has been tested, at one time or another, on every person who's ever been a news reporter for any length of time. In the old days before the whole world became publicity crazy, it was generally someone wanting to keep something out of the paper. Now it is mostly someone wanting to get something in.

On more than one occasion somebody or other tried me, and the most memorable time was in connection with a routine automobile accident involving not-so-routine people.

The situation was, two couples from one of the bigger cities of Florida were cruising South Georgia in the wee small hours of a morning when their Cadillac failed to make a curve and rammed into an apartment building. Now, all of these folks were married, but no two of them to each other. Both the gals had husbands elsewhere, and both men had wives back home. It might also be added than none of them was exactly sober at the time.

Well, there wasn't too much to the accident, but the police had the foursome hauled into the nearest hospital for a general checking over and patching up of various cuts and bruises.

I was the reporter on the story, and was doing a routine telephone check of the emergency room, talking to a nurse, when one of the guys involved in the wreck realized the nurse was talking to the press.

He all but grabbed the phone out of her hand and started telling me how I couldn't put anything in the paper about the matter. He was, he said, president of the main bank back home, a pillar of the biggest church in town, the president of the biggest civic club in town, and had a number of other qualifications as a thoroughly outstanding citizen.

"You can't put anything in the paper about this!" he thundered authoritatively. "You'll ruin me!"

"***I'll*** ruin you?" I said. "How you figure that? I wasn't carrying on with somebody else's wife, soaking up too much booze and running Cadillacs into houses. If there's any ruining going on its seems you kinda done it to yourself."

"All right," he said, "just promise me you won't write anything until I can get down to your office. I'm coming down as quick as I can to talk to you."

It wasn't any trouble to promise that, since it was four hours or so until deadline, and in a few minutes the fellow was at my desk.

At first he blustered and threatened, being obviously a man accustomed to pushing people around and having things his way. All it aroused in me was amusement. Then he began to wheedle, cajole, beg and plead. I could readily see his predicament if the story got into the paper and came to the attention of the folks back home, and in all sincerity I was about ready to make it as easy for him as I could, when suddenly he got mad and turned nasty.

"All right," he said in cold anger, a hand in his pocket. "What is your price? How much do you want to keep this out of the paper?"

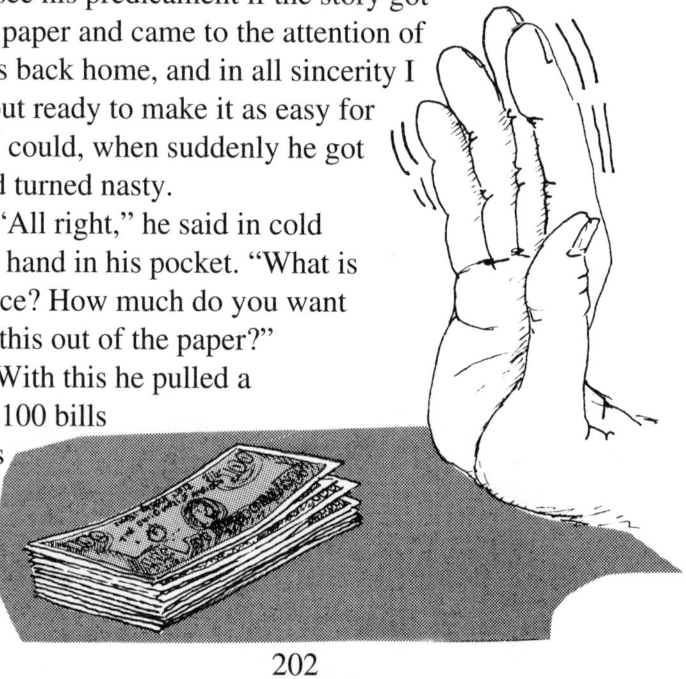

With this he pulled a roll of $100 bills from his pocket that would have, as the saying goes, burned a wet dog. There must have been four or five thousand dollars there, or maybe even more. It probably was the most money that an average $60-a-week reporter like me had ever seen at one time.

I've got to confess that for a moment I almost took the money, before the full impact of what such a course of action would have meant for my future in newspapering. Then I was really furious. At the time I thought I was just mad with the man, but in retrospect I've often wondered if, in truth, I wasn't madder at myself for having considered taking the sop.

At any rate, I was mad enough to throw the guy out of the office and write a blisteringly detailed account of the whole affair, bribe offer and all. The city editor, of course, threw the thing back at me, made me do a straightforward report of the accident and gave me a little lecture about losing my temper over such trifles.

As I grew older and more experienced in the business I found he was right.

*(Poke's about money like Bear Bryant* is about winning — it isn't everything but it beats anything that comes in second.)*

*Editor's note: *If there is anyone out there who doesn't know who the late Bear Bryant was, take our advice and don't ever admit it. Especially in Alabama.*

# Old Charlie Knew What He was Worth

*Charlie the hot-shot ad salesman learned a valuable lesson: Never tell anyone you'll work for whatever he thinks you're worth.*

HOBOKEN, Georgia

I'm nosing around here today waiting for the bluegrass pickers to get in high gear and maybe I'll have more to say about that in the future. But in the meantime, some of the good ole boys were gassing about how much money folks are making these days in various areas, mostly in sports.

All of us agreed that nobody is worth as much as some of these guys are getting, such as $600,000, $800,000, even a million dollars a year for .250 hitting outfielders and 15-game winning pitchers. And they only work six months a year, at that. The only guy I know with a better deal than that is Johnny Carson, who gets $5 million a year and 15 weeks of vacation for spouting stale jokes and making boring "wisecracks" on a television show.

Back when I was a kid I loved baseball so much I would have paid them to let me play, and in all honesty I was better at the game than 90% of these overpaid dolts are today. And, of course, the older I get the better I was as a youngster.

It all reminds me of old Charlie, a guy I knew of back in the Depression days of the 1930s. He had been a real hotshot newspaper advertising man in New York before the crash came.

But, along with thousands of others, he got wiped out and joined that great army of the broke and unemployed. Eventually he beat his way to Florida, where the climate at least fit his clothes, and finally found employment with a struggling weekly paper.

The editor told Charlie he couldn't pay him a regular salary, but would give him 15% of all the new ad business he could bring in. Charlie was a hustler, really knew the newspaper ad business, and he went at it early and late. He did everything from sweep out the place in the morning to cast cuts and hand-set type from the fonts for his ads, and at the end of the first week his commissions amounted to slightly more than $10.

More important, Charlie had sown some seeds and broadened his contacts, etc., and with some redoubled hustling he earned $18 for his second week's efforts. The man paid him, although with a bit of reluctance.

The third week was sensational. Charlie earned the handsome sum of $35.

But on the following Monday, the editor called old Charlie in and told him he could no longer afford to pay him such money.

"Why in the world not?" cried Charlie. "It is all strictly on a commission basis. The more I make, the more you make!"

"I know this," said the editor sadly. "But the thing is, when you cashed that $35 check over at the bank Friday, it created the devil of a stir. You were making more than the president of the bank.

"Now it so happens that I owe a sizable note at that bank. The president called me and said rather frostily that if I could pay people $35 a week, maybe I might better start thinking about paying off that note a bit quicker, since the bank could use the money."

"I see," said Charlie. "Okay, tell you what. Next week you just pay me what you think I'm worth." The editor readily agreed.

The next week, Charlie got a check for $12. It wound up the relationship, since Charlie had by that time hoarded enough of a stake to get a start at some better place.

"It also taught me something," Charlie said ruefully. "Never again did I tell an s.o.b. to pay me what he thought I was worth."

I think there's a lesson there somewhere for all of us.

*(Columnist Poke McHenry says that if you aren't getting what you deserve, chances are you are pretty doggoned lucky.)*

# Pep Talk Ended Layoff by Chickens

*It is a famous axiom that the best means of the getting the attention of a mule is to wham the critter across the nose with a 2x4. Similar or worse treatment, or even the very threat of such, often works with other denizens of the farm, too, including ladies of the henhouse. In the column here, Poke recalls how a little pep talk long ago to a flock of lazy hens brought forth some amazingly quick positive results. Once you get their attention, they've got remarkably potent powers of understanding.*

ST. MARYS RIVER

Sports writer Rick Danis and photographer Ray Stafford* of the Jacksonville, *Florida Times-Union* newspaper did a picture-story published recently about high school boys chasing chickens as a part of football practice, and it sparked an uproar among the be-kind-to-animals folks. Of course, the rattle of chicken bones tumbling into a restaurant garbage can is enough the set up a howl from those benighted save-the-animals souls.

Coach Moses Floyd* of Nease High School in St. Augustine, Florida, told Danis that the chicken-chasing was done to work on developing the agility of his players. But the practice brought several telephoned roars of outrage to the newspaper, including some to me.

Personally, I don't see anything wrong with chasing a few fleet-footed fowls around to improve a fellow's footwork. I'm sure that as a child I probably chased many a pullet or rooster just for the joy of it. I don't think I ever caught one,

**Editor's note: Danis left the paper shortly after the chicken-chasing incident and reportedly went into the construction business on the west coast. Stafford is still with the T-U.*
*** Coach Floyd is still living in St. Augustine but has other interests, having left the coaching field years ago.*

either, come to think of it. So far as I know, no noticeable harm was done to the little rascals.

The pullets generally grew up to lay eggs for gentlemen and, undoubtedly, a few cads along the way, and eventually wound up with a mess of dumplings or dressing for Sunday dinner on the farm. The boy-types mostly got fried young. Many of them regularly went into the ministry, when the preacher would dine with his flock from time to time.

I can, however, understand the concern, however misplaced, of people who think chicken-chasing to develop better football players is cruelty to animals. But who knows for sure?

What if, perchance, the chickens enjoy it as much as the football players do? Who knows but that in the innermost heart of an eager young rooster there lurks the burning ambition to outdo Herschel Walker?

Maybe the chicks even welcome a little diversion from the humdrum existence of scratching for seeds, grubbing for worms and keeping an eye peeled for the fox, the weasel or the hawk — or that hungry fellow or lady with the ax and chopping block.

People shouldn't assume too much, particularly if they haven't talked with the chickens. Probably the safest thing for anyone to assume, all things considered nowadays, is a defensive position.

Anyway, being chased by football players seems to me a fate preferable to that of winding up in a two-piece box with slaw and french fries for $1.69 plus tax. But then, maybe I'm just an old meanie.

Chickens can be talked to, you know. I learned that from personal experience.

Back when I moved to Dothan, Alabama, the house I rented had a chicken yard in the back, which gave me a yen for some fresh yard eggs.

So I got me about a dozen pretty and frisky young hens, laid in a supply of feed and fixed up some nests and sat back to await the goodies.

Sure enough, it wasn't long before I was gathering 10 or 12 eggs a day, enough to supply me and a neighbor or two, and this went on for a considerable time.

But then the production began to wane. I would pick up

four or five eggs a day, then two or three, sometimes one, and, finally, none.

I consulted everybody I knew who had ever had any sort of relationship with chickens, trying to find out what was wrong. I changed the brand of laying mash. I doubled, then tripled the amount of scratch feed.

I laced their water with moonshine, but nothing worked.

I got no eggs, and desperate measures were called for.

So I walked slowly out and leaned on the fence, as the flock scurried up to my feet, expecting another handout, no doubt.

"Ladies," I said. "I want you to listen closely, for I have an important message for you. It is important to you because it has a critical bearing upon your immediate future.

"I bought you and brought you here for a specific purpose: I like to eat fresh eggs. I provided you with the finest in shelter and food and tender loving care, that you might fulfill that specific purpose.

"Now, for a while there, you did your duty splendidly, keeping me fully satisfied in the fresh-egg-eating department.

"But here of late you have failed. You have let me down. You no longer can be counted upon to furnish me with fresh eggs.

"Now ladies, be it here and now understood, once and for all:

*"Either I am going to eat eggs, or I am going to eat chickens!"*

There was a mad scramble as they dashed off to find nests and begin laying furiously, proving the chickens can, at least, take a hint.

Well, maybe that's exaggerating it a bit, but in truth those fool chickens did begin to lay again after that little pep talk.

Of course, it could have been the new laying mash — or the moonshine.

# Pesky Yellowfly Should Realize It Doesn't Exist

*A dastardly villain indeed is the sneaky little yellowfly, a ravenous and persistent cuss who'll find a spot, settle on your defenseless carcass and siphon out your lifeblood before you discover he's in the same county. He's one of the few things in existence that can, and has, chased old Poke off of what he calls a "bass patch."*

ST. MARYS RIVER

Being a fellow who loves to sit around in the cool of the evening — or used to, when there was such a thing as the "cool of the evening" — I have a special sort of hate for those dastardly little whelp-raisers we old South Georgia boys call "yellowflies," I guess because they are mostly yellowish-brown in color.

"I can't find "yellowfly" in any of the dictionaries, so no doubt there is no such animal and they don't exist, but I sure wish somebody would get the message across to the little boogers.

Probably what I call the yellowfly is one of the varied bunch of horseflies lumped under the general classification of "deerfly."

But whatever he is, he bothers me more than somewhat. Of course, I am one of those guys regarded as U.S. prime, table-grade, gourmet pickings for any flying, creeping, crawling, buzzing varmint that stings, bites, gnaws, swarms in the eyes and ears and otherwise makes life dang near intolerable at times. I swear a hungry mosquito, for instance, will fly 40 miles and pass up acres of pulchritudinous sunbathing beauties to help himself to a bite of this old chunk of leathery gristle known as Poke.

But even so, I do believe I can better deal with skeeters than with those insufferable little sneaks, the yellowflies.

There are few things that can chase me off a hot bass patch, but the yellowfly can, and it has proved it on more than one occasion. The first was a good 25 years ago when the late Frank Devane and I were bass fishing on Florida's west coast up the Steinhatchee River, at this particular time in a sort of cove off the main stream.

We hadn't had much luck until just at dusk-dark, when the yellowflies pour forth like the hordes of Attila the Hun and make life miserable for any warm-blooded animal in range, particularly if it's old Poke.

Well, being as dark was approaching, I tied on a black Jitterbug and about the third or fourth saloop, saloop of the retrieve, a three-pound bass tied into it. Whilst I was wrangling with him, Frank put on a Jitterbug himself and by the time I boated my bass, he had one on.

For the next two or three casts the same thing was happening, and then the yellowflies came in like gnats at a August South Georgia dinner-on-the-ground. It was brutal, the way those savage little rascals ate us alive there until we could haul in the gear and cover up with whatever was available. They paid absolutely no attention to two of the finest cussings ever put upon any man or beast, and they had flat stopped me in the middle of one of the best bass-catching spurts I had experienced up to that time.

What got me started on this is that these little pests have been making it impossible all this spring and summer so far to enjoy a cool drink out of doors around my place in the late evening. Insect repellent does very little good against their forays. The other night I put on about three coats of the stuff and one snuck around casing the area for a few seconds then nipped me right on the end of the nose, the only place I'd neglected to apply repellent. But if he hadn't found my beak, he'd have licked off the gunk and made himself a biting place anyway.

The yellowfly is practically noiseless (and altogether noisome) and as for stealth, his touch is lighter than the ashes of goose down. He'll sit down on whatever place he picks out, bore a hole and siphon off a gallon or two of your blood before you discover he's anywhere around the premises.

I don't know why the things showed up in such inordinate numbers this year. Maybe the dry weather has something to do with it, because it does seem the mosquitoes are fewer than usual this time of year, probably due to a shortage of stagnant-water breeding places. Maybe the yellowflies are thriving because of less competition.

Whatever it is, I wish I could find something more tempting for them to gnaw on besides me. If they get any worse, they may run me plumb off, like a bunch of sand gnats did me at Sebastian, Florida, in the long ago.

But that's another story.

# DANDY: HALF THIS, HALF THAT

*Dandy was a dandy from any perspective. He was extremely quick, strong, agile, intelligent, playful — just an all-around adorable little-big dog, a perfect pet. And so different he was one of a kind, so ugly he was charmingly cute. But Poke couldn't keep him, so he had to go away. But he'll always be remembered with that special warmness reserved for great people-like companions. This is his story.*

ST. MARYS RIVER

There is this dog that's been hanging around my place, sojourning until my youngest daughter can return him to Jackson, Mississippi, from where he came to Jacksonville, Florida. His name is Dandy, and he is not your ordinary run-of-the-yard dog.

The reason he is hanging around my place is that my daughter couldn't keep him any longer at her Jacksonville apartment on account of, mostly, he was acting like a dog. You know how dogs act — chase cats, loot garbage cans, go totally goofy over amorous girl dogs, and generally romp around cutting canine capers.

One reason he is no ordinary run-of-the-yard dog is that he is, allegedly, half dachshund and half German shepherd. Now I don't for a minute believe that, but my daughter swears he is the result of a mishap in the kennels of a breeder of both dachshunds and German shepherds. I suppose such a freak could be possible, and I would certainly be interested (for academic purposes, you understand) in knowing which was the mama and which was the papa dog, if indeed this dog is really such a half-and-half combine.

I defy anybody, no matter how expert, to determine what sort of breed this pooch is by his appearance, which in itself defies description. His coloring is a multihued mingling of brown, black, white, tan and varying shades of all of these. He has something akin to half-German shepherd ears, in that they are shaped like a shepherd's but about halfway up their total height they suddenly stop standing up straight and flop over like a guy hit in the belly with a lighter knot. He has a massive head and jaws as powerful, seemingly, as a hyena's. In fact, there is a somewhat hyena-ish look about his head, except for his eyes, which are big and brown and mournful as the lonesome, winter-sundown moan of a roosting dove.

He might be 10 inches high at the shoulders, and his neck, chest and shoulders and forelegs are thick and strong, markedly resembling those of a basset hound. His feet also are broad and big and turn outward like a beagle's, or a basset's, or a slue-footed circus clown's.

His body is long — probably about 2 1/2 feet long — and sleek. He has a tail more like a half-breed possum hound than either a dachshund or a German shepherd. His hair is short and, according to my calculations based upon the pronouncements of my wife, he sheds it at the rate of no less than 10 pounds an hour around the clock, totally and completely covering every piece of furniture in the house and hopelessly matting up in the carpets and utterly defeating the vacuum cleaner's mightiest efforts.

In another two weeks, I'm sure, we'll be up to our eyebrows in dog hair while Dandy blithely keeps producing and shedding additional tons of the stuff. He's a hair factory. Leaves more of it around than you'll find on the floor of a barber shop at an army induction center.

And that brings up another reason he's no run-of-the-yard dog — he's a run-of-the-house dog. Or at least he always has been. And right there he and the lady of the house come to a parting of the ways. She will brook no dog in the house, no matter what his qualifications or how much anybody (including her) might love him.

But withal, this Dandy is an unusual dog in more ways than appearance. For instance, I went over to a neighbor's recently and carefully closed the gate to keep Dandy off the premises, since the neighbor has a dog in his fenced yard. Dandy took a short survey of the situation and, without even so much as a short running start, calmly sailed over the four-foot-high fence with plenty of room to spare. Now, if I hadn't seen that duck-legged mutt perform that act I would have gone to the bank and borrowed money to bet he couldn't have done it. It ain't possible for a 10-inch dog to jump that high.

He is unbelievably quick, too. He can cut and dodge like a tailback in an open field, and I have timed him on those abbreviated legs at more than 25 miles an hour on a straightaway. Just playing, he will catch a squirrel on the ground in a twinkling if the squirrel gets a mite too far from a friendly tree. And if he makes it to the tree, old Dandy's liable to go halfway up the trunk before he realizes the pull of gravity and flops back.

As you can tell by now, I kind of like the little rascal. He is loving and lovable and wouldn't really harm anything, although he makes a splendid watchdog because he has a voice like thunderclaps bouncing off a tin roof. The mere noise of this dog is enough to frighten the most case-hardened burglar bald-headed and rubber-legged. Of course, the uproar more likely than not will be coming from beneath the most distant bed in the house.

Anyway, Dandy can't stay with us, because we can't get used to him staying in the house and he can't get used to staying out of it.

We found him a good home in the country with a nice family, but the daughter couldn't bear to just plumb give him away. So she is taking him back to his former home in Jackson, in hopes that someday she may reclaim him for her own.

It was nice knowing you, Dandy.

# Work Broke Him Down — 'Critters' Lift Him Up

*Serendipity has always been a big factor in the production of many of Poke's better stories. This one is the poignant saga of a lifetime hard worker who, through circumstances he couldn't control or change, might have made him work much too hard and too early in a hard life. At the time Poke wrote of his plight, he was left with nothing much except tender affection for his "critters," whom he attended lovingly and faithfully.*

ST. MARYS RIVER

The other day my granddaughter, Kitti, announced that she wanted a duck.* Now, I have learned to be firm when granddaughters come up with ridiculous notions such as wanting ducks for pets. So I told her in stern and unyielding fashion that I would not under any circumstances even consider buying her a duck. Moreover, I gave her 17 cogent and compelling reasons why it was impractical, irrelevant, incompetent, immaterial, unreasonable, uncouth and otherwise impossible for her to maintain a duck for a pet.

Then, of course, I started looking for a duck — and that resulted in another story. So often does serendipity step right into my path, with positive results!

I noticed this place alongside U.S. 1 about a half-mile north of the Dunn Avenue intersection in Jacksonville, Florida, where the yard looked like Old MacDonald's Farm, or maybe the flocks and herds that old Robinson Crusoe had husbanded so carefully for lo, those many years.

Most of these critters, I discovered, belong to Allen Gay,** a stocky, powerfully built fellow whose appearance

**Editor's note: Kitti is now mother of three, and is experiencing for herself the joys of "I want..." from a parent's point of view.*

*** Allen Gay is now deceased.*

belies his real condition. He has been grounded, at age 48, by a heart condition that won't let him do what he has done for 40 years — work hard and long and steadily.

Gay, born on a farm in Bulloch County in Georgia, was a farmer until 1954, worked nearly 12 years at a concrete block plant in Fort Lauderdale, Florida, then spent 16 years as a mechanic at Key Buick in Jacksonville before being stricken by a heart attack this year.

"When my doctor told me I couldn't work anymore I just had to do something to keep interested in," he explained. "So I started gathering up these 'critters' and watching them grow up and carry on around the yard here. It gives me a lot of satisfaction, just to take care of them and watch them."

He has a lot of things to watch. At last count he had 250 chickens, three geese, three guineas, six turkeys, 25 rabbits, 20 mallard ducks, three horses, seven goats, a hog and three Walker hound puppies, the last given to him by his ex-boss at Key Buick.

Is he interested in selling any of these things?

"Naw, not really — at least not till I get as many as I want, or more than I want," he says with one of the most engaging grins you'll ever be pleased to look upon. "Mostly I just want them around me."

Gay lives on a modest pension and says he has help in feeding all his beasts and fowl through overripe produce donated by a Winn-Dixie store and from the chickens. They produce 18 to 20 eggs a day, he said, which is a help both at the table and with the feed bill.

Hard labor began for Gay when he was 9. His father had a heart attack at that time, and little Allen was the oldest child at home, with several sisters and brothers to help feed, clothe and shelter.

"My daddy would get me up at 4 o'clock in the morning," he recalled, "and hitch a pair of mules to a two-horse cultivator, and many a morning I would have to stand at the end of the field rows until it got light enough for me to see where to start that cultivator.

"Then at 12 o'clock my daddy would bring me some dinner and I'd set under a tree and eat and then get right back behind those mules and stay there until nightfall.

"My daddy would hitch them mules to a tobacco sled and then pick me up — I'd be so tired — and put me on the sled to go back home. And believe it or not, I'd be so tired I'd go to sleep on that old sled.

"When we'd get into the yard daddy would lift me off the sled and bathe me in a big trough by the pump, and sometimes I wouldn't even wake up."

Once while lying in bed late at night, Gay recalled, he heard his mother express the fear that his father was working the boy too hard.

"I'm afraid you're gonna kill the child," she said.

"But what could daddy do?" Gay asks today. "He couldn't work, and somebody had to do for those kids, and I was the only hope.

"But I have thought about what she said a lot of times," he said soberly. "I have thought that maybe she was right, that I worked too hard too early, and too long. Maybe that's why my health just wore out. I don't know. I think about it a lot."

He would still be doing it, though, if the doctor hadn't forbidden it.

"I would go back to Key Buick today and do anything — sweep the floor, run errands, anything — if I could. And I will if I ever get where I can again.

"I have worked hard all my life and enjoyed it. I believe in work, and I'm a mighty poor fellow for sitting around waiting for handouts or hand-me-downs."

If you talk with him, there is no way you can doubt his sincerity.

Meanwhile, he goes on taking delight in watching his critters scratch and scurry, grunt, bleat, nuzzle, nip and sip around the yard that might have inspired the Old MacDonald Farm ditty.

# Channel is King of River Cousins

*This a piece designed to enhance your appetite tremendously with the inside scoop on the king of the assorted catfishes of the world and the best method of preparing him, along with hushpuppies, so that you can delight in one of the world's true taste treats. Don't you dare go through life without experiencing this!*

This bit of enlightenment is coming to you at the requests of many readers, who keep pestering me to give them some details about catfish and hushpuppies, one of the best tasting food combinations the world has ever known.

There's probably nothing in the world of viands I'm any more familiar with than catfish and hushpuppies, nor are there many, if any, things better to eat.

First, a word or two about the difference in various types of catfish. They are by no means all the same. All those inhabiting fresh waters are fit to eat, but some are a great deal

fitter than others. The king of them all is the fresh water river channel cat; there is just no other catfish nor any other fish that can beat him for flavor.

Next to the channel is the blue cat, a close cousin of the channel and very nearly as pleasing to the palate. After the blue comes the catfish the government reportedly stocked in many ponds, creeks and rivers during the Great Depression to help feed a hungry nation. We used to call this one "government speckled catfish," and they're still around in many places and are better than average eating, when small.

Beyond the speckled you get down to the butter cat and the mudcat and various crossbreeds, all of which can be eaten but are more filling than flavorful.

All these are, of course, freshwater fish. There are many saltwater types of catfish, only one of which I consider edible, among all those I have tried. This is the gaff topsail, or "sail cat," and it isn't bad on the table. Might even be considered good by anyone who'd never tasted channel cat out of the Ocmulgee, Oconee, Flint, Alapaha or Altamaha rivers in South Georgia.

Another important factor concerning the eating of catfish is the size. The channel cat of from eight to twelve inches in length is absolutely the tops for eating purposes. This is not to say they are not good in any size, from two ounces to 50 or more pounds; they are just at their delicious finest at the smaller size.

The river channel catfish is streamlined in appearance, with an elongated head as opposed to the broad and blunt look of most of the others. The channel is silvery along the sides when he's about eating size, and some have black specks over the rear portion of the body, some are solid silvery-gray. The flesh is pure white, except for a yellow tinge around the top of the back, and all of this is several notches above delicious on the taste scale. The most distinctive identifying characteristic of the river channel cat is his sharply forked tail. This is not so defined in the larger channels in the rivers and in all the channel cats stocked in ponds.

Incidentally, the channel cat will rarely reproduce in ponds — only in the running water of streams and rivers. They will grow to monstrous size (the Georgia record from a man-made pond is 39 pounds) but only under the most expensive and meticulous conditions can they be induced to make little catfish.

Now about eating these unbeatables. Everybody familiar with them knows the best way is to take them off a trotline or out of a basket, skin them while they are still flopping in protest, salt and pepper them, roll them in corn meal and throw them into a pan of hot grease on the bank of a river. Truly, that is a treat for the gods.

Most folks, unfortunately, will never have the opportunity to do this. So what you can do if you are lucky enough to get hold of a mess of channel cat is salt and pepper the cleaned fish, dredge them in a half-and-half mixture of corn meal and flour, and drop them in hot grease.

The frying utensil can be most anything you have, but a deep iron skillet is better than most anything else. An outdoor-type deep fryer heated by gas is excellent — get the grease heated to 350 to 400 degrees, pop the battered fish in and cook them as quickly as possible. Never let a fish of any kind "sob" in too-cold grease. Cook it hot and in a hurry.

What kind of grease to use? Most anything will do, but peanut oil is exceptionally good, particularly if you are using a deep fryer. But hog lard, shortening or vegetable oil, or any other good commercial product will do the job. In this respect the channel catfish is sort of like an egg — you can hardly make it inedible no matter how you fry it.

I remember once a friend of mine bought a cast iron deep cooker and I borrowed it from him to fry some fish in. I asked him what kind of grease to use and he told me peanut oil, and I went down to the store to get some. When I found out the price of that stuff, I called him back and asked if I could also borrow his grease.

My father had one of the best catfish cookers I ever saw. It was the cut-away end of an old cast iron boiler with some iron legs welded onto it. We had many a wonderful meal cooked out in the yard in that thing. But in those days we used to have channel catfish galore; even had some to sell, cleaned and ready for the frying pan, for about 20¢ a pound. Those days are gone forever, for sure.

Now for the hushpuppies part. Everybody has a favorite way to make these things, and I guess I am no exception. Only thing, I have no formal recipe. I just take an egg, some buttermilk, flour, meal and a medium onion and get with it. I chop the onion up pretty fine, beat up the egg in a mixing bowl, pour in and mix the meal and flour at a ratio of one cup meal to half a cup of flour, or thereabouts, (a tad more of either one won't hurt anything), and stir in the onion and buttermilk and mix until I have a sort of loose paste, just thick enough to stand up momentarily in a tablespoon.

Drop the mixture a tablespoonful at the time into the same hot grease in which you cook your fish, and let brown good all over, and that's all there is to it. I don't know exactly how many this will make, but it is never quite enough. You can make as many as you want by simply increasing the amount of all the ingredients, at the same ratio.. Also, by having no set amount of anything you make 'em taste differently from time to time, which keeps your tastebuds from getting in a rut. You may also, if you wish, drop in eight or ten quarter-inch-thick slices of streak-o-lean, which is salt-bacon, unsmoked, and fry it along with the fish. This makes both the fish and the meat taste better.

I honestly believe that if you have the chance to eat fresh real river channel catfish, fried right, you'll never grow tired of them, even on a daily basis. If you do, just call old Poke. I'll be happy to relieve you of the awful things.

*(Columnist Poke McHenry says he'll add something, even if only a healthy appetite, to any catfish-eating party anywhere, since "things go better with Poke".)*

# Playing in Jail

*Recalling the days of yore when semipro baseball teams traveled to state prisons for tilts with inmate teams. And how Poke once acquired, in exchange for a cheap pair of canvas tennis shoes, a brand new pair of Rawlings state-of-the-art major-league baseball shoes.*

ST. MARYS RIVER

The other day I read a piece in the newspaper about how prison sports is a big thing up at the federal pen in Atlanta, and it set me to thinking about some long-gone days when I used to travel around with a semi-pro (some called us "mostly-pore") baseball team and every once in a while we'd go over to Reidsville and play the Georgia State Prison team.

And thinking of that made me remember that one year a new warden over there announced that for the coming baseball season, the prison team would play road games — home-and-away schedules, you know.

Well sir, that got the greatest turnout in history of candidates for the baseball team. Guys old and decrepit, guys half blind, one-legged aspirants, guys who hadn't picked up a baseball in 20 years, guys who never had picked up one at all, the elderly, the middle-aged, the youthful — everybody was out to make the team. Or, more accurately, the traveling squad There must have been four or five hundred of them swarming over the ball field— they all wanted a chance to get outside on a baseball trip and, of course, take their chances of staying outside once they cleared the walls legitimately.

It was the shortest-lived home-and-away baseball schedule not on record.

The first game was played over around Savannah. I don't remember who the opposition was, but nine members of the prison traveling squad managed to dodge their guards and flee into the wild goo yonder, and it took authorities a month or two to round them all up. That, needless to say, ended Reidsville's policy of allowing traveling baseballers.

I guess they are still playing "home" games over there, and I remember that it was truly a fun experience to play them back in pre-World War II days. They had the finest of facilities, and equipment as good as any major league team. Also, they fed visiting teams royally, and we didn't get much royal feeding in those days. I don't know what the prisoners ate, but every time we went we had excellent steaks with all the trimmings, and all kinds of fresh vegetables from the prison farm. In those Depression days, po' boys like us never got closer to a good steak than some dazzlingly wonderful dream that usually preceded waking up hungry again.

We were, of course, locked inside the bowels of the prison while we were guests. We changed into our uniforms and later showered and dressed in surgically-clean locker rooms, which was a world or two removed from what we were accustomed to. The attendants took all our belts, pocket knives, watches, etc. and locked them away someplace until we dressed after the game. They were taking no chances on some sneaky con confiscating materials for a garrote or other lethal weapon.

When we got out on the field for warm-up, we were greeted by a big crowd of the most wildly enthusiastic and craziest betting fans I had ever seen. Surprisingly, those folks had money, and I mean real money, not chicken feed, and they did bet it on any and every situation that arose in the game, but the biggest bets were made just on who would win.

The prison had a lot of faithful fans who believed implicitly in their "boys" and would not hesitate to put large wads on them no matter what the opposition. And the prison did have a good ball club. It also had some shrewd and astute students of the game, gentlemen who could watch a pair of teams warming up and know beyond any doubt which was best before the first ball was pitched in seriousness.

These sharpies made small fortunes betting against the home team when they were sure it was outclassed by the visitors. In our case, the first time we played there, the wise gamblers took one good look at our players and bet the load on us, and they were right. We won handily. Bets like that didn't come so easily on subsequent visits, but there were always some fans rabid enough to bet on the prisoners regardless.

If there had been instant replays in those days, some of them would have lost money on them.

On one trip there, I went in wearing a pair of new sneakers (we called them "tennis shoes" in those days, although nobody played tennis, and good ones cost about a buck a pair). One of the trusties took a look at my sneakers and said, "You want to swap them for a pair of baseball spikes?"

"Are you serious? New spikes?" I asked.

"Brand new, sir. Still in the box. Same thing they wear in the majors. What size you wear?"

I told him, he trotted off and in a matter of minutes was back with a new pair of Rawlings top-of-the-line baseball shoes. We swapped, of course, and I never have gotten a better deal in my life. It was like somebody giving you, even up, a Pflueger Supreme reel for a Zebco 202, only better.

I wore those shoes through many a rugged baseball battle, and I've worn fond memories of my Reidsville baseball experiences ever since.

*(Poke McHenry is one of those ball players that the older he gets, the better he gets in his mental replays.)*

# Birdies, Eagles… and Geese

*Read all about how in 1979 an irate amateur golfer got in serious trouble by beating a wild goose to death with a putter, and other weird shenanigans participated in from time to time by serious-minded hackers. And why Poke always had a cavalier attitude toward the game.*

ST. MARYS RIVER

Later this month a golfing doctor in Washington, D.C., will go on trial on some unusual charges, to wit: Use of an illegal hunting weapon and illegal possession of a Canadian goose.

This all came about because the good doctor, Sherman Thomas, 66, took his putter and dispatched the goose with an undetermined number of flails with the club. In short, there is no record of how many strokes the doc took to dispose of the goose. Come to think of it, I don't believe a par has yet been established for goose-killing with a putter.

There are conflicting ideas about just what happened. The federal wildlife folks, who do not take kindly to unauthorized killings of Canadian geese, claim the doctor was infuriated because the goose honked as he was putting, causing him to miss and resulting in the subsequent goosiecide.

But lawyers for the doctor claim that the goose inadvertently got in the way of one of the doctor's wild shots and was so seriously wounded as to render it an act of mercy for the golfer to finish the bird off with his putter.

Personally, knowing golfers, I lean toward the "honking-on-the-putt" theory as a motive. If that as the case, clearly it is a case of justifiable goosiecide, since honking on one's putt is absolutely unheard-of in the annals of golfdom. Durn goose deserved to die, if he did such a despicable thing.

Golfers, especially duffers such as the good Washington doctor obviously is, take this sort of thing seriously. Often there is as much as 50 cents riding on the outcome of any given putt, and besides the money there is the principle of the thing.

One of the funniest sights I ever saw on a golf course followed a missed putt. This was a foursome that played together constantly, all of about the same skill, and they usually played 10-cent "skats" and their financial transactions on the links were every bit as important to them as Swiss bank accounts, and considerably more complicated.

Well, on this occasion everybody had holed out except one old fellow who had a three-foot putt that meant the difference in winning and halving the hole. He eyed that putt from every conceivable angle. He lined it up front, back, sideways and otherwise. He inspected minutely every blade of grass anywhere near the projected path of his ball. He took his stance at least three times, only to expel a deep breath, walk around and peer intently at the putt again. All this time, mind you, there was dead silence among the other three members of the foursome, their caddies and a few onlookers such as I. Even the birds in the tress, it seemed, ceased their chirping and breathlessly awaited the outcome of this crucial moment in golfing history.

Finally, the old man stroked the ball. It rolled steadfastly toward the cup, slowed just right, but bent off at the last instant, lipped the hole and settled two inches away. He had missed. For a split second, there was still dead silence. Then a caddie giggled.

With a mighty roar, that old man took out after that caddy, wildly waving his putter and obviously bent on murder, at least. By this time everybody concerned was rolling on the ground in unbridled glee, and the caddy being chased was laughing so hard the old man dang near caught up with him two or three times before the chaser gave out completely after a good hundred yards of hard running.

Most people do take their golfing seriously. I have seen 5-irons rattling around in treetops, putters broken in half, balls beaten into the ground accompanied by thunderous outbursts of wrath, and other such exhibitions of how seriously they take it. Matter of fact, I was once hit on the ankle by a flying club thrown by a fellow venting his frustrations.

I never had that problem. I realized early that I'd never be even a par golfer, let alone of championship caliber, so what playing I did was strictly for fun. If I hit a good shot I gloried in it but if I didn't it didn't matter, because I knew I wasn't supposed to anyway.

Probably the good doc in Washington is one of the greatest majority of hackers who have a tantrum or two when things don't go right.

There have been lots of good jokes stemming from golfing, and one of them I always liked particularly was about the guy who teed up a brand new expensive ball and whaled it over a cliff off to the left of the fairway. He teed up a second shining new ball and sliced this one in a tremendous parabola into a bottomless lake off to the right. He hit a third one into an impenetrable jungle alongside the cliff.

"Look here," one of his companions said to the hacker, "if you are gonna lose balls at that rate, why don't you play with your old balls?"

"Well, I would," said the man. "But I've never had any old ones."

Another favorite was about the guy who teed up his ball, made a mighty swipe at it and missed completely.

"Dang course is six inches lower than it was the last time I played it," he grumbled.

*(The links lost a great competitor when columnist Poke McHenry retired from the game. He never beat anybody, but he was a competitor.)*

# Poke's a Game Saver

*This is the sad story of Poke's old quail-hunting buddy Frank McDearmid, who often shot at random but never could hit even that.*

ST. MARYS RIVER

I am about ready to claim myself a conservation award for this hunting season — since I have conserved all manner of dove, quail, deer, turkey, duck and all the other stuff I used to bag during hunting seasons. But this year I haven't even loaded a gun, let alone popped a cap. Even the rabbits and squirrels have been safe from old Poke this time around, and this is the first such situation since I learned to make a slingshot at about age 6 or 7, or thereabouts.

Over the years I have hunted with a number of folks who were great conservationists, meaning mostly they couldn't hit the broad side of a barn — from the inside.

One of the finest quail conservationists I ever hunted with was my old Albany, Georgia, buddy Frank McDearmid. Frank was a great sportsman and always had everything necessary for a successful quail hunt — good dogs, fine shotgun, access to excellent hunting lands — everything except he just couldn't hit the birds. I think an exception to the rules of good sportsmanship should have been made in Frank's case, allowing him to learn to hit quail by starting out shooting them on the ground. Even then he'd have been no better than an even bet to bag one, especially if he didn't wait till the old bird quit walking around.

You remember the tale about the guy who threw up his gun to shoot at a dove walking along a power line.

"Hold on," a hunting buddy objected. "You aren't gonna shoot that bird walking down the wire, are you?"

"Heck no," said the aimer, "I'm gonna wait till he stops."

Anyway, one of my favorite stories about old Frank concerns the time when he wheedled permission to hunt on a fabulous piece of land which was just teeming with quail. There was but one restriction: The owner told him that next to the area where he had permission to hunt was another tract which was strictly off limits. It was being saved for special purposes.

"I'm going to send my brother along with you," the landowner explained. "To show you exactly where you can and can't hunt. There'll be plenty of birds on the place you can hunt, without your having to get on the forbidden place."

Frank readily agreed to this, so the brother went along, driving Frank and his dogs in a pickup truck. The brother parked the truck, Frank turned loose the dogs and within a hundred yards or so of where they had stopped, the dogs pointed. It was a perfect place to shoot, not an obstruction over waist high for a hundred yards in any direction.

The birds held perfectly and the dogs stayed frozen on point until Frank moved in and flushed the covey, which contained 15 or 20 fat bob whites and hens who roared straight away from our mighty hunter. He blasted off three 12-gauge shots at them and never cut a feather, as the saying goes.

The brother gave Frank a long and unbelieving stare, then said, "Come on, we'll hunt these singles later. I know there is another big covey right up ahead."

Sure enough, within another 200 yards, the dogs had pointed again, and again it was in a perfect place for shooting. And again the same thing happened — Frank flushed the covey, blazed away three times and hit nothing. He was one of those guys who could shoot all day at random and never hit it.

This time, the brother looked at old Frank with utter disgust.

"Hell," he said, "I'm going on back to the house. You hunt anywhere you want to. You ain't gonna do no damage to the birds here or anywhere else."

Frank was so insulted, he said later, that he couldn't hit a thing the rest of the day.

I don't know if old Frank is still hunting quail or not, but I do know he has, in his time, conserved many and many a covey, not to mention untold singles.

*(T-U Columnist Poke McHenry's great-uncle Barker McHenry was a terrific bird dog, but in his old age took to chasing female goats and they had to shoot him.)*

# CHEAP EATS

*A short-lived business venture in the field of restaurateuring is recorded in this column from circa 1978. Also, some other cafe business practices and Florida fruit-juice vending in days gone by. It seems incredible nowadays to think there was a period in our lives when you could get all the fried chicken you could eat for fifty cents. And those were the days when eating fried chicken wouldn't kill you.*

ST. MARYS RIVER

Going down to Jacksonville, Florida, I noticed this sign on a cafe in Callahan, Florida, that read "All the fried chicken or shrimp you can eat, $4.95."

It was another reminder of how times have changed, and also brought back some memories of funny happenings in the "all-you-can-eat-or-drink-for-a-price" places.

In the late 1930s in Albany, Georgia, there was a place called "Adams Inn" where you could eat all the fried chicken you could hold for 50¢, and it was good chicken. Evidently the guy came out all right with the deal, because the place prospered for years, although the last time I went there, if I remember right, the price had gone up to 60¢.

Taking a cue from Adams, a downtown Albany restaurateur a few years later decided he'd offer a similar deal. He contacted an old friend of mine, the late Paul Pryse, a sign painter, and had Paul paint on his window "All the fried chicken you can eat, $1."

Now Paul was a pretty good sized fellow, and had an appetite even bigger. He finished the sign right after the noon hour, and decided he'd be the first customer on the new chicken deal.

"Start frying up the chickens, old buddy," he told the man. About two and a half chickens later, plus all the trimmings, Paul pushed back from the table and allowed as how he had enjoyed that little $1 snack.

Just then, city policeman Jeff Burgamy strolled by and noticed the sign on the window. Old Jeff was an even bigger man than Paul, and with an appetite of corresponding size.

"I believe I will," mused Jeff, meandering in, drawing up a chair at Paul's table.

With sinking heart, the restaurant man kept hauling in fresh platters for Jeff until at least another three and a half fryers had disappeared.

"Pretty good gut-stuffers," said Jeff with a mighty burp. "Specially for just a dollar. I'll be back 'bout the same time tomorrow."

"Well, you won't git no chicken, not for that price," growled the cafe owner grimly. "Paul, get out there and scrape that blankety-blank golblanged sign offa that window. I have just gone out of the all-the-chicken-you-can-eat-for-a-dollar business!"

He meant it, too. His venture into the field lasted for two customers and about six chickens. Paul said the guy even groused about paying for the sign, and he finally had to compromise by trading out the difference in meals.

Another newspaperman friend of mine, Don Kimsey, was cruising through central Florida one time and was intrigued by signs on several places proclaiming "All the orange juice you can drink for 10¢."

It being a hot day and in the days before air-conditioned

automobiles, old Kimsey finally stopped at one of those joints and took them up on the offer.

He plunked down a dime and the attendant handed him a glass of orange juice. He swigged it down in short order, handed over the glass and said "Fill it up again."

The attendant did, then said, "That'll be another dime."

"What do you mean?" rumbled Kimsey. "The sign says 'all you can drink for a dime'"

"That's right," said the attendant, pointing to the glass. "That's all you can drink for a dime." And that's the way it was.

There used to be several places around South Georgia where they had all the fried channel catfish you could eat for reasonable prices, but I'm afraid I personally had a hand (or stomach) in putting some of them out of business. Because there is just practically no limit on how many channel cats old Poke can put away.

I tell you what, I've tried a lot of gourmet food in many places in the world, but I say there is nothing better to eat than a channel cat, freshly plucked from a trotline, cleaned and thrown into hot grease in a frying pan on the river bank.

Now that kind of eating is worth $4.95 for all you can hold of it.

*(Before Poke started eating as a guest of the Army Air Corps in 1942, he considered a pickled egg and a Penrose sausage at Royace Williams' poolroom in Fitzgerald, Georgia, a gourmet meal.)*

# WATERMELON STORY SEASON HERE AT LAST

*This piece carries a good lesson in what not to do if you think you catch someone, or ones, filching watermelons from your patch. A good barroom lawyer can put some remarkable spins on who's guilty of what.*

ST. MARYS RIVER

This being watermelon-eating season, which is one of my favorite times of the year (at my age, all times of any year are favorites), I was reminded anew of it by a letter from Eugene E. Strom of Valdosta, Georgia, who mentioned that his Uncle Leroy used to water his melons with ice water so that he could pick them ice cold.

Strom also said his Uncle Leroy used to plant a chunk of side meat with his peas, so that when he cooked them they'd be already seasoned. Uncle Leroy sounds like my kind of a man.

Old Leroy also said he once planted a whole slew of butterbeans but not a single one of them came up, so after diligent research and study he came to the conclusion that he planted them upside down. Shucks, that being the case, he could have dug them like taters, couldn't he?

But back to watermelons and a classic story concerning them and a long-ago lawyer friend of mine by the name of Francis.

Francis, as he was wont to do most every afternoon, was sitting at a bar along with eight or a dozen or so cronies (including me) who loved the conviviality of a pleasant hour or two over a few cool ones. In fact, Francis was so taken with that kind of pleasure that some said his law practice suffered therefrom, but I don't think it mattered to him even if it were true.

Anyway, one of the guys at the bar was a farmer, and he was telling us how he had turned the tables on some mischievous boys who had been raiding his watermelon patch.

"I caught them in the act there the other night," he chortled. "They took off when they heard me coming and run out of the patch on the other end from where they had left a bicycle and a horse, and so I just took the bicycle and horse on home with me.

"I found out who owned the horse and took him back to the owner the next day and give him somewhat about his boy stealing my watermelons. But I've still got the bicycle, and I might just keep it.

"I got a right to do that, ain't I, Francis?" the farmer asked the lawyer.

That's when the fun began.

"Well, now I don't rightly know about that," said Francis with a deep frown. "It seems to me that there are definitely mitigating circumstances involved here."

"Like what?" asked the farmer.

"Well, for instance, how many watermelons did they steal from you?"

"I don't know," said the farmer. "It was dark and I didn't actually see them, I just heard them scampering away in the dark, but I know they've been in the patch before, and ..."

"Whoa right there!" growled Francis. "You mean to say you have no idea how many watermelons they stole, in fact you can't even swear that they got any, that you didn't even see them in the field? Egad, man, you ain't got no case at all so far!

"How much are your watermelons worth, there in the field?"

"I don't know," said the now-turning-red farmer.

"You don't know!" thundered Francis, who by now had the grinning and undivided attention of the entire crowd, bartenders and all. "Well, were they worth a dollar apiece? A half-dollar? Two bits?

"You don't know how many watermelons, if any, you lost. You don't have any idea what your losses are, or were, if any, and here you have confiscated illegally a bicycle which is probably worth at least $50 and a horse that probably is worth $200. Any old horse is worth $200, if you can ride him at all.

"Did those boys steal $250 worth of your watermelons? Huh?"

"But I told you I took the horse back," cried the hapless farmer.

"Oh yes, you did. And that brings up another question. When you returned that horse, did you take it to the man's front door or back door?"

"The back door, of course," said the farmer. "You don't take no horse to a man's front door!"

"Aha!" snorted old Francis. "You were trespassing! You can approach a man's front door with impunity, but you can't go sneaking up to his back door. That's trespassing! And furthermore…"

"Oh, SHUT UP!" yelled the farmer above the din of the guffaws coming from all over the tavern. "Shut up! I wish to gosh I'da never planted no dod-gasted watermelons in the first place!" With that he stormed out of the place.

I guess Francis was the best barroom lawyer I ever knew, and if he had ever taken up watermelon stealing he would have had his victims paying him damages before the trial was over, provided they ever caught him.

# Real Country Hams, Farmers and Living

*Yearning for the olden days when everybody on the farm had a smokehouse filled with cured pork bellies, hams and sausages. You can almost taste those wonderful meats as Poke takes you with him into a bygone era of good living.*

ST. MARYS RIVER

I don't have any particular hankering for a regular job, but if I did I think I'd want one like old Thornton Hartley's got with the Times-Union daily newspaper of Jacksonville, Florida. Thornton, the newspaper's farm editor, has asked me to write him another guest farm column, 'cause he's taking another vacation. That's three that I know of so far this year of 1978, and if a job with three vacations a year isn't a pretty good deal I don't know what would be.*

But anyway, I'm glad to fill in. I'm always happy to talk about farming, because I think it is just about the best life there is, as Florida's Ray Crawford of Union County farmer so aptly put it when he was honored by county agents as the state's top farmer.

"I don't do it for the profit," said Crawford. "I do it for the living."

Now that, friends, is what farming is all about. Or what it used to be about, before things got too complicated with the world in general.

I've never met Mr. Crawford, but I'd like to. I know he is the type of old-fashioned farmer I knew when I was growing up. The story about him said he started in 1938 with a borrowed $50, a new wife, and a horse donated by his father-in-law. Now he's got a 350-acre farm; raises cattle, hogs and

**Editor's note: Thornton Hartley retired in 1991 and the T-U no longer has a farm column.*

timber; and obviously has no worries about where the next T-bone steak's coming from.

And probably the main reason that Mr. and Mrs. Crawford and their three boys and two girls, all now grown and living away, get together every November is for a hog-killing good time. That is one of the bygone things that I miss very much from the old days — a good old-fashioned hog-killing. I guess it has been 30 years since I was at a hog-killing, but I haven't forgotten the wonderful times and good fellowship they brought about.

Once I was bird hunting up in North Georgia someplace; on a farm that was the doggonedest up-and-down walking I ever undertook. When you'd get up a bird you had to shoot him going uphill, since those going downhill were moving too fast to line up on. I tell you, if that little farm had been flattened out it would have stretched from Chattanooga to Jacksonville.

But getting back to the subject, they were killing hogs that day back at the farm house. It was an old-time community project, with neighbors helping one another in slaughtering and dressing out hogs for the families' tables during the bleak days of winter.

And they were scalding the hogs by a method I had never seen before. They had dug a big vat in the yard and filled it with water, and were heating big rocks (from a foot to two or three feet in diameter) at a roaring fire fed by hickory and oak logs and limbs. When the rocks would get red hot, they'd roll them into the vat, and they got and kept the water scalding hot by adding hot rocks as needed.

Meantime, one of the hog killers was whacking off the tails of the porkers and dropping them into the hot hardwood coals at the edge of the rock-heating fire. Those tails were quickly barbecued right there, and I don't think I ever tasted any better barbecued pork than those tails.

Alas, however, the old-time neighborhood — or even family — hog-killing is, except for rare instances, a thing of the past, more's the pity. It has gone the way of the smokehouse, which used to be as much a part of the farm as the cow barn. Folks cured their own meat in those days, and when you said "country ham" it meant just that.

Wouldn't it be great to find a farm somewhere that had an old-fashioned smokehouse where you could walk in and glory in the aroma of swinging hams, shoulders, sides, and sausages?

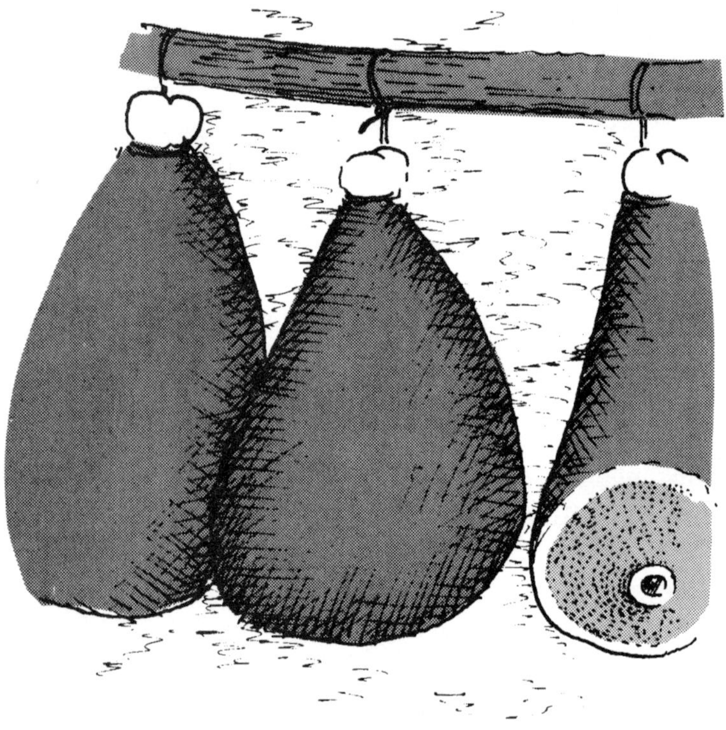

That's the sort of thing Mr. Crawford was talking about when he said, "I don't do it for profit — I do it for the living."

About the only thing wrong with farming these days, I guess, is there just aren't enough Ray Crawfords doing it. May their tribe increase.

*(Only two things keep columnist Poke McHenry from being a successful farmer — laziness and insolvency.)*

# Poke Finds Hushpuppy Link to a Past Full of Fish Fries

*A grand old friend of very long-standing sends her personal recipe for making those great-tasting hushpuppies to accompany those fried catfish, or any kind of fried fish. Hers are wonderfully simple and easy to make, but tantalizingly delicious, Poke says from many experiences.*

ST. MARYS RIVER

A piece I did on catfish and hushpuppies got a great amount of response, and the letter I enjoyed most came from an old friend on St. Simons Island, a favorite person I hadn't heard from in years. Here is the letter:

"Dear Poke:

"I have long been consumed with a burning desire to write you a letter — to join the thousands who but for your column would immediately cancel The *Times-Union* (a Jacksonville, Florida, daily newspaper).

"Hallelujah! Today was your byline!

"Vaguely remembering you whenever you hung out around Groves Station in Acree, Putney and River Bend, (all small communities around Albany, Georgia). I recall your culinary prowess.

"Gee, it was great to read about your catfish and hushpuppy mix. Seems to me I recall a sumptuous fish and hushpuppy jamboree you and your friends served to hundreds on the banks of the Flint River 30 years ago! Or was it 29?

"Yes, I have my mouth watering for your fish and puppies, but frankly as I turn the food pages I actually have indigestion and am completely satiated and stuffed with all the cornbread concoctions.

"Not wanting to be left out and being the modest violet

you remember me — here is my recipe for hushpuppies:

"1. Enough cornmeal to serve enough people.

"2. Enough hot water to make a soupy mixture not too thick, not too thin. Salt to taste. Onion to taste (chopped). Enough white flour (just a tad).

"3. Mix all. Drop into hot grease. If they disintegrate, add meal!

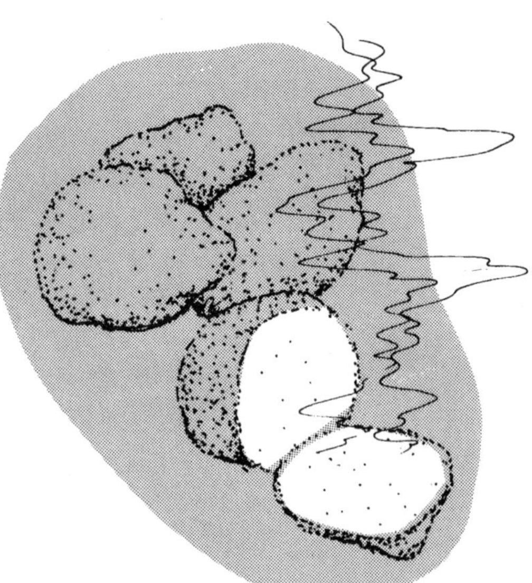

"We used to use Ed Stevens' (a big peanut processor of Dawson, Georgia) peanut oil or leftover bacon fat, but now that there's not much left over I don't know what to do."

She signed the letter "Judith Stiles" — a takeoff on Julia Childs, no doubt — but her real name is Mildred Nix Huie and she is a widely known and acclaimed artist-in-residence on St. Simons Island, Georgia.

Hearing from Mildred did indeed bring back many fond memories. I first knew her at least 30 years ago when she was a member of the school board over at Albany.

I don't remember the particular fish fry she refers to, but in those days we had them fairly frequently and everybody had a wonderful time.

I was really glad to get back in touch with Mildred, who since the letter has promised to roast me some oysters next time I'm over that way. And roasted oysters are but a shade behind fried channel catfish as a taste treat.

*(Columnist Poke McHenry has a standing offer to cook catfish for anybody on halves — he gets half of the fish for doing the cooking.)*

# UNFIT TO EAT

*Poke says a mudfish by any other name still ain't fittin' to eat, even though good buddy Alphin Griffis says he can fix one where it's delicious. And if you ever get a big one in the boat with you, he's liable to throw you out.*

FARGO, Georgia

There isn't a man alive who hasn't tried to eat something awful, some time or other, if he "eats regular." Or even if he doesn't. And, like a bad piece of legislation, you just have to spit it out and remember not to try it again. Like Prohibition, for instance.

One of the worst things in the world to try to eat is a mudfish. It ranks right up there with coot and crow and, even if you're hungry as a boar hog in a groundpea patch, I doubt if you can stomach it.

Turns out that some people say they think it's good, and even a good old boy like Alphin Griffis says he can manage more than a bite.

"Eaten fresh, or fried in small strips, they're rather tasty," he says. Ol' Alphin comes from good South Georgia stock, as anyone who ever knew his daddy Lem Griffis will

attest, but I'm afraid that he's been spending too much time running the elementary school here and not enough time enjoying the better things in life.*

And mudfish isn't one of life's better things.

We catch a lot of mudfish around here. Some folks call them bowfin, some blackfish, a few of the more finicky say "grinnel," but most folks call them trash. If I had my way, we'd get rid of all of them, but folks like me don't get their way too often these days, and I cite the snail darter as an example. That useless fish has held up construction of a multi-billion-dollar dam up in Tennessee** because the do-gooders complained, and even the do-gooders can't come up with a reason for it to be protected. Even an eel won't eat a snail darter.

Besides, if you put a big mudfish in the boat with you, chances are 50-50 he'll throw you out, along with all your fishing gear and half your Vienna sausage.

No matter what Alphin says, don't eat a mudfish. No matter how hungry you are, wait and catch something else. I don't care how fresh the thing is, and I don't care how you fry it, you still won't get a bite worth eating.

The following is somewhat old, but you may not have heard it. If you have, skip on over or ask for your 15¢ back.

It's the recipe for a mudfish:

Filet the mudfish and lay it on a plank of green oak. Cover it with salt, add some garlic, sprinkle with chives and swab the whole thing with A-1 sauce.

Bake for an hour and let cool for 15 minutes. Throw away the mudfish and eat the green oak board.

Of course, there's no telling what goes on among fish-eaters. I know a fellow who works in a fish processing plant and he swears that a lot of the "scallop" you eat is really shark. That's right, shark! The fishermen catch the shark in the

**Editor's note: Alphin Griffis was principal of the elementary school at Fargo for many years and retired sometime around 1991.*

***Snail darter lovers finally discovered there were other places where snail darters thrived, and the dam was eventually built.*

**** Newspapers actually cost 15¢ for the daily edition when Poke wrote this.*

nets, get down to the meat and scoop it out in little balls. I know that the reputable netters don't do this, but you should be warned that not all deep-dippers are reputable. Look at the Congress.

I wish mudfish were good to eat. There's plenty around these parts, and they put up a right good fight. If they were worth a dose of salts, we'd have fishermen from all over the forty-and-eight plus two down here trying for them.

We'd even have a limit, and probably a special license. South Georgia would be as big a tourist attraction as Walt Disney World, and those motel owners on U.S. 1 would be rolling in dough just like they did before the Interstates were laid down.

The mudfish isn't worth eating, but I guess on second thought that the thing is OK to have around. Some folks think it hampers growth of other fish, but I doubt it because I've caught plenty of good stuff while fishing in mudfish-infested waters.

But I think I should give you fair warning not to pay attention to anyone who says that the thing is worth eating. Go on and throw it back, unless you hook it so deep that it takes more than 15 seconds to pull out the hook.

It's not the mudfish's fault that he tastes lousy, and we should respect him for that. You wouldn't kill a coot or crow just out of malice, would you? So throw the thing back and let him give some other fisherman a good tussle while he imagines he's snagged a lunker bass or monster catfish.

And who knows? Maybe the next man will think a mudfish is good eating. To each his own, but I'll be danged if I can eat one of those things.

# A MUSKET CHAMP AND A CHUMP

*This piece comes from the winter of 1979-80, and introduces an off-beat champion and recalls a hilarious incident of long ago when an ignorant squirrel-hunter decided to test an overloaded muzzleloader.*

ST. MARYS RIVER

Not too many people are aware of it, probably, but Jacksonville, Florida, can boast of having at least one world champion. He is Dave Miller, who bills himself as Dave-The-Carpenter and who holds a world title in muzzleloading musket (rifle) competition.

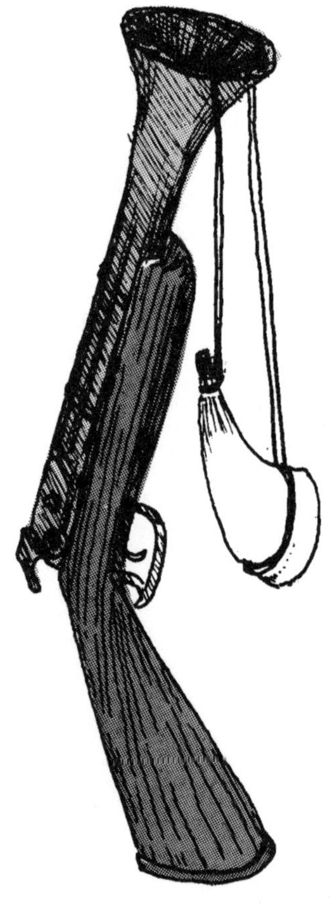

Miller, 43, is a member of the United States International Muzzleloading Team and won his individual championship matches last September at the Quantico (Virginia) Marine Base, where teams and individuals from the U.S. and 16 foreign nations competed for three days. Miller's group took the world team title, and Miller earned his first-place gold medal in the individual shooting by scoring 95x100 in the 50-meter offhand competition, a total within one point of the world record. This means, in plain terms, he put 10 slugs from his 11-pound muzzleloader musket inside a 1 1/2-inch circle from a distance of 50 meters (53 yards.) No rest, either, mind you — just hold 'er steady on the mark through open sights and blaze away.

Miller is a Green Beret veteran of two tours in Vietnam, and has been a muzzleloading enthusiast for many years. He has been shooting in competition since 1965 and is the most knowledgeable authority on muzzleloading weapons I have ever met. He is no stranger to modern weapons, either, as you may have guessed.

It is fascinating to talk to him about muzzleloaders, even though one might be, as I am, thoroughly ignorant on the subject. So being, I will not attempt to pontificate here on any of the technical details of the avocation, but I do plan to learn more about it — particularly since Miller tells me it is possible to plunk around all day with a muzzleloader for a cost of about two bucks or so. This entails buying lead and molding your own bullets, etc. If you love to shoot and have checked the price of commercial ammunition these days you may also want to investigate the possibilities of muzzleloading.

I can remember personally only one sort of semi-close encounter with a muzzleloading weapon, and that was with an acquaintance up in North Georgia. We decided to spend an afternoon in the fall sitting in a hardwood thicket hoping to waylay a few squirrels for supper. I had my old .22 rifle and he dragged along, of all things, a muzzleloader blunderbuss he said had belonged to his grandfather.

He had loaded the thing himself and, judging from what happened when he fired it, he didn't know anything more about muzzleloaders then than I do now.

We saw no squirrels, and after a while an old yellowhammer (for the uninitiated, a yellowhammer is a type of woodpecker) flew up and lit in a tree over my companion's head. He was squatting about 30 yards from me and concealed from my vision by undergrowth.

"Think I'll shoot that old yellowhammer just to see how this thing works," he called to me. I told him to go ahead, since I was sort of curious myself.

Well, I saw the muzzle come poking above the bushes (the barrel was about four feet long), waver slightly, then steady.

I heard what sounded like sort of a click, then a fizz, then a KER-CHUNG! that literally made the ground quiver and shook leaves from the trees. There was a huge cloud of acrid black smoke and bits of flying debris very reminiscent to me of a time when I saw a boiler blow up.

There was a piteous sort of bleating moan from my friend, and of course I sped to the scene as quickly as I could. He was sort of scattered about on the ground, face completely blackened, eyelashes and eyebrows singed off, and bleeding profusely from the vicinity of the upper lip.

The old gun had blown apart when fired, with various pieces of it clobbering my friend in divers places. The hammer — or whatever passed for a hammer — apparently had been catapulted off and sort of hairlipped the poor guy. Fortunately, his wounds, though painful, were generally superficial and he required no more than a first aid-type patching up. Needless to say, it ended forever his association with muzzleloading weapons.

The yellowhammer, incidentally, seemed to stare at the whole proceeding in total confoundment for a few seconds. Then it flew away uttering what I swear sounded like a cackle of pure glee.

My old friend Frazier, the matchless tall-tale-teller I mentioned when toying with the idea of a Poke McHenry Liars Club, knew a bundle of good stories about muzzleloaders. I'll try to recall a few of them if and when we ever get that club off the ground.

# If Rotenone is Really Dangerous, That's All She Wrote

*Here are some reminiscences in a 1978 column about adventures of killing fish with the chemical rotenone, and the true story of how Poke caught the same five-pound bass 15 times and was featured on the cover of a State of Georgia publication outlining rules and regulations for the state's hunters and fishermen.*

ST. MARYS RIVER

Is it or is it not safe to eat fish killed by the chemical rotenone? Seems that the authorities in Florida can't agree on this, and a story from Georgia said that in Georgia such fish are forbidden as food. This must be a recent switch in policy, because it used to be considered perfectly safe to eat rotenone-killed fish.*

Rotenone is a chemical commonly used by game and fish folks to determine the fish population of a given area. It is poured into the water that is to be tested and within a few minutes it paralyzes the gills of every fish it contacts, enabling fish specialists to round up and count everything with gills.

I can tell you from personal experience that if there are any ill effects from consuming these fish, they are a long time in showing up. I first ate some about 25 years ago, when the state made a massive kill in the backwaters behind the Georgia Power Company dam in Albany, Georgia. This was done mostly in Muckafoonee Creek, which is formed by the confluence of Kinchafoonee and Muckalee creeks, all of which

**Editor's note: The labels on rotenone cans advise against eating fish killed by the chemical, and a Florida Game and Fresh Water Fish Commission fish biologist said the state also frowns on the practice.*

adds up to Lake Worth, if you can believe all those names.

Some say the kill ruined the fishing in the area for about 15 years, and it is certain that something did. But I always felt the pollution around the area was more responsible for the poor fishing.

Anyway, it was my first experience with rotenone, and with eating fish killed by the stuff. Apparently it didn't hurt me a whole lot.

Another thing that struck me forcibly about a newspaper report on this subject was the game and fish folks saying the rotenone mostly is used to eliminate rough fish such as gar, mudfish, shad and so forth. It will, they admit, "kill a few game fish."

It will, as a matter of fact, kill the game fish first, and the rough fish, particularly catfish, after everything else has long since gone belly up.

That stuff will kill a few game fish only if there are only a few in the application area. It will kill 10 tons of game fish if there are 10 tons coming into contact with it. In short, rotenone will kill anything in the water that breathes through gills. It paralyzes the breathing apparatus, and that winds things up for anything depending on a breathing apparatus.

Once I went along on a project on one of the deep South Georgia plantations when the state game and fish boys applied rotenone into what appeared to be little more than a mudhole. It was about 40 yards in diameter and not much over waist deep anywhere, but the amount of fish they took out of the place was well nigh unbelievable.

There were three 14-foot fishing boats on the edge of the pond filled to the gunwales, and three No. 3 washtubs were stacked high with bluegills, shellcrackers, crappie and bass, and that wasn't all. There were many gunnysacks (crokersacks) from half to full being dragged away. The state folks said that more than 1,500 pounds of edible game fish were taken from the small area.

I got a generous share of them, ate and enjoyed them. That has been at least 10 years ago, and so far the rotenone has not made me sick. At least not so far as I know. Maybe this pot gut I've put on since I quit smoking is a 40-pound tumor after all.

But the most famous, or infamous, rotenone killing I was in on took place on Lake Blackshear near Cordele, Georgia, where the state boys roped off about an acre and killed off all the fish in it as a part of population tests. They didn't collect much more than 10 pounds of game fish, and less than that of rough fish, in the whole acre, and much of the take was made up by one five-pound bass.

One of the bright state boys from the state outdoors magazine they were putting out in Atlanta then decided to get some action shots of bass fishing, with the stars of the show being me and then-television newscaster Dawson Mathis of Albany, who is now Georgia's distinguished (although for what, I'm sure I can't imagine) Second District U.S. representative.*

So Dawson and I got into one boat, they hooked the bass to my fishing rig and moved off 30-40 feet in another boat and chunked the old dead bass into the water, with a state photographer snapping away as I hauled hard in cranking the fish to our boat. They did this about 15 times, at least, and I "caught" that dead fish until I was plumb worn out before they were satisfied.

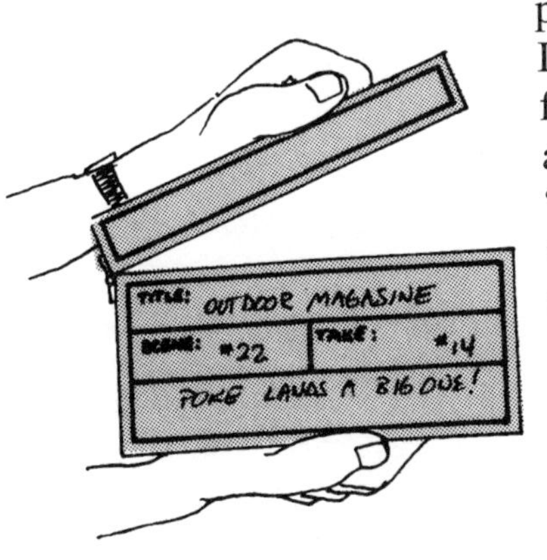


The result was an excellent brochure picture of an outdoors writer and television newsman hauling in a handsome bass whilst enjoying the wondrous bounty one of Georgia's great recreational lakes.

But although the picture was phony, it really wasn't so bad because the good fishing was authentic in most of that lake.

Incidentally, we ate the bass and the rest of the 10 pounds that night. So if rotenone is bad for you, I guess I'm a goner.

*(Columnist Poke McHenry's detractors say that, considering some of the stuff to which Poke has subjected his digestive system over the years with no ill effects, he cannot be considered a legitimate guinea pig concerning what rotenone will do to the normal system.)*

**Editor's note: Mathis served five terms and remained in Washington to pursue other interests.*

# The Worm That Bass Can't Resist

*If you read this 1977 column closely, you might pick up a few pointers that will help you catch a few more bass, bream and catfish. You will at any rate learn that there is no such thing as "conventional wisdom" where fishing is concerned, at least on an every day, dependable basis.*

ST. MARYS RIVER

From time to time I get letters or am otherwise questioned about what's the best bait or methods to use to catch various fish. I guess people ask me when they can't get hold of experts like Charles Waterman and Bob McNally, who are usually off in Canada or Oregon or someplace chasing salmon or shooting bighorn rams.*

There is no doubt that more freshwater fish have been caught on worms, down through the years, than any other bait. And of course there are probably as many different kinds of worms as there are fish.

But for the farm pond-type of fishing that so many Georgians do, the best all-around kind of bait is the worm, and the most fish-productive worm is what I refer to as the "pond worm." This elongated gentleman is sort of pinkish in color, sort of rubbery in tensile strength, and is a favorite morsel of bream, bass and catfish — the mainstays of almost all our ponds and lakes.

The pond worm goes under many different titles: gruntworm, earthworm, grassworm and others, including the latest rage, "Louisiana Pink." A Louisiana Pink by any other name is nothing but a pond worm, and never got any closer to Louisiana than I am right at this moment, which is a "fur piece."

**Editor's note: Waterman is still writing occasionally on outdoor subjects, and McNally still lives in the Jacksonville area and is still free-lancing for several outdoor magazines.*

Other kinds of worms are red wigglers, black wigglers, nightcrawlers and probably dozens of other designations, but none is as effective with as many fish as the pond worm, particularly in the pond or lake. I have taken bass up to 11 pounds on pond worms, and just a couple of weeks ago I lost one in that category after battling her for a long time and from far out in the pond right up to the dam before she finally straightened out the No. 4 bream hook and made off. How do I know it was a she? The males don't get that big.

The experts almost to a man will tell you that big bass lie in deep waters in the heat of deep summer, such as what we have now, and stir but little until after dark. I suppose they do, but there are exceptions. That monster I had on two weeks ago tackled, at 1:30 p.m. on a broiling August day, a pond worm attached to light spinning tackle and fished with a float holding the bait at about 14 inches deep in water about two feet deep. And before the one that got away, I had taken two six-pounders that same summer the same way in the same pond. One struck at 2:15 p.m. and the other at 3. All this proves, I suppose, that bass don't read the papers and outdoors magazines. Or that the bass in that pond were just uncommonly illiterate.

If it is of any use to you, I fish the pond worms two ways. If there is a fairly clear bottom, I don't use a float. Just put on a No. 5 split shot about 14 inches from the hook, stick the pond worm through its reproductive organs (the different colored band around it, near an end) and flip it out with a cane pole or spinning tackle. Move it slightly from time to time if the action is slow. But if there's anything down there, usually you'll get a hit.

The other way I fish the worm is with any sort of

conventional float that will hold the bait and sinker off the snaggy or grassy bottom. I find that, surprisingly maybe, a shallow depth of 14-18 inches regularly gets channel catfish and bass. Bream, of course, will hit at almost any depth, although the shallower the bait, the smaller the fish, as a general rule.

Another generally accepted theory on fishing is that the bigger the bait, the bigger the fish you'll catch. That may be "generally" true, but I have seen the opposite prevail on many occasions. Once I was casting with a Johnson Flasher Minnow spoon at least four inches long, and actually had it attacked by a two-inch bass, which got himself hooked. I thought I had bumped a small twig or something but when I got the line in there he was, fighting that spoon as if he'd swallow the whole thing any minute.

Conversely, there was the time when Jimmy Young of Albany and I were fishing Patrick's Paradise outside Brookfield, Georgia. I was after catfish and was using sturdy tackle and chicken liver for bait. Jimmy was after bream, and using crickets and a light cane pole. So what happens? I catch nothing, but Jimmy hooked and landed a 6 1/2-pound channel catfish that inhaled a tiny cricket!

Well, Jimmy hung the fish but I actually landed him, after he had walked old Jimmy up and down a bank for about 10 minutes, with Jimmy constantly screaming at me: "Don't you lose this fish! Don't you dare lose this fish!"

We had no net, but when Jimmy finally got him near enough, I reached over behind him with one of those folding camp stools and raked him in with it. It might have been the most unconventional method of landing a sizable catfish ever successfully attempted.

*(Columnist Poke McHenry says that when you finally realize you don't know anything about fishing, you'll start to catch a few.)*

# THIS TIME, IT'S THE ONE THAT DIDN'T GET AWAY

*This is the tale of a big bass that was caught twice, boated, then got miles away but was retrieved and finally mounted. The one that almost got away, but didn't quite make it.*

ST. MARYS RIVER

Everybody who's ever done much fishing has a story about the big one that got away, but I tumbled onto a good story this summer about a big one that *almost* got away — and in a most peculiar manner. The story is better because it is, unlike probably the majority of fish stories, true.

Larry Nichols, who is Florida editor of the *Florida Times-Union* daily newspaper of Jacksonville in his everyday vocation, but who is Maj. Larry Nichols at the Florida National Guard Military Academy, put me onto the tale.*

While participating in annual training at Camp Blanding near Starke, Florida, Nichols and the academy chaplain, the Rev. Denton Sumrall of Orange Park, would slip off at opportune times (these times being only at night) to get in a bit of bass fishing. One night Sumrall hung and boated a $6^1/_2$-pound largemouth, which is a pretty fair fish, and this sorta excited the commandant of the camp, Lt. Col. Richard S. Pinson of St. Augustine, who scheduled a trip on Kingsley with Sumrall shortly after the $6^1/_2$-pounder was taken but found he couldn't make it and asked Nichols to go in his place. The colonel specifically forbade the pair to catch anything bigger than two pounds whilst he wasn't along.

Well, the parson cast his grape-colored plastic worm upon the waters in the darkness, and behold, a $9^3/_4$-pound bass

**Editor's note: Nichols is still on the Times-Union Metro Desk and is night editor.*

ripped into it. There was no landing net in the boat, so when Sumrall finally wrestled the monster up to the gunwale, Nichols grabbed it by the jawbone and lifted it from the water.

The fish, however, wasn't through. It made another typical bass lunge-and-twist and broke away from Nichols, plunging back into the lake.

"Right there," Nichols said later. "I'm sure that the chaplain was on the verge of emitting some unchaplain-like language." Sumrall confessed to me that this was so, and I'm in full sympathy and accord with him. I probably would have brained Nichols with an oar on the spot.

However, the fish was still hooked, and on the second chance Nichols hauled it aboard. Then they toured the lake, showing off the big bass at half a dozen places and to many people, including Pinson.

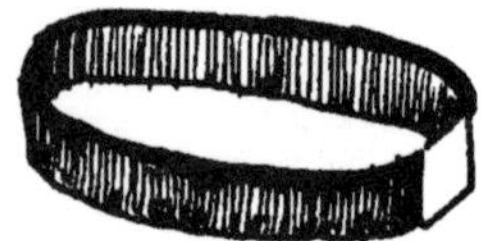

Now Sumrall had a trailer set aside for his use during the time of the camp, and he used it sporadically for miscellaneous things such as taking showers, etc. But he had his personal camper in which he slept. He took the bass and put it in the freezer section of the trailer's refrigerator, thinking to have it mounted when camp was over.

The day before camp broke up, Sumrall went to the trailer — where he hadn't been seen in two or three days — and his fish was gone. Maintenance people had assumed that he wouldn't be back and had left the fish for anyone who wanted it, and some of them had taken it.

This was a Thursday, and Sumrall was in a near-panic.

"I didn't sleep a wink that night," he said.

But the next day he reported the loss to the camp maintenance supervisor and when the personnel reported for duty the supervisor determined which of them had carried the fish away and sent them home to retrieve it. It had been taken to Hampton, a small town between Starke and Gainesville, several miles down the road from Camp Blanding.

"They probably had planned a fish supper that night," said Sumrall, "but happily they hadn't already eaten the bass."

Sumrall, who is pastor of Madeira Drive Baptist Church in Orange Park,* says he has caught larger fish, but decided to have this particular bass mounted because it was such a beauty.

"It was so long and clean and gleaming green-white-looking, coming out of that Kingsley water, that I just couldn't resist having it put on a board," he explained. "And, boy, am I happy that I managed to get it back after it looked as if it had been lost forever."

So there is the tale of the big one that almost got away. It should give the parson a come-backer to top most anybody's "big one that got away" story.

**Editor's note: Sumrall is no longer pastor of this church.*

# A Newsroom Era Has Ended

*Poke tells of the day when reporters and editors threw away their traditional tools of the trade and fell in love with the newfangled way of doing things with computers. Also, the story of an illiterate man worth $10 million at age 35, and what he would have been had he been an educated fellow.*

An era has ended at the Jacksonville, *Florida Times-Union*, the newspaper where I work, and all over the vast newsroom, editors, reporters, writers and even copy boys have mastered a whole bundle of new tricks.

This is the day of the computer — and all the familiar tools of the editing trade such as scissors, glue pot, ruler, eraser, copy paper and pencils, and assorted other paraphernalia have gone to that great musty, dusty, dingy old newsroom in the sky, whence no copy pencil returneth.

The struggle to learn the new method of producing a newspaper has been tough for many — both veterans and tyros — but there is unanimous agreement that these computers and

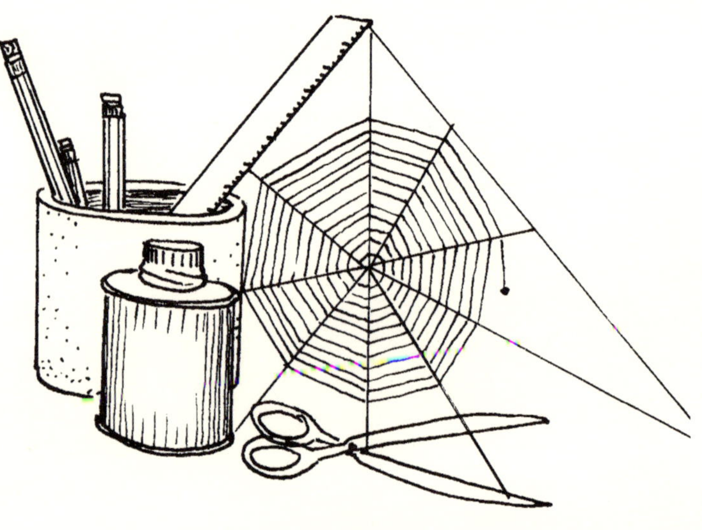

their capabilities are nothing short of pure delight. They never cease to amaze us one and all.

Our resident genius in the matter of mastering these mysterious machines is Dr. Douglas Ripley Hotch, a genuine, 24-carat, bottled-in-bond ex-college professor and late worker in a box factory, who finally got into something where a guy or gal can really have some fun.*

With characteristic cloddishness, the semi-literate among us fail utterly to show the super-educated Dr. Hotch the proper respect, referring to him merely as "Rip." But he's a genial sort, probably of necessity or at least prudence, considering our vast numerical superiority, and never takes umbrage at our verbal jabs.

(Ordinarily, modesty would prohibit my mentioning that I, too, am a "doctor." But while we are on the subject of education, I feel the public should know that I have had bestowed upon me a doctorate of philosophy from the Albany, Georgia, School of Religion, by no less an authority than the Rev. Clennon King, dean. So there.)**

At any rate, these cold computers sneer down their snobbish noses at us mere mortals when we joust with their innards, but when Rip sits down at the keyboard they cower in abject terror and spew forth their innermost secrets. He's trained most of us around the news desk (once long known as the copy desk, but now we have no "copy" as it was formerly known) and still is the man yelled for from far and away when someone gets tangled up and can't get loose.

It all proves, I suppose, that there is no substitute for education, lest it be brains, and Rip has a smattering of the latter.

But education isn't everything, as a departed Irish friend of mine used to say.

"Education," he would say, "is a fine thing. I believe in it. It's the next thing to knowledge a man can have."

**Editor's note: Dr. Hotch was later employed by the U. S. Chamber of Commerce in Washington, D. C. and when last heard of, was living in that area and the author of several self-help books.*

*** In 1992, Poke was also awarded an honorary Doctorate of Humane Letters from Jones College in Jacksonville, Florida*

Which brings to mind an old story about an illiterate young man who was reduced in circumstances to going about from door to door begging work or bread.

He chanced to knock on the door of a house of ill repute, and the madam told him she needed a bookkeeper, but he had to turn down the job because he couldn't read or write. So she gave him a dollar to get himself a meal.

En route to a restaurant, he came upon an overturned banana truck, where the driver was selling bananas for $1 a box. He bought a box, ate his fill, and peddled the remainder for a nickel apiece, showing a tidy profit.

One thing led to another, and within 10 years he had a fleet of produce trucks operating from coast to coast, with many warehouses and auxiliary enterprises, all making money.

He decided to retire while yet young, and called his lawyers and accountants in to liquidate the business. When the paperwork was completed, it was discovered he was worth a net $10 million, after taxes. His lawyer invited him to sign the necessary liquidation papers.

"I can't sign them", said our hero. "I can't read or write."

"Great green gobs of gopher goo," cried the flabbergasted lawyer. "You mean to tell me that at age 35 you are worth $10 million clear of any and all encumbrances, and can't even read or write? What ***would*** you have been if you had had an education?"

"A bookkeeper in a whorehouse," replied the man.

# Sea Mystery Still Haunts Former Sailor

*Poke interviews a Jacksonville, Florida, man who was one of the few human beings to hear the last words anyone ever heard from the actual voice of Amelia Earhart. The famed aviatrix, on an around-the-world flight, disappeared near Howland Island in the Pacific Ocean in 1937. Her disappearance remains a mystery to this day.*

ST. MARYS RIVER

As one of the last people to hear the voice of Amelia Earhart, Charlie Perrotto of Jacksonville, Florida, has a special interest in one of America's great and continuing mysteries.

Several recent newspaper stories noted the 45th anniversary of the disappearance of "AE," as she was known to friends and headline writers. She and Frank Noonan, her navigator, were lost somewhere in the vastness of the Pacific Ocean as they attempted to fly their Lockheed Electra aircraft from Lae, New Guinea, to Howland Island, on a leg of a round-the-world flight.

Perrotto wrote a letter to the editor of the *Florida Times-Union* newspaper of Jacksonville, Florida, briefly sketching his part in the drama, and that sparked my interest. I wanted to find out more, so I visited him.

Perrotto, 67, was born in Brooklyn, New York, joined the Navy in 1931 and has lived in the Jacksonville area since he retired in 1955.*

"I was a member of the crew of the Pelican, a mine sweeper/layer converted into a seaplane tender, at the time of the Earhart flight," Perrotto recalled. "We had been ordered

**Editor's note: Poke found Mr. Perrotto still living in Jacksonville, in good health and about to celebrate his 80th birthday.*

from Pearl Harbor on short notice to sail to Howland Island and stand by for anything we might be needed for."

Perrotto said that his ship was anchored on the sheltered side of Howland Island and that it was the only ship in the area at that time. "You know," he said, "reports had it and books have it that the Coast Guard ship Itasca was at Howland, but it was not."

The Pelican was an 840-ton vessel that crossed and criss-crossed the Pacific constantly, attending to the needs of the Navy's PBY "flying boat" fleet. Perrotto became familiar with such intriguing names as Kingman Reef, Johnston Atoll, Midway, Kure, Howland, Baker Island, Palmyra Island and scores of other remote specks in an enormous sea.

On the morning of the fateful day, Perrotto stopped by the radio shack on the way to his turn on watch. Everybody who had a chance to in those days dropped by the radio shack of every Navy vessel for a brief period of listening. It was the only contact with the outside world, which could seem eons away to homesick lads.

"It was about 9:20 a.m. when I chatted with the radio operator," Perrotto said. "We heard the woman's voice saying something to the effect that a storm was coming up fast. We could see a vast storm to the northwest of Howland, reportedly moving rapidly toward the south/southeast.

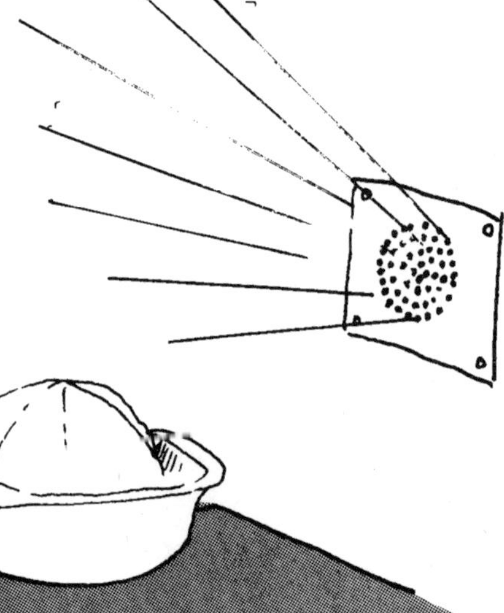

"We could monitor the transmissions from the plane but we could not voice-contact them or the Itasca, which was supposed to be in direct radio contact.

"Then we heard the

voice of the man, believed to be Noonan. He was saying, 'The storm is so big that we cannot get around it nor over it, but we will fly through it.' He especially emphasized the 'will.'

"That was the last we heard, and I believe the last anyone ever heard from the plane. When it was obvious that the plane must be down somewhere in the area, our executive officer, J.T. Trimble, advised the Pelican captain, Lt. A.P. Storrs, that we should launch our search."

They rounded Howland from its south end, sailed northwest and were immediately in the grip of towering seas, raging winds, snow, sleet and rain, Perrotto said.

"I don't see how any airplane could have survived that," he said. "Our main deck was awash and you couldn't see or hear anything."

He said it was unlikely that, as many have theorized, the Earhart plane went down somewhere in the Marshall Islands.

"The storm, wind and ocean currents were moving directly south," he said. "Under those conditions, the plane more likely would have wound up in the Gilbert, Ellice or Phoenix islands, either southwest, south or southeast of Howland. The Marshalls are several hundred miles to the northwest.

"Our radio reception was good for up to approximately 180 miles," Perrotto continued. "And we were receiving the plane messages loud and clear. This indicated to us that the plane was within about 120 miles or so of Howland when last heard from."

He said they searched futilely with scores of other Navy units for the missing plane for more than two weeks.

"We stayed out until we ran out of food," Perrotto said. "They swept the icebox out the morning before we put back to Pearl Harbor."

Perrotto believes the storm engulfed the plane and that, probably, no trace of it ever will be found.

None has, as yet.

# POKE'S BACK

*In September of 1978, Poke underwent a femoral artery bypass operation in Atlanta, Georgia, without informing anyone about it except those absolutely essential to the thing, and the following is the first post-operation column he wrote for the Florida Times-Union newspaper in Jacksonville. In the column, he neglects to inform us that, at age 59 and after 37 years of puffing (and inhaling) the weed, he quit while in the hospital. To date, he has never again smoked anything, including another unfiltered Chesterfield, which was his brand except during the World War II years when he, like every other smoker, smoked whatever he could get when he had a chance to smoke anything. "I come to think Sir Walter Raleigh invented cigarettes," he used to say.*

**EDITOR'S NOTE: Tuesday afternoon Poke McHenry walked into the Times-Union newsroom and set us all straight on exactly where he had been during the past several weeks.**

Well, hello out there, everybody!

Poke, at least what the surgeons left of him, is back.

I just got back this week, and I understand all sorts of wild rumors have been bruited about concerning old Poke's disappearance and whereabouts, and no telling what sort of whoppers have been told on me or what sort of abortions have been wrought under my name while I was out of touch. As yet I haven't had the chance to go back through the papers and see what all I've got to answer for, but rest assured that I'll get around to it as soon as possible and we hope we'll get old Poke back on the right track to stay.

What happened to me was, a blockage developed in a femoral artery and cut off, almost completely, circulation to my left leg. This condition rendered it virtually impossible for me to chase women or flee from jealous husbands, the latter of which could be dangerous to one's health. Any woman slow enough and patient enough to be caught by me might not have been one I would have wanted to catch anyway.

I didn't really mind my condition so much, generally speaking, but when it got to where I couldn't even fish or hunt or even walk more than a few steps in any sort of comfort, I figured it was time something was done. So I went up to Emory University Hospital in Atlanta and the experts up there did some sort of arterial bypass, equipping me with a brand new dacron tube in lieu of a badly-used blood vessel. The thing's snugged in there with some shiny steel staples, too; I've seen them in x-rays.

And what I've been doing for the last six weeks or so is getting myself fixed up in the hospital and then recuperating from the ordeal, which was not much worse than having a baby born with a full set of antlers.

I asked the chief surgeon what sort of guarantee that dacron stuff had and he said it was about 95% as effective as original equipment, and that this job should last "45 or 50 years."

"And just what," I asked, "do you expect me to do then?"

There was a whole bunch of mail awaiting when I got back, and it will take me some time to get around to answering all of it. But let me assure you all that the many kind things that have been said about old Poke are most appreciated. Some of you apparently found out that I have been ailing and sent get-well cards and other tokens of consideration and thoughtfulness, and again I say thank you all.

One of the most interesting bits of mail was an invitation from Charlie Smith to attend the annual barbecue at Scrubby Bluff on the St. Marys River. I just wish I was able to do that one justice, because it really sounds like the sort of thing that is right down old Poke's alley, sho' nuff.

Also, I'm missing the opening session of the dove season, a thing I haven't missed since they've been having dove seasons in Georgia, or so it seems. So if any of you fellows out there have a spare mess of birds, remember old Poke didn't get a chance to get his own this time.

*(There is no truth to the rumor that Poke's operation was delayed while the Wilkinson sword blade folks developed a super blade to cut through his tough hide.)*

# Everybody Has His Price

*Since the advent in the spring of 1978 of the Poke column in the Jacksonville, Florida Times-Union newspaper, the columns had appeared only in the paper's Georgia edition and on no regular schedule. In the spring of 1979, editors of the newspaper decided to run the increasingly popular column in all editions. The following column contains, among several more appealing items, Poke's explanation of why it all came about. Read on.*

ST. MARYS RIVER

I don't know how many Georgia readers of the *Florida Times-Union* of Jacksonville, Florida, or for that matter how many Florida readers, know that there are normally three editions each day. The first is the Georgia edition, the second the Florida edition and the final is mostly for Jacksonville and close-in subscribers.

When I started writing these columns a little more than a year ago, it was almost strictly a Georgia thing, and rarely got into the other editions. But then some time ago, there was a half-hearted sort of attempt to get old Poke in all editions. It sounded like a tarnation amount of additional work for me, and so I didn't make any guarantees. A few of the columns did make all editions, but it was a sporadic thing and so I doubt many readers other than those in Georgia have any idea who Poke is. They aren't, of course, missing much.

To get to the point, I have now succumbed to the blandishments of my esteemed editors and agreed to write a column for the Tempo section every Saturday, and it will appear in all editions.*

I guess you could say that inflation finally caught up

**Editor's note: If you haven't been paying attention — Poke retired from the T-U in 1992. And there hasn't been a "Tempo" section in several years.*

with old Poke. With the price of gasoline the way it is now, fishing is getting downright expensive, if a fellow gads about a good bit as I like to do. So when the ante was upped enough, I said I'd make every effort to have something printable every week. You'll notice that still isn't an ironclad guarantee, but then what is? Read the fine print on the warranty for the next tire, battery or appliance you buy, and you'll see what I mean.

One of the things (besides money) that prompted me to go all editions on a regular basis was a radio show I was on about two weeks ago. The *Times-Union* has an hour-long show on Jacksonville's radio station WEXI twice a week, with Managing Editor Fred Seely as host.* His guests are reporters, editors, advertising and circulation folks, columnists and others associated with the newspaper business.

Fred invited me to be his guest on June 29, and we had a grand time. Many good folks called in while the show was under way and were highly complimentary of the Poke columns they had read. One man assured me that if ever I write a book, I can count on him as a buyer.** Another gentleman said he had heard every one of the shows and that ours was the best of them all. Still another said I should be on the editorial page every day. (He's obviously got great taste.)

One lady called and wanted my opinion on football, which, I suppose, proves folks think old Poke knows everything. They're right, of course.

**Editor's note: The newspaper stopped this practice several years ago, and Fred Seely is now Chairman of the Eye Research Foundation in Jacksonville.*

*** If you know who this person is, let him know Poke's ready to take him up on his offer.*

I told one old joke on that show that had Seely laughing so hard he couldn't speak for about half a minute. It was about the old man who, when he reached his 100th birthday, was being interviewed by a reporter from the local paper. The old boy was obviously on his way out, as he was bed-ridden, senile, half-blind, nearly deaf, and generally in the last stages of life.

When asked the inevitable question of to what he attributed his longevity, the old man replied in a quavering, high-pitched whine that he had always lived an absolutely clean life, had never touched tobacco or alcohol in any form, had always been one to go to bed and get up early, had always been faithful to his dear wife, and so on along that line.

While he was talking, a tremendous uproar broke out in the next room. There was loud cursing and shouting, the crash of breaking furniture, the shattering of glass and a generally terrible din.

"Good heavens!" exclaimed the reporter. "What in the world is all that?"

"Oh, don't pay no attention to that," wheezed the old man. "That's just Daddy. He's drunk again."

The joke most people got the biggest kick out of seemed to be the one where I said I had proposed to my wife over the telephone. I explained that I called and said "Honey, will you marry me?" and she replied joyously, "Oh yes, of course! Yes! Who is this?" I wish I could claim that joke for my own, but it probably originated before I did, which was a spell back. I tell you one thing, though, my wife didn't think it was a dang bit funny the first time I pulled it on her in a party crowd.

At any rate, I'll be coming your way regularly, I suppose, with comments, opinions, tall tales, funny and unfunny stories and whatever else happens to cross my mind as being possibly entertaining.

*(Columnist Poke McHenry isn't worried about the high cost of rent or electricity, but when gas is a dollar a gallon and bait shrimp cost $3.50 a pound, he figures something should be done.)*

# Barrier Isle Unspoiled

*This 1979 column is about Poke's trip to secluded, restful and practically unspoiled (at that time) and altogether beautiful Sea Island, little known barrier island off the coast near Brunswick, Georgia. (Remember, this column's information is almost 15 years old.)*

LITTLE ST. SIMONS ISLAND, Georgia

On the map, this place looks like an ice pack draped over the heads of St. Simons and Sea Islands — two of the better-known barrier islands off the Georgia coast.

For a long time, I had been itching to take a close look at Little St. Simons, and I finally got the chance. I can recommend it as well worth the effort to visit. And it does take some effort to get to it, since the only means of access are by boat or plane, unless you're a better swimmer than I am.

There is a brochure on the place informing that "Little St. Simons Island is a privately owned, unspoiled barrier island with over six miles (actually, about seven miles) of undeveloped Atlantic Ocean beach. It is located near Brunswick, Georgia, approximately midway between Savannah, Georgia and Jacksonville, Florida."

The pamphlet goes on to point out that the island has been preserved for nearly a hundred years as a family retreat by its current owners, the Berolzheimer family.*

There is no question that this island, along a coast teeming with high-rise condominiums and other developments, and with more constantly following, remains virtually pristine. The last commercial project on the place wound down in 1906, when the Eagle Pencil Co. stopped cutting island cedar from which to make its writing instruments.

There is a rustic lodge and a couple of cottages and,

**Editor's note: Little St. Simons Island is still owned by the same family and continues to be open to visitors.*

while the accommodations may look primitive, they are indeed most comfortable, in addition to being spotlessly clean.

Retired Eastern Airlines pilot Buddy Hasell and his wife, Jackie, who live on St. Simons, manage the Little St. Simons property for the Berolzheimers. On the island, naturalist John Crawford greets visitors and conducts hikes through woodlands and trips to the amazingly unpopulated beaches, in addition to briefing folks on the whats, whys and wherefores of the island.

To get to the place for a $25 day tour, one rides a barge from a landing on St. Simons Island. The craft wends its leisurely way for 20 to 30 minutes through the Hampton River and Mosquito Creek marshlands to tie up at the Little St. Simons dock. The boat leaves St. Simons at 10 a.m. and gets back at 4 p.m.

I was one of a group of a dozen or so people making the trip, and the first thing we did after landing was check out the lounge and get a briefing from Crawford. Then we went for a walk among some of the oldest and biggest oak and pine trees in this part of the world. These were scattered among magnolia, red bay, cabbage palm and many other varieties of trees and shrubs.

Crawford, who proved to be one of the most knowledgeable naturalists I've ever known (my knowledge of naturalists is rather limited, I'll admit, but he's a bright and well-informed lad, nonetheless) promptly answered fully and understandably every question any member of the group had.

We found a great many little green frogs, most of them about the size of a man's fingernail, on some of the undergrowth. "Good bass bait," I remarked.

Looking up quickly, Crawford replied with a smile, "I prefer to look at them as little bug-eaters."

After this, the agenda called for lunch at the lodge, and it was quite good.

In the afternoon on the beach, some kid in the crowd discovered a pile of glunk that had just washed ashore. The most charitable way I can describe its appearance was that it looked like something you definitely wouldn't want to step in.

But it didn't faze Crawford, who immediately identified it as "sea pork" and told us it was a colony of small animals considerably more advanced in their development than most of the strange living creatures of the deep. I believe I can do without further acquaintance with the lesser-developed creatures.

At the lodge, European fallow deer strolled around the premises and grazed almost within reach of the tourists. One female, a pretty white creature, actually eats cookies out of the hands of visitors.

There are no telephones or televisions on the place, which makes it much more attractive for me. I like everything about television except the commercials and the programs, and telephones I love to do without at every opportunity, although in fairness, they are necessities. Televisions ain't.

The island does have electricity — it is piped in by underwater cable — and the artesian water is excellent.

This is the way the concluding sentence of the previously mentioned brochure begins:

"Little St. Simons Island is not just another seaside resort. It is an exceptionally beautiful, secluded, unspoiled island..."

That says it all.

# AFTERWORD

From the time I started pecking out the Poke columns for the *Florida Times-Union* newspaper in Jacksonville, Florida, it was always in my mind to maybe someday put them, or many of them, into book form.

But I doubt very much, being the world-class procrastinator that I have always been, that such a thing would ever have come to pass but for the persistence and insistence of my daughter, Vicki Smith.

"We are going to get you published," Vicki announced to me at almost the exact minute my retirement from the Times-Union became official on January 2, 1992.

When Vicki makes up her mind that something is going to be done, it is. No amount of world-class procrastinating, whining, wheedling, malingering, excuse-manufacturing or other attempts to dodge the work necessary to produce this thing you are now holding in your hands could ever dissuade Vicki from her dedication to the desired end; from her undeviating and undaunted determination to achieve her goal of getting Poke published. She did it in spite of my prodigious propensity for loafing.

This was vintage Vicki. She applies the same principles and qualities to everything she does, and she does everything in keeping her Jacksonville marketing and public relations firm of Smith and Daniel humming successfully along.

It takes a remarkable amount of work and dedication to produce a book, but Vicki has never flagged or faltered in her mission with this one. She has been my editor, chief proofreader and general motivator, and such a relentlessly formidable ramrod on this project I would have been the worst kind of ingrate not to have cooperated with her fully and thankfully.

And now that we are over the major hump in getting the first one out, despite all the struggles and pitfalls, we look forward eagerly toward the next such volume, which is already underway and should be a lot less trouble and fewer headaches. In it, we will try to cover most of the 1980s through Poke's eyes and words in "Poke II" or whatever we choose to call it.

And if I am still hitting on most cylinders, there'll be a "Poke III" or, again, whatever we decide to call it.

It is our sincere hope that our first effort has met with your enthusiastic approval, and that those to follow will render you purely euphoric with delight, and that you will drop everything and rush out and buy them in great quantities at a furious and lasting pace.

This in turn will render me highly emotional, and cause a great big lump to arise in my throat, not to mention my billfold.